ENGELBERT

What's in a Name?

MY AUTOBIOGRAPHY

Engelbert Humperdinck
with Katie Wright

Virgin BOOKS

6 8 10 9 7

First published in the United Kingdom in 2004 by Virgin Books

This edition published in the UK in 2012 by Virgin Books,
an imprint of Ebury Publishing
A Random House Group Company

Copyright © EH Productions Inc. 2004

Engelbert Humperdinck and Katie Wright have asserted their right under the Copyright,
Designs and Patents Act 1988 to be identified as the authors of this work.

www.randomhouse.co.uk

Addresses for companies within The Random House Group Limited can be found at:
www.randomhouse.co.uk/offices.htm

The Random House Group Limited Reg. No. 954009

A CIP catalogue record for this book is available from the British Library

Penguin Random House is committed to a sustainable future for
our business, our readers and our planet. This book is made from
Forest Stewardship Council® certified paper.

MIX
Paper from
responsible sources
FSC® C018179

Printed and bound in Great Britain by Clays Ltd, St Ives plc

ISBN: 9780753541104

To buy books by your favourite authors and register for
offers, visit: www.randomhouse.co.uk

DEDICATION

To my mother and father, who made me strive for perfection.

To Patricia, who made me realise what love is all about.

To Louise, Jason, Scott and Bradley, who bring me great joy.

To my wonderful friends around the world, who have kept all of this going.

INTRODUCTION

When my father passed away in 1984, I was absolutely devastated, so overcome with grief that, when I was given the news, I regressed to childhood, went into a frenzy, threw myself on the floor and began to pound the carpet. Dad, although he had not been well of late, was OK the night I left Leicester. I was off for a run of shows which started in Lake Tahoe and was scheduled to run throughout Canada, but I had only just completed my first few breaths on the cabaret stage in the hotel in Tahoe when he breathed his last.

Even though I could not possibly have known that he was about to die, I cursed myself for being on tour, for not being there for him – with him. The truth is, knowing he had not been well, I had *wanted* to stay with him, but there hadn't seemed to be a real need and I didn't speak up. I'd assumed that he'd be there for me to visit as soon as the pre-booked tour ended and, as always, I didn't want to let my fans down. Likewise, I was responding to a long-established, inner need to present an infallible exterior to the outside world and keep my private life and personal relationships *very* private. All these were factors that sent me winging off on that plane to step on stage and continue my life as a performer.

I don't suppose anyone is ever *really* prepared for the death of a parent, and I proved to be no exception that night.

'Oh, God, no, I'm not ready for this,' I kept crying out in anguish when I received the news at Bill Harrah's home. Whenever I performed at his hotel, Bill always arranged for me to stay at his house and even hired a butler, a cleaner and a Rolls-Royce for me, as well as a boat to take out on the lake. He was a very generous man who was like this to all the artists who performed at Harrah's, but he was also a great friend of mine.

If I had to receive such tragic news, it certainly helped to receive it in Bill's home, rather than in the anonymous surroundings of a hotel room. At least I wasn't left to pound the walls and chew the carpets alone but, gutted as I was, I couldn't stop repeating, 'I'm *not* ready for this, *not* ready to cope with such a loss . . .' My father was the pillar of my family – my rock. I couldn't imagine life without him.

A friend of mine who was acting as my stand-in manager at the time, John Smythe, went off to place the necessary calls for the cancelling of my show business engagements, and I began getting the word around that I needed to bypass a lot of other appearances on stage in order to spend some time with my family, followed by some time gathering my thoughts and putting the pieces of my heart back together.

Having spent the first ten years of my life in Madras, in India, where my father was stationed during the Second World War, courtesy of His Majesty's Army, I decided very soon after the funeral that I wanted – *needed* – to go back there. So, the year my dad passed away, I returned to my boyhood town to honour him – and my past – by visiting my first home and looking for some suitable venues where I might be able to do some performances.

As I stood in Madras in the incredible heat of the midday sun, breathing in air that always seems to be laden with the scent of exotic fruits and spices, I glanced up at our old house, which was situated in the area by the harbour, and I was amazed. I was only too aware *before* I had arrived outside the gates that when you're a child everything seems enormous to you and that my memory, which had been telling me that our old house was absolutely gi-normous, was probably way off the mark. In truth, I was really expecting a tiny dwelling, where my mum, dad and we ten kids must all have been packed in like sardines – and this conviction was further endorsed by the fact that the route to my old home was totally poverty-stricken. Whenever I looked out of the car's window, the surroundings looked utterly different from anything I remembered from my childhood when British occupation had spit-and-polished certain areas, and the front gates to our house were protected by militia and manned by servants.

When we rounded the bend of Spring Haven Road, however, I gasped at what I saw. By then, I had become used to being in other people's big houses, but this house – my first home – was bigger than anything I'd ever been in, or lived in since, and there it was larger than life.

'Good on you, Dad,' I murmured when I'd recovered from the shock.

With the surprise confirmation that my memory was actually correct, I realised I needn't downsize the impact of any of the experiences that life had brought me thus far, whether they related to my career or personal life.

My childhood *had* been like a fairytale, one in which I was lovingly tended for, hand, foot and finger! And, from the time of my return visit to Madras, I began to recap my early life, beginning with a daredevil moment when I fell several feet off the garage roof. My sister Dolly had to tend to my sliced foot, which was bleeding profusely. I also recalled the times when my siblings and I played on the seesaw or swings of the children's playground, which had been erected in our garden.

Such thoughts – and the emotions they engendered – were very new to me. I had lived through so many years when I had donned privacy's armour and kept certain memories to myself that key moments were in real danger of fading, and what *really* shaped me – made me who I am today – was likewise in peril of being modified by the image of myself that I read in press interviews.

I guess all genuine sentiment and reactions get accidentally modified over time, leaving small handfuls of significant moments to turn into key memories that seem to define who we are. It makes sense that the past is muddled by our present station in life, and I imagine this happens to everybody, even those of us who are not in the spotlight and on the paparazzi's hit list, and who do not, therefore, struggle to separate their two worlds – public and private – in order to keep their private life *private*.

Standing outside our old house in Madras, with my uniformed friend British Airways pilot Captain Brian Wallace alongside me, but with no other uniformed authority of yesteryear holding the gates closed, I allowed my mind to open up and expand and, for the first time in my life, I began to process certain events and consider their effects and significance. This outing back in time in my head, which brought new understanding of what went on inside me, felt good – *healing, empowering.*

'Perhaps in future I'll prop ajar the door of my life,' I thought, 'and put all the *real,* life-changing events and momentous experiences on paper, inviting anyone who's interested to have a look inside.

At that moment, as these thoughts were running through my mind, the people who now lived in my former home and who were unaware that I'd been coming for a visit, caught sight of me. Having recognised me, they approached the gate and – very tentatively – asked if I would like to enter.

'Yes, thank you kindly,' I replied, only too aware that, just minutes after getting out of the car to stand at the end of my boyhood drive, this full-grown man, who was me, had taken on the appearance of a hunch-shouldered, wide-eyed, insecure boy. 'I'd like that very much – I'm ready now.'

And, straightening up, I unhunched my shoulders and strode into my past – and into the pages that would one day become this book.

Engelbert Humperdinck

CHAPTER ONE

Madras, in India, now called Chennai, where I spent the first ten years of my life, while my father was stationed there courtesy of His Majesty's Army during the Second World War, was – and still is – a truly hot spot, chock-full of historic treasures and holy places, such as grand temples and shrines, and magnificent forts and palaces. Even then, before I'd reached the age of ten, I knew I wanted to be a *somebody* in the entertainment business, and I used to bite my nails and fret that I would never make a name for myself if I had to bring along my face and very unfortunate body!

I was a fat kid, with a flat nose that was so adhered to my face, it seemed impossible that my nostrils could be in working order; and the only thing I disliked more than my thick, car-bumper lips were my teeth that protruded way beyond them. In fact, my teeth stuck out so far, I could have eaten an apple through the strings of a tennis racquet. In those days, the 1940s, nobody thought of orthodontia; you got the teeth that came with your head and *that* was *that*. For three years I slept face-down, my mouth clenched over my closed fist, willing my teeth to move back and stand in line, or at least adopt a more presentable position. Every night when I went to bed, I hoped I would wake up a better-looking boy, but all I saw when I opened my eyes was a set of very sore, chapped lips and tooth-indented fists.

One of ten children, I believed my siblings – Olga, Dolly, Tilly, Arthur, Bubbles, Celine, Peggy, Irwin, and Patricia – were the lucky ones who had harvested all the good genes from our parents, Mervyn and Olive Dorsey, and that was why they had turned out as good-looking as our mum and dad. I, on the other hand, who had entered the world on 2 May 1936, was a runt who had cropped misshapen looks that could only worsen as I grew.

Although, in my heart of hearts, I knew from a very early age that looks should not matter if you had a real talent for hire, I was convinced I would always appear as a spotlight repellant that would quash any dreams I had of fulfilling my then-ambition to become a big-band leader. I really fancied being in control, dressed in sophisticated clothes. For years, refusing to believe that a nose is just a nose, I tried to take matters into my own hands by spending endless hours pinching, pressing and massaging my face, trying to sculpt it into the kind of profile I craved or, at least, into a look that was a closer match to the one I imagined myself possessing whenever I was daydreaming about my future on stage. Each night as I pulled upon my nose and pinched my cheeks, I willed it to 'stand' up and become more elegant and, however many times I was disappointed, I just had to keep those beauty rituals going. Bandleaders, I believed, were a dapper lot; men of charm and cheekbone, whose handsome facial features were only surpassed by their musical talent. I knew audiences adored stars like Sinatra for their singing, but I also knew that it was thanks to his looks that Sinatra's adoring fans called him 'Ol' Blue Eyes'.

Nose aside, I still hoped I might be in with a chance. After all, my mother was an absolutely stunning brunette. Standing 5 ft 3 in, she had a beautiful porcelain complexion that remained flawless until the day she died. She was a great violinist well worth listening to and, oh, how I hoped I'd inherited some of those genes, and that I'd become as talented a musician as she was. As well as playing the violin, Mum had an operatic voice with a range that was capable of cracking crystal and shaking chandeliers, and our party guests were forever asking her to sing for them.

My father, who was always my hero, was an engineer with a brilliant mathematical mind and stern, Victorian ideals when it came to bringing up his ten children. A great entertainer, with an unlimited store of wonderful anecdotes, he was also very amorous – sexual – in the way that he interacted with my mother – and our female guests! I guess, in my case, some people would mutter 'the apple doesn't fall far from the tree,' but more on that later!

There was never a dull moment during those years. Our home was a large red-bricked house with a veranda running round it with balconies on each floor and numerous bedrooms. It had a flat roof on which we would sit at night, playing the guitar, or listening to the sound of the tropical wildlife, and watching the ships in the nearby harbour. I remember the sky and stars always seemed so close that you felt as if you could just reach out and grab the moon.

Dad hosted massive, lavish parties for all the British and American troops, and he presided over these in a *perfectly* pressed suit and *perfectly* arranged bow-tie, and at 5 ft 10½ in, with prematurely grey hair, he looked quite debonair. He had a muscular physique due to the fact that he was a superb athlete, always playing football or hockey or going deep-sea diving.

As his hostess, Mum looked equally sophisticated. Her evening gowns were wonderful and the shoes she wore had such high heels that I used to gape at them in astonishment, trying to work out how she could put one foot in front of the other without landing on her slim bottom. She really was supremely elegant – and the two of them were always perfectly coiffed with a wonderful kind of poise that I found enchanting.

At family get-togethers, Dad would often gather us kids in the garden, or the parlour, to sing for the guests, and there we would stand in a neat, orderly, Von Trapp *Sound of Music* sort of way that all the adults seemed to approve of and love. During one of the parties, though, I let the side down by picking up a half-full bottle of rum and downing some of the contents. I honestly didn't realise I was drinking anything potent. I don't think I had that much of the stuff before I was discovered in the act, but I still ended up running amok among the guests, picking up garden chairs and balancing them upside-down on my head. It was probably the only time in my early years that I wasn't at the mercy of my shyness and trying to hide behind a piece of furniture or blend in with the wallpaper.

At these get-togethers Dad, who obviously thought I had a good voice, would single me out and say: 'Come over here, Son, and entertain these people. Come and do a song for them.'

'Daddy,' I would reply, wriggling and overcome by shyness, 'I will. But can I sing from over here – behind the curtain, or underneath the table?'

'Sing wherever you like,' he would call back chuckling.

So, shrouded in linen curtains, or hidden beneath the heavy, dark oak table, sing I would. Even as a very young boy, my voice was strong and masculine, but I would always try to make it sound even more manly. The guests, as a result, were more entertained by my determination to sound like a grown-up man than they were by my voice. I wanted to be *somebody* – anyone other than my ugly self, even then – and, when the guests were gone, although I was still unable to reach the forte pedals on the piano, I would do a boogie-woogie. In those moments I was always in complete command of my imaginary audience, and I would sing and make grandiose gestures. The inanimate objects in the room *really* loved me!

Even though singing for real people – our visitors – made me feel uncomfortable, I felt much more at ease at home in those days than I did when I had to put my daydreams on hold, venture out to school and witness real life on the Madras streets where the temperatures often rose to 37°C. The riots of pre-Independent India were under way and producing some pretty horrific events and images and, before Independence was finally achieved in 1947, these inspired a whole string of terrifying nightmares that often disturbed my childhood slumbers.

I was just eight years old when I saw my first beheaded policeman lying in the dust and dung of the roadside, and before my next birthday had come around I'd seen a dozen such sights. Our school, St Kevin's, a Catholic school run by nuns and priests, was located within a compound and we would often see mutilated, dismembered bodies, minus heads, eyes and limbs, and other spoils of the riots, placed in rolled-up mats on either side of the gates that led into it. Witnessing terrorism at any age is very traumatic, and as a young, sensitive boy it took its toll on me and made me retreat even further into myself.

I was a loner. The kids used to call for my brother Irwin, who was eighteen months older than I was, but they never called for me, and I felt rejected and left out. I was small for my age, while Irwin was well proportioned and very good-looking. I ardently wished I could look more like him. Appearances aside, though, I could never *really* resent anything about Irwin. Without him, I would not be here now – he saved me from a horrendous fate that would have resulted in a very short life.

Our house was situated in a harbour that was always teeming with colour and life, and right opposite was a railway line which ran alongside another small, watery inlet that lapped directly into the ocean beyond. A servant used to take us on a late afternoon stroll there most days, but on one memorable occasion we escaped her clutches, crept off unaccompanied, and got ourselves into near-fatal trouble.

The inlet housed timber logs that the ships used to drop off and, as kids aged between five and six, Irwin and I and other local kids loved playing on these. It was obviously a potentially dangerous activity for the unwary, and that evening, when Irwin and I were there with a whole gang of kids, this proved to be the case. Playing the daredevil – showing off – I started to walk out much further than usual, stepping from one slippery floating log to another. Naturally, I lost my balance, slithered sideways and, as the log began to swivel and turn, I plunged into the water.

In seconds the intense, blinding brightness of the Madras day disappeared and turned to hellish dark; moments later, I found myself sinking beneath the logs into the murky depths of eight feet of water that was steeped in wood splinters and contained a shoal of jellyfish. I had never been taught to swim, and with the logs blocking my way, it was impossible for me to surface.

All the children that had been with us – about a dozen or so – had run away. The only person that was left was my brother, who could not swim either. Crying and screaming, 'My brother! My brother!' he was brave enough to crawl over the logs and risk his own life in order to save mine.

Holding on to a cluster of logs that were tied together, Irwin splashed around until, by the hand of fate, my own hand popped up and he was able to grab it and pull both of us up and out to safety.

By then, the life was ebbing out of my body and I had swallowed enough water to sink a small ship. My mouth and lungs were full of painful wood splinters and every inch of my skin had been stung by jellyfish.

Once he'd got me to the bank, Irwin, young as he was and acting purely on instinct, sat me up, spread my legs and kept forcing my head down between them. As he repeated this action, I began to struggle and choke, and all the water came gushing out in great torrents. Slowly, but surely, I found myself able to breathe again.

There is a postscript to this near-death experience.

The next evening, my dad, having made sure that Irwin and I – and all our servants – fully understood that we were *never ever* to visit that place unaccompanied again, decided that a return visit would lessen the trauma and help us boys to feel less fearful of water in the future. This was a bit of child psychology that backfired! In the event, we ended up *more*, rather than *less*, traumatised by the experience.

As the servant, Irwin and I stood on the small bridge that crossed the inlet, staring down at the dark water where I had disappeared into the depths the night before, we caught sight of something huge, black and very sinister moving just beneath the surface. Then, suddenly, there was a tremendous heave and splashing that sent us and the servant reeling back, and the water parted. Moments later, we could clearly see the outline of a large shark dislodging the clutch of logs that Irwin had clung on to when he was pulling me from the water.

The shark, which was open-mouthed and displaying a wondrous set of pin-sharp teeth, was frenzied, obviously panicking at finding itself trapped between the logs in the bay.

Looking on in horror, we knew without expressing it, that if that frightened giant had been there the night before, Irwin and I would have been shark meat for sure. We had been even luckier than we had thought.

Later when a local fisherman informed Dad of what had happened, he was sorry he had given Irwin and me a bedtime belting the day before. He was truly overwhelmed by our good luck and only too thankful that we had been spared and had come home to him and Mum.

I might have been lucky to avoid being shark fodder but, even though I'd avoided losing a few chunks of myself, I still didn't feel lucky in my looks. Every time I looked in my bedroom mirror, there was no improvement and my terrible shyness and lack of self-confidence only increased. While I accepted what I was always being told that my legs would grow and I would be able to reach the piano pedals, I was in a tearing hurry. I had to, I felt, get a more suitable, more *accessible*, musical instrument to master if I were to have *any* hope of a future life on stage. If I succeeded in that, I decided, I might be able to demonstrate sufficient natural talent to distract people from my dreadful looks.

I despaired that my name would ever be announced on any radio show or uttered by the people who mattered in show business, however talented I might turn out to be. I was, it seemed, doomed never to see my name – *ARNOLD GEORGE DORSEY* – lit up in neon lights, twinkling in my parents' home city of Leicester. And, as for Liverpool or London, *no hope*!

CHAPTER TWO

When the time came for my father to move us all back to his native Leicester in 1946, I was really happy about it. Dad had brought us up to be proud that we were British and had told us such a wealth of stories about life in England that I had absolutely no regrets. In fact, when I watched the lights of ships coming into the harbour in Madras, I'd always imagined that they were coming from England, teeming with the kind of goods – and rich experiences – that could only be gleaned there, and I wanted to board ship!

Now, on hearing we were about to sail across the ocean and land on her shores, I started fantasising about the new life we would have when we got there. Every day, during the late afternoons, I would sit swinging in a hammock on the terrace, daydreaming about this during that magical hour when the sun is setting, but the heat of the day lingers on, causing the overripe fruit on the trees to smell extra sweet and wet, and the tropical birds to quieten their singing as the bats begin to dart about the air.

Across the ocean, I imagined there were would be plenty of jobs for a boy with show business ambitions and any number of musical instruments waiting to be bought – and played. 'All the world's a stage,' I had learned in my schoolroom studies of Shakespeare, but I was sure this applied more to the Bard's birthplace – England – than anywhere else in the universe.

Once there, however, England required a bigger adjustment than I'd ever imagined. We had moved into a detached house which, although quite large, was by no means as grand as the one we had just left. I used to play football in the street with other children who lived in the same street, and go hunting for money in the grilles which covered the coal chutes. There were no servants to wait on us hand and foot; we had to do everything for ourselves! It was also a big shock to my system – *cold* and *wet*, rather than sunny and dry, and frequently gloomy rather than bright; and, while oranges and bananas were plentiful where I'd come from, fruit was scarce and food and clothes were rationed.

Nevertheless, although everything seemed rather drab and dreary after all the teeming life and the sweltering heat of days spent living by the harbour in Madras, it was still wonderful to be in my homeland. I had been taught that there was a time when 'the sun never set on the British Empire', and I was very aware that I was now living in a country the world had respected for centuries.

Although I realised that even necessities were in short supply, I kept begging for a musical instrument. By then, I was absolutely desperate to prove that I had something to offer and I was convinced that I could do this if only I was given a chance. But times were hard for my parents, who had ten kids to clothe and feed, and I will never forget the day I was sent on my bicycle to pick up our egg ration. Having put the sixty eggs inside my jacket to protect them during the ride home, I hadn't got very far when the whole lot slipped out and – *splosh* – created an uncooked omelette all over the road. Can you believe that? Two weeks of breakfast for the entire family now running down my bicycle frame in sorry *glops* on to the street and into the gutter.

'Oh, no,' I wailed, looking at the colourful, gooey mess, 'I'm *done* for! Oh, God!'

My chief despair, though, as the yellow yolks continued to streak off in all directions, was the realisation that I now had no chance of persuading my father that I deserved – was *responsible* enough – to own an instrument.

So, for a short time, after this dreadful event in which we all went egg-free at breakfast, I accepted my fate and stopped asking and moaning and complaining.

Within the year, however, Dad surprised me with a gift of a secondhand saxophone. As an ex-military man and engineer, Mervyn Dorsey may have ruled us all with the proverbial 'iron glove' but, as a father, he had a heart of pure gold, and was always ready to dip into his pocket for friends – or even strangers – who needed help.

The sax was not in good shape – the bell, in particular, was very dented – and it was probably only worth about £5, but I was thrilled. I knew that Dad, in his heart of hearts, wanted music to be my hobby *not* my career, yet he had done this for me anyway. That made the sax, whatever its condition, very special.

Dad, brilliant man that he was, could make the most marvellous toys out of wood and metal, and he could figure out mathematic equations in his head faster than most people could manage on a calculator. I was always aware that he wanted me to follow in his footsteps and become an engineer. Years later, when I was a budding singer and going out with Patricia Healey, who was to become my wife, Dad took her aside one day and muttered, 'Why don't you tell him to stick with a *proper* job?'

That moment, though, when I first raised the saxophone's mouthpiece to my lips, while he was standing there, hands thrust deep in his pockets, watching, was *very* touching. The first note I made the instrument sound was a good solid note and, although the sax was old and battered and terribly difficult to blow, I managed to play a song immediately, and could play 'My Blue Heaven' all the way through within an hour.

Flashing me a satisfied smile, Dad said: 'OK, Son. Practise on this one, and maybe we'll get you a new one later.'

I was up for the challenge – more than ready to prove at eleven years old that I would deserve that 'later on'.

For the next four years I did a morning paper round, earning, come rain, sleet and snow, a weekly pay of 4 shillings, the exact cost of a single saxophone lesson with Mr Parker. His place was a long, chilly walk from my home in winter and, since you can't play keys with frozen fingers, I'd strap the sax around my chest in order to keep my hands tucked in my pockets and protected from the cold. Despite this, every Saturday, I would arrive, fingers chilled to the marrow, and Mr Parker would meet me at the door, saying, 'Come and have a warm-up,' before leading me to his living-room fireplace, where there was always the good, cheerful glow of a fire burning in the grate.

The unspoken understanding between us was that my fingers would always arrive cold – and he respected the reason why. He knew I couldn't afford to buy mittens without sacrificing a few weeks of my classes with him. So, ignoring the chilblains on my hands, I would play whatever tunes I'd been practising and, although he always told me he was pleased with the progress I was making – and he could tell I had musical talent – he would add: 'But I *don't* want you to play like *that* – I want you to play the way I teach you. Don't try to do anything by ear. That is not the way to learn an instrument. You need to learn in the practical, sight-reading way that I teach you.'

But I loved playing by ear and was always fretting that the weekly lessons were not bringing me any closer to my dream of becoming a Tommy Dorsey-type bandleader, able to command an audience with a trill of a horn and a flash of a hand. While Mr Parker never seemed to worry whether I really had the ability to reach a professional standard or not, I did.

When I was fifteen, I left the Melbourne Road School for Boys and Girls and began work as an apprentice at an engineering firm. My father approved of this move, but I wasn't very happy. I had no wish to follow in his footsteps, because I had my own ideals, but I did want to earn sufficient money to buy myself a better musical instrument and some better clothes and shoes.

The plan, though, didn't really work out for either of us. My moans and groans were so deafening and the money was so minuscule – 28 shillings a week – that, by the time my sixteenth birthday came round, I'd got shot of that job. I'm not sure which one of us – Dad or me – had the last laugh, though. My search for another job, with better pay, landed me in yet another engineering factory!

On my first day there, I worked from eight in the morning straight through to six in the evening, gathering a few shillings extra for an hour's overtime. At the day's end, I was handed £2, which was more money than I had ever held at any one time. I couldn't wait to show Mum. Feeling very pleased with myself, I ran all the way home, never slowing down once over all three miles, and headed straight into her room. Once there, I opened my fist like I was performing a magic trick.

'Oh, good boy,' she said. Then, as was the custom, she added, 'Now give it all to me to pay for your room and board.' But she then handed me 5 back, and I felt like a rich man. Those five coins, cupped in the palm of my hand, had real weight and not just because they were big money for me to squander.

'Some,' I thought, 'can go into savings, some for the pictures, and what's left over can buy me a bite to eat.'

Over the next year I earned a little bit more and, by the time I was seventeen, I was earning £4 a week. This was 'Big Time' for me, and I was able to buy some clothes on a weekly hire purchase basis and to dress a bit better.

I have always been proud of the fact that my parents taught me self-discipline and how to support myself, thus allowing me to become my own person. They always used to say to me, 'civility costs nothing', and if you respect yourself you will respect others. An easy ride and a free meal ticket presents no challenge to young people to get up and go; and hard work and good grooming has always been of the utmost importance to me. Being able to improve my appearance with smart new clothes works wonders for my self-confidence when I venture out on stage.

In those early days, however, my self-confidence was hard-earned even in new clothes. By then I'd discovered some local clubs in Leicester where I could play my sax or sing. I wish I could have joined in with the bands there and gained some experience, but I lacked the self-confidence to so so and thus it never came to pass.

Autobiographies tend to pinpoint a moment in a person's early years that reveal the future's compass: the potential vet saves an injured bird, the likely Olympian outruns a bully, the barrister-to-be wins an argument; and each, having experienced one of these subtle moments, is set upon a path that has a specific direction. The life I was searching for – and hoping for – was sitting right under my nose, but I was utterly blind to the clues that I *could* succeed in what I so desperately wanted simply by shifting my focus. I wanted to be an entertainer, a band leader and, while I had been singing harmony by the age of five and performing for an appreciative audience (albeit my father's guests) even before I could lace my shoes, I was still clamouring for success as a saxophone player, the instrument I had started to play at the age of eleven.

Somehow it never occurred to me that I had an instrument all along, and that it was nestled right there within my larynx and voice box.

All this changed, however, the night I got a standing ovation when I was singing for the first time on a real spotlit stage in a little club in Bond Street, in Leicester. My face, Irwin told me later, was an absolute picture! As I stood there in the golden spotlight (*real* stage boards beneath my feet!) I looked like a taken-aback, gob-smacked guest-of-honour at my own surprise party. In that split second, as I fully took in that the eyes of every smiling cheering person were focused directly upon me, I blushed to the roots of my hair, then beamed back at each and every one of them.

I do believe in the saying 'what will be will be', and I hadn't gone to that club on that Friday evening to do a turn and hopefully be discovered. A few months short of the legal age to drink in public places, Irwin and I had found our way to this particular venue because some factory lads had told us that this was a place where the barman did not query your age when you were craving a pint. Given that I had got up on the stage without even noticing that the club was hosting auditions for working men's clubs, destiny for me, it could be said, came served up in a pint glass.

So it was, then, that having enjoyed some illicit sips of ale, while I watched a variety of people taking turns at the microphone, I downed my own pint of bitter and then got up on the stage to sing. Turning to the guy sitting at the Hammond in the corner, I said, 'Do you know "Your Eyes Are the Eyes of a Woman In Love"?' Fortunately, he realised I was referring to a song title!

Obviously a man of few words, he replied by swivelling back to the keys and playing the opening chords of the number. By then, the courage given to me by the liquor was fading fast, but I knew I could not back down without looking a fool. Once centred in the spotlight, I gave him the 'off' nod and did my very best to look and sound like someone other than myself – like Frankie Laine of 'I Believe' and 'Answer Me' fame.

Most beginner-singers start by copying other artists and I was no exception. Provided we follow the original singer's phrasing well enough, we remind the audience of the hit performer and get a warm reception. That night, I obviously pulled off my rendering of Frankie's 'Your Eyes Are the Eyes of a Woman in Love'.

'Wow!' I thought as I looked around the smoke-filled room at all the people holding their hands above their heads and clapping, 'I would never get a reaction like this playing my saxophone. This is magic – *wonderful!*'

I could see Irwin on his feet, swivel-eyed and proud as Punch, smiling as broadly as I was, but before I could get to him, I was surrounded by some gentlemen in suits who seemed somewhat over-dressed and over-coiffed for such a club. Collectively, all smelling of hair lotion and aftershave, their reaction was, 'That was good, lad', and they fired the same questions at me in unison:

'Who's your agent?'

'Who are you working for right now?'

'Have you any vacancies in your book?'

I told them I hadn't even realised I had entered an audition and I certainly did not know that there was a pre-arranged order for people to take their turn on stage and perform.

'You didn't know this was an audition?' the nearest suit scoffed. 'Oh, come on, lad, pull the other one, I *don't* believe you.'

'You *must* have known,' said another. 'It was surely obvious this was an audition for people who want to perform in working men's clubs. *Right?*'

Wrong!

The bafflement I had caused was pure magic – a seminal moment for me. I may have garnered my initial courage from the pint of ale, but the boost to my confidence that followed came from the men-in-suit's disbelief that I had not already labelled myself a 'professional singer', or let a music label, or an agent, do so on my behalf.

I did *not*, thanks to this experience, become a professional singer overnight, but my destiny was sealed. I was *hooked*! I no longer wanted to be a sax player or a big-band leader, I wanted to be a singer and get 'high' every night on repeats of that standing ovation. That said, it wasn't just the audience's reaction that made me decide I wanted to add song to my sax-playing skills – and sing, it was the feeling of the performance experience itself. Holding the sax had always given me confidence, and now, as I moved on to become a singer, the microphone became my crutch.

I had just quit another job – this time at a factory manufacturing boots and shoes, because I was convinced that the required labour would, sooner or later, impede any hopes I had of becoming a successful bandleader. This bout of nerves had come about when I heard that another bloke had left the factory early one afternoon because his hand was so badly mangled – reduced to mincemeat

– after becoming trapped in one of the machines, and he had needed to be hospitalised. That was a fate I didn't want to share. How could a saxophone player play if he only had half his fingers – or was missing a hand?

Having left the factory – and seeking to earn more money in a less hazardous way – I tried my hand at selling televisions. That didn't last long. I wasn't very good at convincing people they should let me enter their homes with this still comparatively new amusement box and show them how I could plug it in and provide instant entertainment.

Who could have known then that, in the oncoming years, I would enter their living rooms on those television screens? But if any of my ex-customers did witness their former salesman performing when they were gathered around the television, this must have taken place at a neighbour's home, because I never sold a bloody TV in my life.

What little money I had in those days, I spent on sheet music, which I then took to a piano player called Kathy Boonham, and had her instruct me in what key to sing the song in, how to go from here to here, and how to get back to the coda.

'I'm *not* in the business,' I had warned her when we first met, wanting her to realise that she needed to be very explicit in her directions.

Once I felt I understood a number, I would carry the pages to a local club and ask the pianist to read the notes in the margin, and then accompany me in the one way, the only way, I knew how to sing the song. By then, 1953, I'd practised the songs and singing styles of the hit-recording artists of the day that I'd heard on radio, and, among others, I was endlessly singing Frankie Vaughn's hits of the day, gaining comfort from singing that even more loudly whenever I got the chance to stand on a stage, however rough the surroundings.

Lo and behold, at the age of seventeen, something at long last had started to happen to my looks! My nose began to unflatten itself and stand up on its own accord, and my Bugs Bunny teeth retreated to a more proper place behind my lips. As a result, I was becoming much more self-assured. So much so that, when I went out on my very first date, and the girl asked 'What do you do,

Arnold?' I replied, 'I'm a singer,' testing how it would feel to say such words with a modicum of confidence.

'*Really*?' Her lovely blue eyes with long black lashes gazed into mine and she was obviously impressed. 'Sing something for me,' she added.

I could have kicked myself! I should have anticipated such an obvious request and planned how I would deal with it, but I hadn't.

'*Sure*,' I said, trying to sound cool, but suddenly overcome by my usual shyness and having to resort to my usual solution. 'But I hope you won't mind if I turn my back on you.'

She didn't protest, but her eyelashes ceased to bat and her flirtatious smile faded and turned a wee bit wary.

Standing with my back to her, I sang, '*Wanted, someone to kiss and hold me closely* . . .' in my best possible bravado way, with Lothario-like gestures, the whole bit thrown in.

I have no idea how long she remained looking at my back before concluding I was absolutely round the bend and started to plot her escape, but by the time I turned around again she had buggered off and made a beeline across the park and was already at the bus stop. So my first date passed off without even a hand-hold, let alone the hoped-for goodnight kiss. Apparently, a serenade *isn't* a turn-on if your audience is asked to enjoy the show via the back of your head. I'd have to work on that one.

Elsewhere, too, my shyness always seemed to fracture my fragile self-confidence and, although my facial features were definitely on the move and improving, I hadn't quite achieved the height I'd always hoped to reach. I was still a bit of a titch – only 5 ft 7 in – and, oh, how I was *longing* to stand taller in my shoes.

CHAPTER THREE

I grew up in the Army, literally. By November 1956 when I was coming to the end of my two-year stint of National Service, I was 6 feet 1 ½ inches tall, a full two inches taller than I had been when I arrived as a new, eighteen-year-old recruit in Germany in 1954. But, even more importantly, I had matured in every sense of the word while living on the Army base.

At the time I was drafted, my search for a showbiz life was proving somewhat elusive, and I wasn't really worldly enough anyway to cope with the bizarre, free-for-all lifestyle that often goes with it. In the Royal Army Service Corps, however, I learned self-control and discipline, qualities that are essential for any human being who wants to stay on the rails. The Army routine kept me on the straight and narrow and, by the time I was demobbed, I had a much greater respect for myself, for others – and for life.

I was, nevertheless, very lucky to survive the experience! After eight weeks of 'bull', 'square-bashing' and unbelievably manic training, the draftees were gathered on a square in Borden to await their assignments. When the Sergeant Major blew his whistle, we had to fall into three columns, so that he could count us into batches of young men destined for different parts of the world's territories.

When the whistle blew, I started to move, praying that I would be selected for a post in Cyprus where one of my schoolfriends, Ivan Tibbles, who had lived in the same street as I did in Leicester, was already stationed.

As I stepped forward, though, I noticed to my horror that my bootlace had come undone, an unforgivable sin in the Army. Although the count-down for the next group of 24 soldiers had begun – 'one, two, three, four, five, six, seven, eight, *Malaya*' – I bent down to tie my lace, pulled down the gaiter, checked to see that my trouser leg was British Army-perfect and then ran to fall into line.

The Cyprus grouping ended just one lad before me, and I had to bite back my disappointment. Moments later, I was the first of the next batch to be assigned to Mulheim, Germany.

It was while I was en route there that I discovered that I had missed a certain-death experience. Word came through that the troops headed for Nicosia, in Cyprus, had never arrived. They had been ambushed after touching down on Cypriot soil, and all 24 of the young soldiers present had been killed.

I had trained with those recruits, knew them all personally, had shared their young hopes and dreams, and even performed for them. I'd entertained them with my impressions of different artists, such as Frankie Vaughan and Jerry Lewis. Corporal Johnny George, who was in charge of them, had played Dean Martin to my Jerry Lewis, so the sudden death of the entire group punctured my heart, gutted me and opened my eyes to how vulnerable life can be.

Once at the base, I learned to respect orders – never to arrive late for breakfast and, as a result, suffer famine and two-hours' boot shine; and never to mess with Sergeant Sam Chapman, known either as 'The Bull' or 'The Animal'.

It was a lot for a kid to learn and, although the Second World War was long over, being in the Army could still be a frightening way to come of age. On a number of occasions I had to ride a motorcycle through the night on an urgent delivery assignment, and I remember finding the long journeys on the lonely roads of Germany quite taxing on the nerves. As well as the *autobahn*, I was terrified of the total darkness of the cobbled side roads. I would be riding with my eyes wide open, but with my body flattened low against the bike, just in case one of those dark areas still had a war-time wire stretched across it or a missed, unexploded mine. I had a vivid imagination, had probably seen too many war films, which is not helpful in such circumstances, and the images I painted in my head were awful. My bent-over body also ached something rotten from the way I would ride. I was, however, certainly alert and, as a quick thinker, I made quite a good soldier. In a comparatively short time, I became an excellent marksman with a rifle and sten gun and a driver who was capable of handling military vehicle wheels even after long stretches of sleep-deprivation drills. Once, when we were out on manoeuvres, which lasted three days and three nights, only twelve out of the two hundred truck-drivers completed the arduous route, and I was one of them!

My attitude was: 'If I'm going to be a soldier, I'm going to be a *good* soldier. If tomorrow I find myself in a war zone, I will want to be able to do what I've been taught to do.' So I took my assignments seriously, and even though I didn't want to become a regular – and ultimately turned this opportunity down – I was proud that my attitude and skills led to an offer of a field commission, based on my ability 'to act instantly and without hesitation in dangerous situations'.

They say that in the face of extreme danger, people react with a 'fight or flight' mentality and, in 1954, the face of extreme danger for me belonged to Sergeant Chapman. As for fight or flight, I chose both.

The entire platoon feared Chapman's scowl, so I'm not quite sure what made me think I would be able to bang him up the backside and get a laugh out of him, or why – failing that – I should be daft enough to knock the wind out of him. There are some situations, I learned, where you can never win, even if at first you think you have – or can!

One day, when we were headed out on yet another manoeuvre, driving to a wooded area to enact a mock war, Chapman was in the jeep leading the convoy. As the driver of the second vehicle, who was following in his tracks, I misjudged the distance from the back bumper of his jeep and, when he pulled to a stop, I bumped into his vehicle. It was only a little bump, but I was about to learn you don't make such mistakes in the Army! Peering through the canvas flaps of the back of his semi-covered vehicle, I could see the back of his head, but I couldn't tell how he had taken it. I wasn't left in doubt for long. When he stepped out of the vehicle, he launched a tirade straight at me.

'*COME OUT HERE, YOU LITTLE BUGGER. I'M GOING TO TAKE YOU RIGHT HERE,*' he bellowed. '*I'M GOING TO TAKE YOU APART!*'

Now this was a man who was a talented wrestler, who had a reputation for knocking people on their arses before they even saw his fist coming.

'I'm *so* sorry, Sarge,' I replied, but it was clear from the way he was rolling his shirt sleeves up his thick, trunk-like forearms that he was not in a listening mood and was going to give me a real pasting.

I was actually capable of defending myself rather well. When I was a kid my dad used to put me in the ring with my older brother and allow each round to last well beyond the standard three minutes. I would be crying, absolutely bawling my eyes out, taking a beating, but he thought it would toughen me up and teach me self-defence.

It did.

As Chapman began to take a mighty swing at me, I blocked it with my bunched up fists and then smacked him one right in the stomach, sending the air gushing out of his lungs through his mouth, nose, and eye sockets, in an audible *WHOOOOOSH* like a puncture from a lilo. Then, before he could straighten up, I took off running.

Lying flat on my stomach in the soft, damp earth of the surrounding woods, I held up the convoy and instigated a two-hour search party. He was, I was sure of it, going to kill me, but I knew I would have to go back and face him in the end. This guy was one of the best motorcycle riders in the Service; he could do *anything* on a bike – bump up and down full flights of stairs, or ride with one wheel on the kerb, the other on the street. He was bold, courageous, and full of confidence and I looked up to him as a man and a soldier and I hated the thought that he was probably now looking down on me for being a 'yellow belly', for running off like a scared rabbit.

'Sarge, I'm *really* sorry. I didn't mean to do that,' I said when I gave myself up and stood trembling in front of him. 'It was an instinctive reaction, honest, and I was scared. I'm *sorry*.'

For a moment, he didn't move a muscle, just stood there, looking me straight in the eye. Then: 'All right,' he said, 'forget it. Get back in your lorry.'

And *THAT* was *THAT*.

Apparently he hadn't ended up hating me and, after that, we became good friends; and, still, all these decades later, we send each other Christmas cards every year, and he and his wife attend my concerts whenever they are in the vicinity of one of my venues.

When I ran into him about ten years after my demob from the Army – just as was I becoming a *BIG* success – he even offered to be my bodyguard.

'If you're looking for someone to drive you around, I'm your man,' he said.

He was still a massive man, definitely big enough to make anyone he protected feel they had nothing to fear while he was around.

'If I do ever take up your offer in the future, I'm certain I'd feel safe with you at my side,' I replied.

'Oh, I'd look after you all right,' he smiled.

I enjoyed the fact that I was able to look up to the British Army personnel. There was one officer in particular who was idolised by most of the platoon, who thought he was the cat's whiskers. His name was Captain Dick Otley and he was a fun-loving man who would tip us all out of bed whenever he came home with a few drinks inside him. He was a great athlete – and he had a lot of compassion for his men.

Those days in the Army were the first time I was really able to mix with such a diverse bunch of people and make a lot of friends, and I found that just wonderful. We would go into the Mess, where they had a jukebox, and just socialise and get to know one another. Elvis, who was also stationed in Germany, was often on the juke box – or in the news – and, what with 'Heartbreak Hotel' and 'Blue Suede Shoes', he was thought of – and treated – like a President, Royalty.

I had never given up on my dreams of being in show business and, even in the Army, I'd practise my saxophone in the billet and sing a bit to myself. One day the officer in charge of entertainment overheard me rehearsing for my future, and said: 'Come to my office. I need to speak with you.'

Putting my sax away, I duly reported, without having any idea of what was on his mind and what I might be letting myself in for.

'Listen,' he said, 'we're putting on a concert and I'd like you to perform.'

'What would you like me to do, sir?' I asked.

'What do you do best?' he replied.

'Well, I can play the saxophone, and I can sing, and I'm a bit of a comic as well. I think I could get by on a few impressions . . .'

And the matter was sealed.

But, *boy*, did those Mess Hall concerts prove to be a tough learning curve for me! The lads piled into the room and all personnel who tried to take the stage as entertainers were given a baptism by fire in which they risked 'raspberries', constant shouts and heckles, and getting booed off stage if their various performances did not quite come up to scratch! It took brave hearts – or thick skins – to face that lot! So, when I did my first fifteen-minute spot, I kept in mind how important it would be to win them over with a laugh, and I started with impressions of Dean Martin and Jerry Lewis, who were constantly featured together in movies during that time. I also continued to make fun of myself, before and after I sang, so I wouldn't get hissed with, 'Oh, look at him trying to be "Mr. Romance"' and, as a result, I earned their respect.

That was *great*. And this, of course, all added fuel and fire to my dreams and fantasies. I was in the Service, I didn't have to clock on in a factory, and I had plenty of time to work at honing my stage presence and performance skills because my military duties were often reduced to allow time for rehearsals. Thank God for that! Sometimes, my responsibilities were also lessened in order to let me sleep on for longer. More than once, I didn't arrive in the canteen for breakfast, and my superiors would explain they had assigned me to some sort of bunk detail in order to justify my absence. The real reason for my vacant seat, though, was exhaustion. I'd been up half the night with a bunch of them – and they knew they could trust me to keep my mouth shut. They often chose me as their driver when they went out to party at pubs, and bordellos (don't forget we were in the army) and they would thank me on red-eyed mornings, when it was time to get up when I'd barely put my head on the pillow, by allowing me to stay in my bunk and miss the drills that sergeants required of privates.

Quite often I would be absent from parade and our platoon officer would come along to find out what I was doing in the billet. When one of the officers, Lieutenant Danks, came to try and wake me up to report for duty, I asked him, 'Do you think you could tell the Sarge that you've detailed me in the billet?'

'Oh, very well,' he replied.

Those late nights spent visiting bars and brothels – followed by my late mornings staying in bed in the billet – became quite a habit.

* * *

Young servicemen, very much at the mercy of their raging hormones, *crave* women's company, but there is not much opportunity to form long-lasting romantic boy/girlfriend relationships. Unable to spend too much time shopping around for somebody who's willing to offer sweet comfort and companionship, I soon discovered that the quickest and easiest form of relief was to buy it.

Totally naive – and innocent – I didn't know a thing about a woman's body because, singularly lacking in curiosity, I hadn't ever got around to being inquisitive about the opposite sex when I was at school or thereafter. For example, I had no idea what a woman's breasts felt like because my first date (when I had hoped to establish this!) had passed without so much as a kiss.

Although visiting a brothel felt like a very wicked seedy thing to do, the other lads were talking about it so much, I figured I needed to join up and find out what all the fuss was about.

The first time was *scary* and I didn't really finish what I had started. You do not, I discovered, romance a prostitute. You are not even allowed to kiss her. The room, although softly lit by one red bulb, was charmless and totally basic. It looked like a shabby, low-priced hotel room in a down-market area. There was a washbasin in the corner which the red-haired prostitute, of ample body, pale flesh and indeterminate age, filled with tepid water before asking me to lean over while she gave me a quick, rough-handed wash down. That done, she pulled a rubber out of a packet and put it on me. It didn't even fit properly. I ended up pulling it off – and taking off – in an awful hurry. I hated the whole dreary, loveless, empty experience and, worse, it cost five marks, which I could ill afford at the time.

I am not, though, one to give up and, as it is important to me to be the best I can be at everything I do, whether it's playing golf or cricket, fencing, throwing darts or performing on stage, I saved some money, went to a nicer establishment, and gave it another go with a better-looking, slimmer, soft-skinned prostitute. This time, I got a glimmer of what all the fuss was about. It was not until I went to Antwerp in Belgium with the troop, however, to play cricket – and I met this 23-year-old Brigitte Bardot lookalike – that I *really* got the message.

My Brigitte Bardot was absolutely gorgeous. There was a dance in a local establishment after the cricket tournament, and that's where I first caught a glimpse of her seductive pouty lips and lovely dark hair. She was dancing with a decorated officer, but I somehow summoned up the courage to saunter over to her and mouthed, 'May I have the next dance?' without her partner seeing. She nodded a yes, so I backed off and waited until the dance ended. Then I quickly went up to her and said: 'Would you like to go for a walk?' and off we went for a stroll by the water's edge. She was wearing a flared skirt, and as I picked her up and placed her on one of the bollards along the jetty, the wind lifted her skirt and I could smell her perfume – body and bottle fragrances – and it was the most wonderful perfume I had ever smelled, coming from everywhere. It was *so* intoxicating, *so* arousing, it coursed through my whole being.

Later, after exchanging some truly passionate kisses, as we walked past a chapel, she said, 'Why don't we go in and say a prayer?'

I *am* a religious person, but prayer was the last thing on my mind at that moment – and I do hope I've been forgiven for the fact that prayer was not the only act of worship that took place inside that chapel that night.

As if making extramarital love in such a place was not sacrilegious enough, she then pouted her lips and confessed that she was a *married* woman. The whole event, though, was unbelievably romantic as well as sexually exciting. She was the first woman I was truly aroused by, and I remember her address to this very day!

About three months later, by which time my feelings for her had cooled, her Volkswagen Beetle showed up outside the gates of my barracks.

'You're in *big* trouble, young man,' a guard informed me, smirking. 'There's a young lady, who's been looking all over the place for you. She wants to tell you she's in *the club* – pregnant.'

I couldn't understand why she hadn't mentioned this in one of her letters. I was only eighteen and so naive I didn't think I could get anyone pregnant on the very first time we had sex.

'The young lady' continued to appear outside the gates for a whole week, but I never went out and faced up to her. I let the guards deal with her for me.

She had scared the daylights out of me. I didn't want to take on the responsibility of a child – that may not have been my child – at such an age, and I was very scared as to what my parents might think of me. I was not worldly-wise and didn't know what to do, so I did nothing.

'If I try to go out on the town,' I thought, 'I will be done for. I'd have to exit out of the front gate, which would mean passing her.'

As I was terrified of a confrontation – and kept going hot under the collar every time I thought of her – I stayed in the barracks. All sorts of thoughts kept coming into my head: 'Perhaps she's not pregnant at all. Perhaps she's just using that as an excuse to trap me – to get me to stay with her.'

Looking back, though, I think she was a genuine girl who felt for me in the same way that I had felt for her when I first met her, but any feelings I might have had re-kindled, changed when she showed up at those gates.

There may be a chip off the Arnold George Dorsey block living somewhere in the world. I do *not* know – and I have never wanted to know. What I *do* know is that the whole scenario seeded my 'Casanova' status – a reputation that followed me throughout my days in the Army and forever after.

After 'Brigitte Bardot', there was a German woman, a farmer's wife, who enticed me into her bed with a sob story and a sweet.

There I was innocently idling away the time in my royal Army vehicle, parked on the outskirts of her land, when she opened her front door and, holding out a dish of strawberries covered with lashings of cream, said: 'Are you hungry?'

'No, I'm fine, thank you kindly,' I replied curtly, but I did accept the fruit she held out.

Watching me as I dipped the spoon into the bowl, she began to tell me the tragic tale of her child who was in hospital with some kind of awful wasting disease. Her husband, she kept sighing, obviously suffered from some kind of genetic problem and was incapable of producing a healthy child with her, which was rather sad really.

'This would not be a problem for you,' she informed me, smiling. 'With your green eyes, the same colour as mine, you look like a *very* capable young man. You are the kind of man I would like to have a child with. Why don't you come in?'

We were still in her rumpled bed – pillows adrift, empty dish and spoon upturned, and clothes that had missed the back of the chair lying about all over the place – when we heard the dogs barking, signalling her husband, the farmer's return.

I dressed in such a hurry that I put both my feet into one leg of my pants, and then made the weights at the ends of my trousers ring the strawberry bowl like a bell. My Frau, on the other hand, still found time to reprimand me for my clumsiness while twisting hospital corners in the battered sheets. Obviously well practised, she had finished making the bed before I had even located my left boot.

Shooing me into the next room, she pointed to a chair, shoved a cup of cold coffee in my hand, and threw a checked blanket over my lap. So, there I was, sitting in the corner by the fire, looking as innocent and as boyish as I could manage, trying to give the impression that there was no dodgy business going on, when the farmer made his entrance. A tall, burly guy, carrying a shotgun over one arm, he did not immediately bring to mind the adjectives 'inadequate' or 'incapable'. Throwing me a look that could have frozen the coffee I was holding, he even managed to hush the dogs with a deep bellow.

Reaching out to touch the arm that wasn't acting as a gun rack, his wife proceeded to explain the situation, and her convincingly, casual tone was certainly tailor-made to give the impression that there was nothing naughty going on. I only understood a little German, but I caught the gist of what she was saying: 'The soldier, such a *young, homesick* lad, was *very* cold outside, so I brought him in to warm him up.'

The poor bugger who was unlucky enough to be her husband did not have a clue just how she had gone about warming me up.

One way or another, then, Germany helped me to grow up, and I made some everlasting friendships with a lot of my fellow servicemen. At a recent show in Southend, Essex, for example, I was chuffed when I was leaving the venue – a full two hours after the show ended – to find a Mulheim buddy, Willie Williams, and his wife waiting to say hello to me and compliment me on my performance.

I hadn't seen this man for 47 years, and we instantly began reminiscing about our days on the base, recalling stories in such fine detail that it was like they'd happened just a few days ago.

He reminded me of 'discharge days', when dressed in our newly pressed uniforms, with our boots so polished we could see our faces in them, we would all say goodbye to the groups of officers or corporals who had just finished their years of service. To this day, I still have one Army buddy – Bob Blevins – who e-mails me on an almost daily basis. He became a very good friend of my parents, often visiting them when I was away and chatting to them for hours. When my mother died, he sent a wreath and attached the white cap that he always used to wear when he visited her. He was a brilliant boxer, with the best set of biceps you could ever hope to see in a ring, and I admired him. Besides that, it was good to have a boxer on my side in the Army, in case I got into trouble, especially as 'trouble' could break your nose, realign your face, or mess up your sax-playing hands!

One night on the base, I was Orderly Corporal, which meant that I was in command of the night duty. On this particular evening, a guy called Ronnie Hart, who was one of the hard men was playing up a bit, throwing plates at people and so on, and I had to deal with him and then get the orderly officer to straighten things out. So, for revenge, he challenged me to a fight in the ring. Ronnie was a real tough nut and I knew if I let him get close to me he'd give me a 'Glasgow kiss' or two, that is, nut me with his head harder than I could ever punch him with my fist.

I tried my hardest to box him according to the rules, but Ronnie was a 'dirty' fighter who succeeded in pinning me against the ropes in the corner and, although I put both my hands up to protect myself, he went *thump-thump-thump* and nutted me. My nose was busted – and there was blood cascading down my face.

'Come on, Gerry!' he yelled, using the nickname I'd been given after doing my Jerry Lewis impressions, then he continued to pummel his fists into my face. Moments later when he brought his knee up and smacked it into my groin, I doubled up in agony and, taking a step back, I pulled off my gloves off and stood there swaying, unable to see anything for the blood in my eyes.

I was beaten, but only because he was a hard case and a 'dirty' fighter who was not interested in boxing by the rules. Later on, when I told my friend Bob Blevins, the champion boxer, this story, he took that guy in the ring and beat the living daylights out of him. Bob has been my friend ever since. Actually Ronnie became my friend as well, but some years later I heard he had been involved in the Great Train Robbery and that he eventually went to prison for killing a man.

During those two years in the Army I really missed my dad and mum and, although they were still young then, I kept thinking I must get home soon because they were getting old! Young people have a very strange perspective on age. I was totally dedicated to my family and, when I came out of the Army in November 1956, I went straight back home to live with my parents and got a job working in an engineering factory. By then, instead of being called Arnold, my first name, I was encouraging everybody to call me Gerry, the nickname I had earned in the Army. The new name appealed to me because it made me feel as if I was entering a new phase in my life, and also because my sister Bubbles had a boyfriend called Jerry, who I looked up to and who always seemed to know exactly what to say and how to act.

My thinking was: if my demob from the Army meant leaving behind all the wonderful times I had experienced performing for the lads in the canteen and having to take life more seriously, then the least I could do was to cheer myself up and sport a new name. This would be a daily reminder of what I was still determined to be, an entertainer who would charm bums off seats with brilliant performances. It was all a far cry from my new job in a Leicester factory, but I was still young, and the young live in hope!

CHAPTER FOUR

'God damn it, your tan beats mine hands down.'

As far as chat-up lines go, at least this was original – and so it needed to be. When I first laid eyes on the very pretty brunette Patricia Healey at the Palais de Danse, in Leicester, in 1956, when I was just twenty, I knew at once that I wanted her to find me mysterious and irresistibly attractive! This was a time when I enjoyed making things up and playing different characters. Army life had done me a world of good, but I was still painfully shy and, that night, my new-found self-confidence seemed to desert me just when I needed it. Even though I kept reminding myself I was 'Gerry Dorsey, Man of Self-assuredness and Bold Backbone', I could not quite manage to summon up the superhero that resided within me! Better, I decided, to let my friend, Ivan Tibbles, make the opening gambits – and, having shooed him off to ask Patricia if she would dance with me, I stood in the shadows, watching and waiting for her reaction.

'To win this girl's attention, I have to be somebody,' I was lecturing myself as Ivan returned with Patricia in tow. And, panicked into coming up with a somebody, I disguised my British accent, took on a GI drawl and came out with that chat-up line to compliment her on her gorgeous tan.

'Jesus!' she exclaimed. 'Where are you from?'

It was not quite the reaction I had anticipated.

'In-di-ana,' I drawled.

Why I decided to pretend I was American, I will never know! I'd never been across the pond and knew nothing of the great Wild West apart from what I had seen on the big screen. All I knew was that I felt an urgent need to put on airs and graces, and pretend to be somebody – anybody – other than who I was. Patricia, the woman who was to become the love of my life and who would one day become my wife and the mother of my four children, fell for the whole caboodle.

Or did she?

Later I found out that she had 'smelt a rat', so to speak, and, although she agreed to come with me on a date to the cinema the following night, she told her friends she didn't quite know what to make of me.

'He's a handsome, swarthy, well-tanned fella,' she told them, 'who looks smashing in his white suit – and he has a great smile – but there's something odd about him!'

She should talk! When I walked her home, after the dance on that first night, she threw me when we arrived at the entrance of the muddy lane that led to the house by pausing and reaching about underneath the hedge.

'What on earth . . .?' I began but, before I could finish the sentence, up she popped with the pair of wellies she had stashed there at the beginning of the evening when she changed into her dancing shoes.

'Hey,' I drawled, 'you don't need those now that I am here,' and, with no more ado, I hoisted her clear of the mud onto my shoulders. As we walked up the lane, leaving Patricia's wellies under the hedge, her sister, June, accompanied by her boyfriend, Derek Whitehead, shot past us on a motorbike. Needless to say, their jaws fell open at the sight of us.

Apparently, June rushed on ahead into the house and said, 'Mum, our Pat is coming down the road with somebody in a white suit, and she's sitting on its shoulders!'

'ITS'! Can you beat that?

But, perhaps that's why, when Patricia came to meet me for our first date at the cinema, she arrived half an hour early and hid by the café across the street. By doing that, she could get another look at me and see what she was letting herself in for.

As for me, I soon discovered that Patricia was one of the most uninhibited people I had ever met in my entire life. This was a girl who never flinched, who spoke her mind, and who, when my sisters encircled her to size her up, endeared herself to my entire family by taking on all comers. This included my father who, at that time, was always grumbling about my showbiz dreams and saying, 'He should get a proper job'.

'No, Dad, he will do whatever he wants to do,' Patricia retorted. 'He's got a mind of his own.'

That's how she was then – and that's how she is now!

When she was seven, Patricia used to scale the fruit trees in local orchards at night with her friends and expertly consume the apples without even removing them from the branches. They called themselves 'The Black Hand Gang', and would chortle, 'The Black Hand Gang Strikes Again.' Then off they'd go, leaving perfectly eaten cores hanging, like weird Christmas-tree ornaments, from the boughs. This behaviour continued until a neighbour caught them at it, red-handed, and forced them to jump down into a patch of stinging nettles!

She had a lovely family, although sadly her parents were separated. But by coincidence her father had also been stationed in India as had my dad and her mother, who was such a support to her when I was away on the road, used to work in a café. I realised immediately that Patricia, whom I nicknamed Popea (pronounced Popia) on the night of our very first date, and whom I have called the Pope in the years since – was quite a catch.

After I left the Army, I was determined that my life should remain dual, that although I needed to work during the week in Cannon & Stokes's engineering factory, which was responsible for turning out Rolls-Royce airplane parts, I would still do the club circuits in Nottingham or Derby at the weekends. Civvy street was not, to say the least, an easy transition. I had enjoyed the camaraderie of the army – and loved the evenings that I had spent entertaining the troops in the canteen – and I now hated with an equal passion the drudgery, the everyday sameness of being in a factory. The oils used in the job were a constant peril to life and limb. They coated us as well as the machinery and were nearly impossible to remove. All the workers ended the days with hands that were coated in black grease, and arms splattered in spots of oil that had spluttered from the lathe. The only way to clean up was to steam your arms and hands over a boiling kettle, and wait until the oil was hot enough to wipe off before it started to burn the skin off beneath. It was to say the least a painful business and I was terrified that the cleaning-off-oil ritual would damage my hands and put paid to my sax-playing days – and that the factory fumes would wreck my vocal chords just at the moment I had started singing in the local clubs.

Nevertheless, needs must, and, Monday to Fridays, I would work at the factory and then trip off to Sheffield on Saturday to do three shows at working men's clubs in the evening, followed by three shows on Sunday afternoon and three shows in the evening, and then return to Leicester at the crack of dawn on Monday's milk train.

If I had enough money, I would get board and lodging in digs on Saturday nights but, for the most part, I could not afford to do this, and I ended up sleeping on railway-station benches, or in telephone boxes (not an easy feat when you are as tall as I am), or even in public lavatories. Unsavoury is not really an adequate enough word to describe the latter experience!

The nights in the telephone boxes, however, were the worst. They were always freezing cold and I had to sit on my case or lean against the chilly glass while I tried to get some shuteye. On such occasions, I always reached up and unscrewed the light bulb so that the passers-by could not see me shivering to death inside. Curiously, I was never disturbed by anybody wanting to make a short- or long-distance phone call – and nobody tried to urinate in them while I was inside!

Throughout this period, I always kept the suitcase containing my stage clothes and grooming gear in pristine order, and I somehow managed to give myself such a thorough squeaky clean wash 'n' brush-up that nobody in the audience ever guessed that I had spent the night on a park bench, or in a telephone box or a public convenience.

The much-repeated press story that I used to sneak out of dressing-room windows in the working men's clubs after giving a performance has now become legendary. The truth is I had to escape in this way not to avoid paying my bills, but to preserve my good manners! Club audiences often honoured performers by buying them a drink and, if the entertainer was worth his salt, he would then be expected to reciprocate by ordering the next round. I just couldn't afford to squander my hard-earned money on appreciative audiences. So, not wishing to appear mean or rude, I would disappear to the dressing-room, where I would wash my shirt for the next day – and do any necessary grooming for the night – then I would open the window, drop my suitcase out and crawl through after it. Luckily for me, I was never asked to perform in a two-storey venue.

Inevitably, during these days, I often missed the train home, or I got back so late on Sunday that I overslept on Monday. As a result, I was perpetually late arriving at the factory, which was a three-mile run from my house. My legs, which became rail-thin white stalks from all these exertions, were in such sharp contrast to the well-tanned, muscular upper body that I'd developed performing manual tasks in the Army that Pope used to say I looked like a mushroom.

The factory boss's son, Tony Baldwin, would try to save my arse by clocking on and starting my work for me at the factory, and he would even meet me at the front door to try to block my entrance by walking in front of me. This kind ruse, however, never really worked. I was taller than Tony and, even when I crouched down to shunt along behind him, I could still be seen. As if that wasn't enough of a giveaway, the other workers would bang their tools on their machines, which made one hell of a din and caused the boss to look down from his office window to see who was being tardy. Despite this, every single Monday morning, Tony, who knew I could not afford to lose out on the first fifteen minutes' pay, would attempt the same sneaky routine.

Popea, worked in an office and earned £10 a week, which was a small fortune in those days. Even after paying her mum for her board, she still had enough to buy a motorbike on HP (Hire Purchase). When she heard that the Isle of Man was hosting a talent contest, she bought me a new pair of shoes and a packet of ciggies and off we went to try my luck. When I won the £75 prize money – and a free holiday to the Isle of Man – we were thrilled to the marrow.

It was 1959, not as yet the so-called permissive 60s, known for free love, and unmarried couples were never allowed to sleep together in respectable premises. When we set off on that holiday on Patricia's motorbike, which she always allowed me to drive, it was bucketing down with rain. Absolutely soaked, we knocked on the door of an impressively big house that had a B & B board swinging outside.

When a kind-looking woman, a Mrs May by name, came to the door, I swallowed hard and, indicating Patricia, who could have been a man, dressed as she was in motorbike clothes – nylon trousers and anorak – and still wearing a crash helmet, I said: 'Could my mate and I get out of the rain and stay the night?'

There was a brief pause, while Mrs May eyed Patricia up and down, but then, as we held our breath, she said: 'OK – there's a summerhouse in the garden that's got two made-up bunk beds in it. You can sleep in there if you like.'

The next morning when I was in the kitchen alone, paying the bill, just for the bed not the breakfast, she couldn't resist letting me know that she knew Patricia was a girl – and that she hadn't had the heart to turn us away.

After that, we used to go back there quite regularly. But we never graduated from the summerhouse to the house!

On another occasion when we went away for a weekend, we borrowed my brother's motorbike, but the damn thing broke down on the way there. Having wheeled it into a garage, the mechanic said, 'I won't be able to get that fixed until tomorrow.'

'Oh, Lord!', I muttered desperately. 'We haven't got any money to stay another night.'

'Then you'll have to come back to my house and sleep in the front room,' he said, as if this was the most natural response in the world.

That's how people were then – generous and open and so much less fearful of strangers than they are now. Some people say they were also much nosier because they used to ask so many questions. But they weren't; they were just more interested in other people's lives then. The Pope and I met so many people who took a liking to us. Maybe it was because we were so happy and open ourselves and had honest faces. Later on in my career, one of my landladies, who ran digs, really took a shine to me and named her dog Engelbert after me! She had two friends, Percy Simmons and Ronnie Dorsey (no relation), who were dubbed 'the two Robin Hoods' and, to this day, Percy still calls and visits us. They were all larger-than-life characters, who were always happiest when they were helping people out and doing something for nothing.

Winning that contest in the Isle of Man gave my confidence a tremendous boost and added fuel to my growing conviction that I was ready for the next step: that it was time for me to leave

Leicester and go to London to prove my mettle on stage there. By then, I was going down really well in the local working men's clubs and, although my dad knew and was proud that the members really liked what I was doing, he was not happy with my announcement that I was off to London and he gave me dire warnings that I could end up on the streets. Whatever I said in reply, he made it abundantly clear that he disapproved of my decision to quit a solid job at the factory for a mere fancy and a dream.

As it turned out, however, I didn't have to quit my job. After a weekend talent contest, when I arrived at the factory late yet again for another Monday morning, the manager at Cannon & Stokes said, 'It's okay, lad, you don't need to run to work any longer, you're FIRED!' Then, creating a scene that was designed to make me look just like a 'dead man walking', he gave me my last pay packet and led me down the corridor, out of the door and into a NEW LIFE!

CHAPTER FIVE

During my very first performance in London, knickers were everywhere! The stage looked as if it was covered in panty confetti and, offstage, there were plenty of half-dressed women milling around the dressing-room. But all this was to be expected – I was singing in a strip joint!

The plan was that I'd get a manager and a spot on a television show right away, and my career would immediately start taking off. I had not, however planned on sharing a dressing room with all the strippers at The Gargoyle or the Windmill, where 'taking off' was certainly a nightly theme, yet was not a command directed at me and had little to do with my career. Still, I had no complaints! It was nice work if you could get it and the strippers and their antics were forever creasing me up and making me laugh.

The girls really were very nice to me – and not just because I propped open the dressing-room door for them when they darted off stage – 'Hold the door, darling! Just going for a pee!' – or because I didn't bat an eyelid when they pulled a knicker leg aside and used the washbasin as a makeshift commode, they liked me and enjoyed my singing!

One night, I slipped on the step outside the dressing-room and, as I landed with a thump on my bum, one of the more genuinely well-endowed, Dolly Parton-type girls hurried over to give me a helping hand.

'Come on, darling,' she said, smiling sweetly at me, 'let me help you.' And as she bent down to give me a yank up, I got a wonderful face full of her substantially deep cleavage and a breast in my ear. I began to think that in show business, it was easier to get a boob in the ear than a foot in the door. Such moments made the days spent getting shot down at auditions a little less unpleasant!

Before I left Leicester I intentionally saved enough money to spend that first week in London, £5 a night, at the plush Grosvenor House Hotel on Park Lane. The idea behind this was that I could do the rounds of managers and agents, in the hope that I would find one who would want to represent me, and that he would be so impressed by my temporary accommodation and Mayfair telephone number that he would add me to his books straightaway. My game plan was to get a spot on a television show so that my career would be given a mega boost and take off before my money ran out. Well, I was young – and very foolish, too!

I obviously couldn't afford to stay at the Grosvenor for more than a few nights, and I was very lucky to meet Jean Young when I was singing at The Aster Club, where, a few years later, I would say to the booking agent there: 'This guy, this friend of mine, is a great singer. He's going to be a big star, and you should book him.'

Who was I talking about? Myself? No. It was TOM JONES, the Welsh ex-miner who made it to No. 1 in February 1965, swivelling his sexy hips and belting out 'It's Not Unusual'!

When I told Jean I was looking for a place to stay, she phoned her mother, who invited me to board with them in Holloway in North London. When I eventually left them, though, I very nearly starved to death. I had got into the habit of being spoilt by Mrs Young with her fabulous breakfasts. She was so good to me and I have never forgotten the smell and the taste of those wonderful egg, bacon, sausage, mushroom and fried-bread fry-ups. They were unbelievably good.

It was Jean who, in all innocence, introduced me to a gay agent, who tried to hit on me!

As a general rule, I have always believed that a person's sexual orientation – and preferences – are their own business, but in those days many of the most influential people in the entertainment business tried to make their preferences our business, whether we, the would-be performers, were up for it or not.

Along with countless others, I soon learned the sad truth that refusing such sexual advances had an impact – and took its toll – on any success we might have enjoyed in the business. We were all only too aware of this problem and we all knew if you put your foot down, you'd never get a leg up on the competition!

The agent Jean introduced me to was the kingpin of a very successful and highly regarded theatrical agency. Renowned for his 'hits' on the unwary, desperate hopefuls, he always made a point of screening new talent in his very posh, opulently furnished, Mayfair apartment that was dripped with chandeliers and other crystal artefacts. Thankfully for me, however, he made the fatal mistake of removing his coke-bottle, horn-rimmed glasses before trying to chase me around the bed. Moments earlier, he had set the specs on a little nightstand as he pulled a tube of K-Y jelly out of a drawer.

'Come over here,' he murmured.

I desperately wanted a job, but I was having none of it. Turning to face the opposite direction, I headed towards the door.

'I'm sorry,' I muttered as I did so, 'I really must go.'

But his blood, so to speak, was UP.

'No! Don't do that! Come here. Come here!' he uttered, starting to run around the room to block my exit.

Fortunately, as he was as blind as a bat without his glasses, he went one way around a settee, while I went the other – and out of the door.

'Damn him!' I muttered as I headed for the tube.

Needless to say, I never heard from him again and I never got any work from his agency, although his office did refer me to another agent, Sidney Myers, who was based in the same building.

But it would not be the last time I had such close encounters.

This, to say the least, was a humbling, trying time for me, especially as I had departed Leicester with such high hopes and the conviction that I was about to get the BIG break. Now, instead of living it up and being able to phone mum and dad and Popea, who was living back at home in Queneborough, proud as Punch, I was down on my heels – busted.

Every single audition ended in agony. I failed over and over again to get any work. I should have taken more note of the casting directors when I appeared for an audition on the then popular TV show, *Opportunity Knocks*, the show that gave so many performers their big break into showbiz. My audition judges, though, either sat there yawning or actually winced throughout my rendition of Pat Boone's 'Love Letters in the Sand', and it would probably have been even worse if I'd chosen to sing Pat's 'Friendly Persuasion'. As it was, I continued to sing, 'My broken heart aches . . . with every wave that breaks . . .' and I flopped.

Many years later, when I met Pat Boone at a golf tournament, I said: 'You know, Pat, I loved your singing and your performances and your records so much that when I was trying to get started I took one of your songs to every audition and every time I bloody failed. I just couldn't sing the songs like you, no matter how hard I tried.' He just smiled, but I could tell he was pleased and flattered!

Times, then, were actually getting perilously tough, and the money I had saved was rapidly disappearing. When I was sixteen, my sister Olga had bought me a Martin saxophone, which was an upgrade from the one my father had kindly purchased for me when I was eleven. I really prized the new instrument, which I took with me to Germany and practised on so often in the barracks and played so often on stage that its pads ended up falling out. One of the officers in charge of me, Captain Dick Otley, took pity on me, a mere lowly-paid private, partly because he wanted me to continue performing for the troops, but mostly because he could see how much I cherished that horn, and he dipped into his own pocket to have it repaired when it was no longer playable. Since those days it had always been my constant companion, always at my side, but when the hard times arrived in London and I couldn't afford to pay the rent for my room, I had to pawn my saxophone in order to survive and get a few shillings for my rent.

'I'll be back to collect this shortly,' I kept saying to the bloke behind the counter. 'I'll be back very shortly – as soon as I've got a bit of money.'

But the timespan was not as short as I had hoped. By the time I returned to collect my beloved sax, I was too late. It had been sold – and my heart was broken. Leaning against the wall outside that shop, I had to put my fist in my mouth to fight back the sobs and the waiting tears. At last, when I had got enough money in my pocket to redeem it, it was gone. My old friend was doing the rounds elsewhere – was lost to me forever.

It was 1958, when I was twenty-two, before I finally got a real shot at the entertainment business. I managed to get a 42-week Tuesday-night spot on a TV show called *Song Parade with the Grenadiers* thanks to my agent, Sidney Myers. On this show, I sang the hits – whatever song was topping the charts that week or had been the week before. Standing there in the spotlights, with the fabulous dancing Grenadiers sashaying behind me, I sang my way into many a British home. Television, which I truly believe is *the* best form of exposure to get us showbiz people known, certainly left me feeling that I was on the verge of making it, and that Gerry Dorsey would become a household name after all.

Prior to my appearances on *Song Parade*, Sidney Myers of Foster's Agency recognised that I had a certain appeal as a pop singer and offered to become my agent. Foster's was one of the biggest theatrical agencies in the business and Sidney, who had taken a real shine to me, also offered me a room at the elegant apartment, which he shared with his wife Stella Hartman on the Edgware Road in Maida Vale, generously offering to accept a deferral of the payment of rent at the same time.

By then I was very grateful to have the offer of a roof over my head; I kept saying: 'I've no idea how I'll ever pay you for everything, Mr Myers.' He just shrugged, looked at me kindly, and replied: 'Don't worry about that. If you become a success, my son, you'll pay me back tenfold.'

Sidney, an immaculately dressed man with a very big heart, took me out for lunch the very first afternoon he met me. I will never forget the moment at the end of the meal, when he held the bill with one hand and reached into his pocket with the other, and pulled out a thick bundle of notes that were even more perfectly pressed than his suit.

Good God, I thought, he must be rolling in it! I had never seen so many clean, crisp, new notes – no creases in them, no corners turned up, all seemingly unused. They looked as if they'd come straight from the Royal Mint.

Thus far, it seemed, I was destined to be a 'kept' man! My dole money, in between the meagre jobs, did not go far and Pope, bless her, who had never lost faith in me, had been paying for just about everything. Now, however, the meticulous Mr Myers – the longed-for theatrical agent who, thank the Lord, was 'straight' – was taking me out to get my hair cut and my nails done.

'Yes, please,' I had said when he offered to take me for a manicure, although I had no idea what that was. Thank heavens he had not offered a pedicure – I wouldn't have wanted any girl to get up close and personal with my feet, which were displaying a fine array of corns and blisters from all the trudging around I had been doing from one audition to the next!

And, oh, how I ate at his house! Stella prepared nothing but the best – splendid fry-ups of lox (smoked salmon) and eggs, and often there was a dish of juicy bacon set by my plate. As practising Jews they didn't eat bacon, but they went out of their way to provide it for me. I stayed with them – stretched out in the lap of luxury – for a very happy six months.

Stella was a fellow singer who performed in summer-season shows, and it was she who helped me do the rounds of the different recording studios. I am certain the people in those studios only gave me a chance because she made it so clear that she doted on me and my voice. In the event, she proved to be the only one, though! Everything I recorded, from an early attempt with Decca even to the ones I did for EMI with Norman Newell, the brilliant songwriter and impresario, was a total flop.

Going into the recording studio in those days was somewhat different from how it is these days, mainly because the technological advances have been so great. Nowadays, all the music is recorded separately and you usually lay down the vocal tracks on a different occasion. Back in the late 50s, early 60s, everything was recorded together, so it was vital that you concentrated in order to give as professional a performance as the orchestra playing behind you.

When the records I cut with Norman didn't become immediate hits, I had to hit him for a loan.

'I need some money, Norman, to pay my rent,' I stated, thinking that what I was about to say was normal business practice. 'Can you let me have an advance on my royalties?'

'What royalties?' he guffawed.

There weren't any – not even one.

'But, Norman, how am I going to survive?' I wailed.

This was the moment for Norman to reveal his true preferences. Falling in line with some of the other managers and agents I had met, he grinned and suggested, 'You know you don't have to live this way, you could come and live with me.' Unlike the others, however, Norman is far too much a gentleman to try to coerce me into believing that 'a roll in the hay' could be a dandy way of taking the kink out of my financial straits.

'You don't have to live this way,' he cooed. 'I have space enough and money enough for both of us.'

'Oh, stop it, Norman. Cut that out,' I retorted smiling.

I wasn't worried that this particular man would take a rebuttal of his advances badly and hold it against me. Norman was different – generous and kind-hearted – and he turned out to be one of the most important people in my life. When everyone else in the business was slamming doors in my face, he never failed to come to my rescue.

'All right, all right,' he said laughing aloud. 'I'll write you a cheque for seventy-five pounds. Yeah? Will that do for now?'

It saved my bacon – and covered my rent for three months.

A decade later, when so-called 'overnight' success finally swept me off my feet, I remembered his unfailing generosity and decided to pay him back by recording some of his songs for my albums. I felt – and I think he would have agreed – that it would have been tacky for us to sit down with a calculator and chequebook attempting to tally the true figure of what I owed him from the old days. Besides, what he had given me then was not calculable in pounds, shillings and pence. He was a true friend when I was in need – in every sense of the word. Nobody could have been more thrilled than I was, when, during that period, millions of my records sold and he regained his money – a thousand times over – and I regained my pride. I have never taken advantage of anyone's kindness, and Norman was one of the kindest. Pope always refers to him as 'an absolute sweetheart' – and he was. It wasn't just the artists, like Judy Garland, that loved him – all the girls flocked to him like he was the bee's knees.

One day, Sidney sent me to audition for an appearance on Jack Good's TV show, *Oh Boy*, which was a great success throughout the 50s and a shop window for many up-and-coming artists who succeeded in getting a spot on it. At one time or another, every major star who came over from America did guest appearances on the show, and home-grown stars, such as Cliff Richard and Tommy Steele, were regulars.

Following the audition, 21 February 1959 proved to be a truly special, lucky day for me. Jack Good added *my* name to his list of people who had guest spots and he invited me to give a rendition of the very popular Harbach and Kern number 'Smoke Gets in Your Eyes' on his show.

On the night, totally unfamiliar with television productions, I went into a blind panic backstage when I heard the studio audience screaming their heads off ecstatically at the performers who had gone on before me. I'd been instructed to make my entrance by appearing at the top of a flight of grand white stairs, then descend in time to the song's intro. I was then supposed to begin singing the first note of the song the moment my shiny, slippery-soled shoes touched down on the stage. But, to my horror, I realised there was *no* way I would be able to hear or count the introductory bars over the manic screams and shouts of the audience. Having broken out in a cold, clammy sweat, I grabbed Stan Jones, a member of the Dallas Boys' singing group, the show's veterans.

'I'll never hear the introduction over that din,' I gasped. 'I've got an eight-bar intro and I have to walk down all those stairs and . . .' I broke off, trembling from head to foot. This was such an important night for me and I couldn't afford to screw up.

'Tell you what,' Stan said, trying to console me, 'I'll stand by the camera and count those bars on my fingers. Then you can watch me instead of trying to listen to the music.'

There was no alternative – I had to agree – but I was still so nervous that another of the Dallas Boys literally had to push me on to my mark and propel me down the stairs. There I was, my BIG moment, at the top of the grand steps, trying to be debonair and look like a showbiz natural while I gaped at Stan tapping out his finger down below.

God help me!

At the bottom step, I barely heard my cue note, and I could only take off, praying that I'd inherited some of my father's mathematical skills and that I'd come in on target.

'They-y-y-y asked me how I knew . . .' I began and, miraculously, it was right on cue!

The audience probably did not appreciate what had gone into this amazing feat, as they just continued screaming in ecstasy from the beginning to the end of the song. In fact, there was such a din, I doubt that they could have heard a single note I sang, but I am sure the people watching at home heard, because the microphone was linked directly to the recording desk and the sound flowed straight into the homes of what I hoped would be my new-found fan base.

I wanted to be heard by everyone, of course, but I didn't mind the screaming one bit. It was my first introduction to such ear-piercing shrieks and I was overjoyed to be the cause of some of them. I found the screaming girls very arousing, very exciting, and I hoped this was something that would follow me throughout my career. Just like the roar of the crowd at a football match, screaming fans charge your batteries and boost your performance.

The higher we rise, we are told, the harder we fall, and in-between jobs, the time actors call 'resting', was tough – and far from restful. At the very least, however, thanks to my appearances on *Song Parade* and *Oh Boy*, I felt more at ease in myself and more worthy of being in the company of other young performers, many of them destined to be the major players of the future; and, although it was tough for me as an entertainer who had not got a hit record under his belt to survive on the merit of a few television shows, at least I was able to go on tour with Adam Faith, known for his hit 'What Do You Want', which he sang as 'Vot do you Vant?' and Marty Wilde of 'Donna' and 'Teenager in Love' fame. And, on these short but sweet tours around the country, I continued singing the hit pop songs of the day.

By then, I had given my all to landing a hit record myself, but I had only succeeded in making five flops with five different labels, which included 'Mr Music Man' with Decca and Johnnie Ray's 'I'll Never Fall in Love Again' with Parlophone.

It was while I was on one of the steamed up, smoke-filled tour buses that I met two people who would become very important in my career – and my life. The first was a piano player called Les Reed, who, along with Barry Mason, eventually wrote 'The Last Waltz', which was a No. 1 for me, and 'Les Bicyclettes de Belsize', and 'It's Not Unusual', a No. 1 for Tom Jones. Barry and Les turned out to be more than just dear friends; they were my saviours.

The second was Gordon Mills, who was then on tour with The Viscounts, the all-male singing group who had two chart hits, 'Shortnin' Bread' and 'Who Put the Bomp (in the Bomp, Bomp, Bomp)'. Gordon went on to become an agent/manager and started to represent Tom Jones and, later still, me.

We had some fun times together moving from here to there in shabby old buses that always smelled of our aftershaves and hair creams. The only entertainment on offer as the miles sped by came in the form of card games and gambling – and when I indulged in this with the members of the John Barry Seven an English group, it got me into heavy debt and cost me my entire wages on that trip! However ghastly the journeys and the tours were, though, I still felt I was making some headway – moving along.

When I wasn't on the road, I sought out any local club gigs that were on offer, and Tony Cartwright, someone whom I met through Gordon Mills and who later become my roadie (road manager), used to help me find my way around Tin Pan Alley. This name, which was originally given to a district in New York situated between Fifth Avenue and Broadway, where many music publishers, songwriters and composers, such as Irving Berlin, Jerome Kern, George Gershwin, Cole Porter and Richard Rodgers, were based, had also taken a flying leap across the Atlantic and taken root in Denmark Street in London's Soho. We used to hang out at a place called the Giaconda Café, where we'd have a coffee or a cuppa with the likes of John Lennon, Keith Richards and Mick Jagger, and we'd all sit around for hours, sharing showbiz anecdotes and our dreams of becoming stars.

In our Tin Pan Alley there used to be all these vans lined up along the side of the road, where various groups and solo artists who were trying to make it in the business were camped out.

'If you didn't start at the bottom,' was the attitude, 'you'd never get to the top.'

We were not proud and it all made sense to us young musicians, who were touched by fire, to sit around on our butts and wait for something to happen.

In those days, solo artists like me didn't make much money, but if we had a band we could command between forty and fifty quid more. That aside, we also had a lot more fun on the road when we were singers with our own bands; and, if we didn't have a band, it was important to gather one together. What used to happen was that Tony would go knocking on the doors of all the vans, saying cheerfully, 'D'you want a few gigs working with Gerry Dorsey?' and, invariably, he would return with some who did. Although I didn't have any steady work, I was feeling pretty good – broke, but good.

A month after my first performance on *Oh Boy* – a very long month in which I could only wait and hope – I was invited to return for a second appearance; this time my name, GERRY DORSEY, appeared at the top of the bill. Thank God, I had dropped the Arnold all that time back! A top-of-the-bill spot was very special and I really thought that this time there was no going back, that I was in with a chance. What more could I ask!

After a heady performance, in which the fans screamed even louder, a very pretty brunette asked me for my autograph. It was the first time I'd ever been asked and I was so excited I could barely steady the pen.

By now I was on such a 'high', I genuinely thought I was home and dry. How wrong could I be? There was another casting-couch event on the horizon, which meant I was about to be in for a very long rest period.

When a guy named Larry Parnes, who represented some of the biggest names in the business, and who had a rock'n'roll tour, smiled at me and said, 'I'd like to take you out to dinner to discuss a few things,' I really believed he had a business proposition in mind. Flattered – and very eager to get my name top of the bill again – I accepted with great enthusiasm. Larry was a major player in the business, a promoter and impresario, who had become so affluent, he enjoyed living in the lap of luxury. I was very excited that he had singled me out and I had absolutely no idea that I was about to lose all the ground I had gained thus far.

On the night of the dinner, the comedian Jimmy Tarbuck, who eventually became master of ceremonies on *Sunday Night at The*

London Palladium, joined us at the Lotus House on the Edgware Road, one of those posh, white-linen Chinese restaurants that serve finger bowls containing warm water scented by lime wedges. I was not a particularly worldly person – I couldn't afford to be! – but I was astonished when Jimmy started to pour salt, pepper and soy sauce into his bowl and then take a sip. This set the agent and me off, and we ended up laughing so loudly that all the other patrons turned to look at what Jimmy was doing.

Unperturbed, Jimmy kept bellowing: 'This soup has NO taste whatsoever!' To this day, I have no idea whether he was serious or kidding, always a joker, Jimmy – who turned out to be one of Britain's most prominent comedians and television hosts – kept on trying to season that 'soup'. Hey, Jim, were you serious?

Towards the end of the meal, Jimmy suddenly announced that he had to go. By then, I also needed to make a move because the restaurant was five miles from my digs and, unable to afford a taxi, I needed to catch the last bus home. As the agent picked up the impressively expensive bill, however, he said: 'Hold on a mo, Gerry. I want to show you my lovely apartment. It's just across the road, a couple of places down.'

It was a lovely apartment all right, one of the most opulently carpeted and furnished places I had seen, on or off the big screen.

'This is very nice,' I said, without sitting down.

'Sit down, Gerry,' he replied, pointing to the plump, middle cushion of a sleek leather sofa. 'Sit there. Would you like something to drink?'

'Whatever you're drinking,' I said nervously, reluctant to take the seat he had indicated.

'You can have whatever you want, Gerry. What do you really, really want?'

Nothing that he wanted, I was beginning to suspect!

My choice of drink back then was whisky and Coke, which he mixed and handed to me before dipping the lights. Then, angling a spotlight directly into my eyes, he stood looking down at me and cooed, 'You're really quite wonderful to look at.'

By now, I was very nervous and getting more and more anxious to get up and go.

Bugger him for keeping me so late, I was thinking. I'll miss my bus.

'Relax,' he murmured as he came and sat down beside me on the sofa. Then, glancing over his shoulder, he called out: 'Hey, sweetie – darlin' – can you come in here a mo?'

A bedroom door opened down the hall and a good-looking, lanky guy, who was obviously his live-in lover, responded to the call and came sauntering towards the sofa. 'Sweetie, will you explain to Gerry that I'm a nice man – a very nice man,' the agent said.

'Yes,' the poor bloke replied, batting his eyelids and delivering an automatic response. 'He's a nice man, a very nice man,' and then he was dismissed with instructions to sleep in the spare room as I would be joining the agent in the master bedroom for the night.

OH, NO!

That was the moment I gave up trying to be diplomatic in order to advance my career.

'Oh, no,' I said, finding my voice at last. 'No way! I can't sleep double. If I stay as you've suggested, I'll have to sleep on my own somewhere.'

'Very well,' he said shrugging as if that were my loss not his. 'Then, dear boy, you can sleep in that room over there. There's a single bed in there.'

'Fine.'

He was acting as if our sleeping arrangement did not matter one way or the other to him, while I was sitting there feeling awful that I had not once mentioned Popea. By then I was in the habit of keeping my relationship with her a secret, thinking I had to appear single – footloose and fancy free – for the sake of my career. 'Fans,' we were always told by people in the business, 'liked to feel they were in with a chance – they didn't like "fixtures" around.' When I did mention Popea, I told everyone she was my sister so that I could justify having her around without provoking any awkward, embarrassing questions. Later on, when I started to go on tours, girls would approach her and say, 'I really fancy your brother. Could you put in a good word for me? Help set us up?', and Popea would smile and have to take all this in her stride.

Having managed to fend off the agent's advances, I thanked him for feeding us so well and said a hasty goodnight. Once in the bedroom, I wiggled the bolt very carefully so it wouldn't make a sound and then locked the door.

It was just as well I battened down the hatches! In the middle of the sleepless night, he tried to get in and was absolutely furious to find his way blocked by a lock.

'Do you have any idea who I am, or who you're dealing with?' he yelled, incensed.

I kept my mouth firmly shut and said nothing. Then, at about five in the morning, I got up, put on my clothes, opened the bedroom door very carefully and sneaked out the front door.

As I trudged the five miles back to my digs in Holloway, I watched my feet, moving further and further away from an upmarket area into a downmarket area, and I felt every footstep was predicting the direction my life and my career were about to take. Sure enough, the next day, the agent removed me from my current show, instigated the proverbial blacklist, and lengthened my time on poverty's path.

CHAPTER SIX

I had just come off stage after appearing in a charity concert in Manchester and I was feeling absolutely awful – really ill. While I stood there, swaying, feeling as if I were dying on my feet, I had to admit to myself that I'd been feeling way below par for a few weeks. Even so, there had been nothing until now to indicate that I was about to be hospitalised for six months, and that this stay on the wards would be followed by the need to convalesce for a whole calendar year. In fact, on the night of the charity gala concert in Manchester, I hadn't been feeling that poorly and, while on stage, I'd sung my heart out.

And my lungs, too, apparently.

'Are you all right?' somebody nearby me in the wings asked in a concerned voice.

Ever the optimist, I replied, 'I will be when I get back to the dressing-room.'

The moment I was back there, however, I suffered a terrible bout of coughing, the kind of fit where you hold one hand over your mouth and press the palm of the other against your chest to keep your insides from rattling around. The pain was horrendous and, when I eventually got in my car and began the drive to Leicester, I was starting to spit up blood. That was alarming – and I actually drove the 150 miles home with my body draped over the steering wheel for support.

The next morning, still feeling really grotty and still bringing up blood when I coughed, I told my mum about my symptoms, and she shunted me off at once to see a one-eyed doctor who looked in even worse condition than me!

'Open your mouth and say "Ah",' he instructed wearily.

Then, having looked down my tonsils, he announced, 'Hm, nasty throat infection'.

'I am not happy with that diagnosis, doctor,' my mother declared. 'He's coughing up blood – I want him to have an X-ray picture – now.'

My mum was a woman of great grace and character, and she had the kind of resolve when necessary that people did not question. So it was that moments later, I found myself headed to the Radiology Department. Five minutes later, I was in shock.

'Go home, collect a toilet bag and a few belongings, and come back at once,' I was told. 'Prepare yourself, my boy, you're going to be out of commission for quite some time.' An hour later I was admitted into the sanatorium at Leicester's Groby Road Hospital.

That was just what I needed right then – months and months of being out of a business which is famous for forgetting faces, however good the performer, overnight!

The ground-floor ward of the sanatorium was spacious, painted clinical white, and divided into separate little cubicles. Many of the residents of these nooks and crannies were serious cases, but some were said to be only 'temporary'. Were these the ones who died? If so, we were not allowed to see the bodies being removed and we were never told.

During my first hour there, being a Catholic, I was honoured to have a priest come and visit me for a bedside chat even before I had finished unpacking all my things.

'How nice,' I thought, 'that he should come and visit me just as I've arrived.'

'I will be saying some prayers for you,' he told me, in a grave voice.

'Thank you very much, Father, I appreciate that,' I replied.

It wasn't until eight weeks later when I had been declared negative from my disease, that my mother put me right on that event.

'My son, my son,' she said, taking my hand in hers, 'that priest was there to give you the Last Rites.'

The disease, which was highly infectious and responsible for countless deaths at that time, had really got that kind of stranglehold on me before it was diagnosed – and it was only because I was young, and all my vital parts were strong, that I survived.

By the time of my enforced stay in the sanatorium, I had appeared on television a number of times and toured the country and, as a result, some of the other patients and medical staff recognised me and treated me as a bit of a celebrity. I liked that! My ward mates called me a 'star' and the doctors asked me to autograph their clipboards. I allowed them all to believe I was a big success and a wealthy man. In truth, I had nothing. After appearing for those 42 weeks on TV, the work had drained away, leaving me with only a few low-paid touring jobs in the pipeline. One of my biggest regrets was that the house I had bought for my parents, for which I was paying the mortgage with my income from *Song Parade* and my variety performances, had to be repossessed and meant that Mum and Dad had to go and live with my sister Dolly in her house.

I did, however, still have the car I'd put a deposit on from my television earnings, and I was now keeping this, covered in tarpaulin, in the hospital grounds so that the finance company I'd got the hire purchase money through wouldn't be able to find it and nick it back.

One night, promising the lad in the next cubicle a decent Sunday dinner at Popea's brother-in-law's, I persuaded him to make a break for it with me. As we sneaked out of a window, loped across the lawn, crept around the back of the building and uncovered the car, we felt like World War II heroes.

Now, when you have TB, you are not supposed to lift or push anything heavy because this can set you off coughing and make you bring up more blood, but the two of us braced our thin shoulders against the car, got it rolling downhill, then jumped in as the engine kicked over at the bottom where the hospital staff could not hear it. We got a few miles down the road when I must have run over a nail because we got a puncture in one of the back tyres. We had no choice but to shuffle around in our dressing-gowns and carpet slippers until we found a telephone box where we phoned Popea's family for help. Her sister's husband came to our rescue and changed the tyre, but, given the time, we could only drive back up the hill to the hospital, where we re-covered it in the tarpaulin. Then, deflated and defeated, we crept back through the very same window we had crept out of earlier. Our escape in search of a good Sunday roast – Yorkshire pudding, horseradish sauce and all – had not gone well!

With hindsight I think the night staff turned a blind eye to our antics that evening, probably thinking the psychological boost of our bid for freedom would be as good as any rest cure.

The majority of the staff were, in fact, extremely kind and some of the nurses who were on visiting-hour shift even brought a glass of milk for the Pope when the two of us crept off into the tree-lined grounds pretending we wanted to enjoy the fresh air and a picnic! By then, she certainly needed something to top up her strength!

Some of the nurses even seemed happier than I was when handfuls of my fan-mail came through the post. There was, however, one exception to this – a pretty young nurse, who pretended to be nice to me, but who also seemed to get some S & M pleasure out of administering my daily injections. I was convinced she was only happy when she was using the lumpy bruises from the previous injection as a bull's-eye target for the next. In the end, after some careful plotting, I got my own back on her – and had the last laugh.

The bed next to me was empty, and large coils of surgical tubing and medical dressings were left there, ready for use on the patients. By this time, I was getting some strength back in my limbs, and I wasn't as easily winded and not experiencing as many moments fighting for my breath. So, one morning, when she arrived, brandishing the needle, while gesturing me to adopt the usual bum-up posture for the next injection, I threw back the bed sheets, leapt up and, catching her off guard, forced her backwards on to her rump on the empty bed. She must have thought she was about to suffer a fate worse than death – some amorous advances! But, taking a long length of the tubular dressing, I taped her arms and legs together. Having tied her limbs to the underside of the bed, I then climbed back into my own bunk. She was lying there glaring at me and saying, 'I'm going to get you' in her soft Irish brogue. It was *so* satisfying!

She was still there, bound hand and foot, looking like an Egyptian mummy in a nurse's cap, when it was time for the doctors' rounds. That was a priceless moment, the one I had been waiting for. The doctor came in, all the other staff in line behind him, took one look at me, one look at the lump in the next bed then, to my astonishment, proceeded to examine my chart as if no mischief whatsoever had been committed. Obviously used to outrageous medical students' rags and antics, he returned the chart to its usual hanging place at the end of my bed, and said: 'How are you today – doing OK?'

'Fine, thank you doctor, fine,' I said, trying to be serious over the issue.

Then, leaving her there completely at my mercy, he continued on his rounds, still followed by his wide-eyed, gob-smacked staff.

Only when he had completed checking every patient and their charts and had left, did I, reluctantly, release my captive. She immediately began her ranting and raving. And, oh boy, did she have a go at me and continued to do so for days afterwards. She never saw the funny side of it – she was really peeved and upset with me. On the next occasion she appeared to give me a jab, I called out in panic: 'Staff can you get another nurse to give me my injection, please?'

A really nice fellow, the staff nurse replied: 'All right, calm down, I'll give it to you myself.'

He was the best at giving injections anyway; he used to take the needle off the syringe and ease it into your buttocks very gently before reattaching the syringe to administer the dosage. They were huge needles and my arse was black and blue and covered in bumps and punctured skin. When you have an injection from a big, long needle every morning for six months, it's tough.

My antics that morning when I took the nurse captive must have convinced the doctors that I had now recovered sufficient strength to be discharged – or maybe they didn't want to risk any mischief I might get up to next! Either way, I was freed from the hell that was normal life in a sanatorium; and, although the nurse had been very angry with me initially, she gave me a leaving hug.

'You were a very bad boy,' she muttered, still wanting to cut me down to size, 'a very bad, bad boy.'

'I don't know about that,' I said with a wicked wink. 'I could have been a lot worse!'

After six months in the sanatorium – and another six months convalescing on medical orders – I couldn't wait to get back to work and use my vocal chords for something other than uttering the word 'ouch'. Temporarily living back in Leicester, I would sing every day – whenever there was nobody around to tell me to take it easy – trying to get my lungs strong enough to belt out ballads in the way I had before.

When, eventually, I returned to London and got a gig with the John Barry Seven, John told me I needed a repertoire of four songs for my return appearance and I ran all the way round to Les Reed's apartment to seek his help.

'Les, I have no money for you right now,' I stated, out of breath, 'but, if you'll write the music for four charts, I promise I'll pay you back as soon as I've done this gig.'

Considering Les had just become a dad – and I had to make my plea in front of his newborn baby girl – I felt very guilty about making such a request. My lack of funds, however, didn't even give him pause for thought. He just agreed on the spot to compose the arrangements for me. He was a very generous man.

When I got to rehearsal, I handed the arrangements on their sheet-music pages to John Barry, just expecting him to glance at them and approve, but I was in for a shock. He instantly recognised his ex-piano player's handiwork and it became abundantly clear the next moment that something was wrong between the two of them.

'I'm not playing this pony shit!' he muttered, and dramatically tossed all the papers up into the air.

As they fluttered down on to the stage, I got down on my hands and knees to collect them and, as I did so, I noticed that my skin was breaking out in a bright red rash.

'Oh my God,' I thought, 'I'm having a relapse.'

As I crawled around the stage in front of people who had gathered there for the rehearsal, I really thought I was watching tuberculosis breaking out again right in front of my eyes; and, as I stood up, placing the last recovered page in order with the rest, I couldn't even bring myself to make eye contact with John. How could he? I was choked. I couldn't believe anyone could have been so insensitive as to treat a very recently recovered invalid like me, one who could obviously have a relapse and land back in the sanatorium, in that way. But I knew I needed to remain calm. I desperately needed the money that was on offer for this particular gig and there was no room in my life for disease, let alone pride. I simply had to tuck my tail between my legs.

'What would you like me to do, then, John?' I asked in a conciliatory voice.

'Just do two numbers, instead of four, and the band will busk it without written music,' he snapped, still seething. 'I'm not playing this shit.'

For me, every arrangement Les Reed had ever done then – and everything he's ever written for me since – has been absolutely first class. By this time he had achieved success worldwide – so I knew there had to something personal going on between the two of them that had nothing to do with me.

I did as I was told, went on to perform just two songs and, despite the fact that my set had been abbreviated, I managed to do well that night. We were performing in Coventry Theatre and, aware that many in the audience had come to see me perform, my making a decent go of it was very important to me. It was even more important to get paid – I really was desperately broke.

I was also very angry – incensed – with John and that night I made myself a promise.

'If I ever make it in this business,' I told myself through gritted teeth, 'if I ever become a star, I will ask John Barry why he thought it was OK to humiliate me like that and make me crawl around the stage on my hands and knees in front of people, picking up the scattered pages of my sheet music. I'll ask what made him believe it was all right to treat a physically and emotionally weakened man like an animal. And, if he can't give me a satisfactory answer, I'll return the humiliation by slapping him across his face. There's nothing more humbling for a bloke than a good slap!'

Many years later, when I had made it in the business and I was on holiday in Barbados, someone said as I got off the plane: 'Oh, you're the second celebrity to come here this week!'

'Really?' I said politely, 'who was the other one?'

'John Barry,' he replied.

Bingo! My promise to myself had not faded with time.

As I checked into the hotel, I said politely: 'Do you know where John Barry is staying?'

'At Coral Reef, on Settler's Beach,' was the reply.

I had stayed there on a previous occasion, so I knew where it was and I hired a little jeep, put the top down, and drove round to the hotel.

'Excuse me,' I said to the staff in reception, 'is John Barry here?'

They had immediately recognised who I was. 'If so, I'd just like to talk to him,' I lied.

'The strangest thing,' the pretty, young receptionist replied, 'is that he'd only just arrived and taken one phone call, when he came straight back down again and checked out.'

I can't be sure, of course – there may have been another reason – but I like to think that word had reached him that I was looking for him and he had guessed that I wanted to ask him some pretty tough questions. In the 36 years that have passed since then, I have never set eyes on him, and as time goes by, my feelings have mellowed.

So, I would just like to add this: 'If you're reading this, John, I apologise.'

Throughout those days, I was sharing such a tiny room with my manager, Gordon Mills, on Charleville Road in West Kensington, London, that our beds stood end-to-end and our feet used to touch in the night. It was only too obvious that we needed a better place to live, with a significantly larger space for sleeping arrangements. This, however, posed a problem. We didn't have enough money to move to a nicer place and, what's more, we already owed more back rent than we could pay on the present one.

'We'll have to do a moonlight flit,' said Gordon, 'and get out of here.'

For a moment, I thought his use of the word 'we' meant we were in this together, but then he added: 'I've got something I have to do tonight, could you do the moving for us?'

'Gordon,' I protested, 'I can't carry all our shit down those stairs myself (and it really was shit we didn't have nice things). The bloke that owns the house will hear me bumping the suitcases around.'

We didn't have much, but what we had was too much for one man to manage. Nevertheless, that's what happened. I ended up taking all the cases down the twisting, winding stairs on my own and getting a cab – a real luxury then – to go to Cleveland Square,

Paddington, where Jo Waring, Gordon's future wife, was living. I was sweating when I arrived to move in, not only because of the arduous activity but also because of the sheer terror of having to get out without being heard by the owner of our digs.

How he could have let me do such a thing on my own – one of the worst things he ever did to me – I would never know. But I forgave him and, when Popea came down from Leicester on her usual visits at the weekend, we all got on famously and used to go out for drinks with Gordon and Jo, and Johnny Gentle.

The house we were all living in then was huge and we called it 'Rock 'n' Roll House' because there were a number of other show business people who also had flats there, such as Terry Deans, Joe Brown, Dickie Pride and Duffy Power, and we had some really great, fun times there. Our pockets may not have had much money in them – and were often completely empty – but we were full of life.

When Gordon finally left the room we were sharing there to share one with Jo, I had to move into a smaller one. All this had was a bed – the toilet and bathroom were on the landing – and all I had in it, apart from the bed, was a kettle and a toaster. I did have access to a little balcony, however, and that was great. People-watching when I was too broke to go out and do anything else became my total pleasure. I'd go out on to the balcony, look down at the street and watch the passers-by greeting each other, standing around smoking their roll-ups, or entering the pub across the road. The balcony was as close as I could get to that pub – I couldn't afford to join the revelry – but I could smell the smoke and ale wafting from out of its doors and I took in deep lungfuls of that.

The smell of dinners cooking in the other rooms of the house, however, was a different matter – absolute torture. The scent of a hot meal – when you haven't had one for days – goes right through you and pinches your stomach into tight little balls. Often I would take a long way around the passages of the building to get to my room, purposely going past people who left their doors open when they were cooking. Sometimes when they saw me pass by, I'd strike lucky. I'd greet them courteously, saying: 'Hello there – how are you doing?'

'Oh, hello,' they would reply, 'how are you? Have you eaten today?'

'Oh no, I'm fine,' I would lie.

'I'm just cooking supper – would you like a bite to eat?'

'Oh, no, thank you kindly.'

'Oh, go on, come in and have some eggs and chips.'

'Oh, OK,' I'd reply casually. 'Thank you very much.'

Those were wonderful meals!

I particularly remember Michael Lloyd, who used to sell dresses. He was obviously doing OK financially – and always ate very well. He was a friend who'd invite me in whenever he saw me.

On the rare occasions I had a bob or two, I would go into the bar across the road, buy half a pint of beer, and just keep sipping it until somebody noticed me and said, 'Do you want a drink?'

'Oh no, thank you,' I would reply.

'Oh, come on, I can afford to buy you a drink!'

'But I can't buy you one in return so . . .'

'That's OK – have one on me anyway!'

People were very kind – true friends in deed – really great in that way.

Just as I was beginning to despair that I would be hungry forever, always dependent on the kindness of comparative strangers, a job came up. I thought I was home and dry, out of trouble, but I was about to discover that there are more troubles in life than long, 'resting' periods. And some of these troubles, which could land you in deep anguish, you could bring down on your own head.

CHAPTER SEVEN

The job I got in 1962, when I was twenty-six, was in a summer-season cabaret at a hotel in Les Arch, Jersey, playing alongside two dancers, two soubrettes and three musicians: piano, bass and drums. When the two very attractive dancers ran off stage for a costume change between acts, I used to help them out of one outfit into another. I was always happy to lend a hand on such occasions!

After the show the girls would just sit around the dressing-room in their birthday suits. They could afford to be so free and uninhibited – they had superb bodies. Having worked in strip clubs, seeing them sitting there naked was nothing new for me but, this time, perhaps because I felt more like a name – more self-important to the show – it seemed different and things went to my head. I had a fling, was unfaithful to Pope, and, having given into temptation, I discovered I had risked everything that really mattered – everything I held dear – and lost Popea.

'Many a slip between the cup and the lip,' was one of my mum's favourite sayings and, now that I had slipped, and the Pope had put two and two together and found out, she had gone missing – had absented herself from my life. I soon heard through the grapevine of our friends that she wasn't angry so much as determined that she was not going to spend the rest of her life with a man she could not trust. She knew she was young enough and pretty enough not to have to settle for this. So, having said, 'It's over between us – all o-v-e-r – there's no going back,' she broke off our relationship and went to stay with her friend, Ronnie Collis, and his wife Jean.

I was a mess, an absolute mess. For six months Pope would not take any of my calls and, when I went round to the Collis home, Ronnie would put his head out of the window and say, 'Go away, Gerry! She's not coming out.' (Later, Ronnie would teach me how to tap dance on his kitchen floor.)

Although she told her girlfriends that, in spite of it all, she still loved me, I heard that they kept telling her she would be mad to tie herself down at such a young age to a man she couldn't trust and who made her unhappy. She, in turn, always ended up agreeing with them that she should leave things alone and that, given time, she would get over me.

In despair, I went to see my manager, Gordon Mills, whom I was sharing with Tom Jones, who was destined to take the world by storm three years later, in 1965, with his sexy rendering of 'It's Not Unusual', and I asked Gordon and Jo, who was soon to be his wife, for their help.

'This is the girl I want to marry,' I kept on wailing. 'I can't accept it's all over.'

They, in turn, went to Popea's mother's house, where Popea was now living and starting life anew without me, and they told Popea everything I had said: 'He wants to marry you. He's utterly miserable and wretched. He can't live without you.'

It was all too true and, finally, Popea listened and agreed to a meeting at my sister and her husband Norman's home. Once there, and at last alone together, I had my long-hoped-for chance to win her forgiveness and re-win her love. And, to our great mutual joy, I succeeded and we were reconciled. That night, after Popea had accepted me once more into the greatly missed comfort of her arms, she let me kiss her over and over again passionately and, in between, I rejoiced and we both cried.

'I love you, really love you, and I can't live without you,' I kept repeating between sobs. And, overcome by the sheer ardency of my passion – and her own – we made love.

We also made something else that night – our first baby.

What needs to be understood here is that it was truly awful for a girl – especially a Catholic one – to get 'pregnant out of wedlock' at that time. Girls who did were 'disappeared' from life by their families, banished from the localities where they were known and would bring shame on their parents and siblings, or packed off into nunneries with no choice to marry anyone but Jesus and God. As a result, for over four decades, Popea and I kept her pre-marital pregnancy a secret, and gave the dates of our marital nuptials as 18 April 1963 rather than the true date 18 April 1964.

Popea did tell Louise – the daughter we conceived that night – though. As soon as Louise was old enough to understand –

thirteen-ish – Popea explained in a heart-to-heart how she had come into being, but neither of us ever asked Louise to lie about her age just to protect our secret. The rest of our family, our three sons – Jason, Scott and Bradley, who followed in 1965, 1968 and 1974 respectively – were not told until I decided to tell the whole truth and nothing but the truth when writing this autobiography! So, suddenly, in 2004, our forty-first wedding anniversary became our fortieth! When, around this time, we informed Bradley, who is an aspiring pop singer, he took it very well. Turning to Popea, he said with a wide grin, 'Mum! So that means you were very naughty.'

Popea has never forgotten how to blush!

Also, when I decided to write this book, Popea called her sister, Mary, who lives in Australia, to tell her that my autobiography was going be an 'honest tome', in which we would 'tell all'. Mary was horrified to hear that we were going to open up our private life and reveal previously hidden truths. 'The fans in Australia don't even know about Enge's history of womanising – or any of his affairs – let alone the fact that you were pregnant before you got married,' she exclaimed, deeply concerned.

'I know, but it has to be done,' Popea replied. 'It's time to come out with it all – and the fans in Australia and elsewhere will have to understand, and I'm sure they will. We want to be honest; there's no point in Enge writing a book about our life if all we're going to do is cut-and-paste together what's already been printed in the papers. We can't waste this opportunity to fill in the gaps and reveal the real emotions behind everything. I think people will appreciate it if Enge is really open and forthright, not just in Australia but around the world.'

It is true, though, isn't it, that although we may want to be open and pretend we are tough and couldn't care a monkey's about what other people think of us, inside we do care. We are all very human, in the same boat, wanting other people's love and approval. I'm no different from anybody else – and I've certainly come to believe in that saying, 'He who has not a good memory should never lie.' Too often, over the years, I found myself fumbling and taking a few seconds longer to answer questions about my personal life and anniversary dates. I often needed a moment to make sure I'd got the story straight in my head before letting the answer come out of my mouth.

Likewise, although people might assume that keeping our secret became easier over the years, it never did – not for me or for Popea. Just recently, when Pope was filling out a form alongside my assistant and friend of 29 years, Bill Strasburg, she didn't notice she had accidentally penned in our true wedding date until Bill looked at the document and said, 'No, that date can't be correct, Patricia, your daughter, Louise, was born in 1964, so that means you were married in '63, right?'

Wrong!

In our youth, it would not have made any difference if people had been told that we had been courting for seven years before Patricia became pregnant, or that we had every intention of getting married at some time in the future. My poor Pope was too frightened to even tell her mother, and she was terrified that others would think we were only getting married for the benefit of the baby. Luckily for her, nobody could see she was pregnant just by looking at her. Her tummy remained flat-as-a-pancake for weeks. But she knew – and she was so afraid of the then-inevitable stigma and so consumed with guilt, we nearly didn't get married at all!

Before marriage then – and probably now – you were expected to go to the church to discuss the union-to-be with the priest or minister; and, in our locality, you had to ring the bell to alert him that you were waiting. So there we were, standing outside his closed front door, just waiting and waiting, until the Pope turned to me and said, 'Oh, well, I guess he's not in and we should be off.'

Taking her hand in mine, I said gently: 'Darling, I know you're feeling all mixed up and terribly nervous, but I saw what you did just now. You only pretended to ring his bell because you couldn't bear the thought of facing up to him.'

The truth was that my love was so traumatised by what had happened to us, she was suffering anxiety attacks and having nightmares when she'd dream that all her teeth were falling out or that she'd arrived at our wedding in plimsolls – tennis shoes. She was convinced that something terrible would happen because she'd been naughty!

Both sets of parents were happy when we told them that we were going to get married, but we did not mention at that moment that we were expecting a baby! 'Well, you've stood the test of time and you obviously love each other very much,' was the gist of their response. But I think, deep down, they knew there was something else going on. After having ten children themselves, they would have known the actual look of a pregnant girl.

At this time we were living with Jo and Gordon. As Jo was now a top model, she had been able to acquire a small but splendid flat in Westbourne Grove, in Bayswater, and, knowing how badly off we were, they allowed us to sleep on the floor. She also made the wedding dress and veil by hand, and took care of decorating the church hall we had rented for £3. She and my wife-to-be were up until three in the morning the night before the ceremony, making sure everything was perfect. It would have been, but for Elvis, Jo and Gordon's cat! Unlike his well-known namesake who was gentle and kind, Elvis the cat was a vicious little thing.

Jo had hung the gown and the veil on a door, ready for the next day's ceremony but, early that morn, Elvis attacked the long veil, quickly re-modelling it into a short one by ripping most of it to shreds. Popea took one look at it but, instead of bursting into tears, decided it was just as gorgeous as it had been; and we were all able to relax again when we discovered that the cat's revamped version still fitted her head perfectly.

Like me, in that very first moment when I had to deal with all the studio audience's eyes upon me on the set of *Oh Boy*, Patricia Healey wasn't altogether comfortable with being in the spotlight. A wedding day is supposed to be the bride's day but, given her personality and the situation, she really needed a hefty push to set her off down that aisle.

Barry Mason and Les Reed played a key role in the ceremony and also in my heart, by agreeing to be our ushers; and my friend, Tony, who had a small band that didn't seem to take issue with the fact that they'd only be paid for their efforts in slices of wedding cake, took charge of the music. None of us had much money just yet, and although the entire wedding only cost me roughly ninety pounds, that was a lot of dosh for us!

Our family and friends turned out for our big day and had a great time, even though we couldn't invite any of the family members' children as we needed to keep the numbers down and the cost as low as possible. For us lot, though, who didn't know any bigger or better, it was a successful, wonderful occasion that was just perfect. Patricia looked absolutely ravishing in her wedding dress and, when I stood at the altar gazing down into her eyes, her beauty positively shone right through her remodelled wedding veil.

After the ceremony – in which the words 'for richer or poorer' had special significance!, – Pope and I were far too nervous to eat anything, but our guests enjoyed the food, drink and cake on offer at the reception in the hired hall.

Gordon and Jo's wedding present to us was amazing – a honeymoon trip to Paris. This, however, began as a total disaster. Having arrived safely at the airport, our first realisation as husband and wife was that we were utterly famished. Having checked in, we headed off to a restaurant in the terminal, ordered steak and chips (courtesy of Gordon and Jo again) and sat there devouring them. We were enjoying the food so much, we didn't once think to glance up at the clock or Departures' board. So, we satisfied our appetites, but missed the flight.

Luckily, Gordon and Jo came to our rescue and arranged for us to take a later flight, while we ran around the airport trying to see if we could catch up with our luggage. We couldn't! It had *not* missed the flight and was well on its way to see the Eiffel Tower without us.

Once in Paris, we stayed in Pigalle, which was said to be the seediest and sleaziest of areas then because it housed so many strip clubs and dark, dubious-looking nightclubs. We didn't mind that – our hotel was cheap, clean and cheerful and very French! Now she was married, Pope relaxed into her pregnancy and allowed herself to breathe out and loosen up! Her tummy finally started to show the very day we arrived. The whole experience – being married and wandering, hand in hand, exploring the different pavement cafés in the different quarters of Paris – was totally exhilarating.

Our hotel room, which only cost 22 francs a night, had something inside it called a bidet, and we had no idea what that was used for. Like many before and after us, I thought it was for washing one's feet. Luckily, I didn't mistake it for a drinking fountain! The room also had twin beds, although one of these, of course, remained unused. As we sat down together on one of the beds, we took a deep breath and felt so happy and relaxed. That didn't last long – our eyes caught sight of a rat the size of a bandicoot running along the ledge outside our cracked, dirty window.

'Oh, my God,' my new wife squealed. 'I'll never sleep in here.'

'Don't worry,' I said with a cheeky wink, 'you won't have to!'

The very next morning, as we were leaving our room to go down to breakfast, the maid, a cheeky young Parisian who spoke broken English, took one look at us, smiled and said, 'You darlings.' The implication in her voice was that we were young lovers enjoying a clandestine affair.

'We're married,' I said, proud of Pope and proud to be a young husband. Then, not wanting to appear a novice, somebody on their honeymoon, I went the extra mile and added: 'We've been married for ages.'

Turning her head on one side, she shot us a smile that implied she knew otherwise.

'No, no, no,' I said, acting as if this was a preposterous idea. 'We really have been married for a very long time.'

She finally accepted this, but not for long. As I reached in my pocket to rearrange my top handkerchief, I sent confetti that had become trapped in there the day before flying about like pastel snowflakes all over the place. In seconds, the carpet was speckled with it.

Oh, shit, that's torn it, I thought.

The dimensions of the girl's smile had increased somewhat.

'You darlings,' she said, as she bowed out leaving us with egg on our faces.

Almost as soon as we got home, I used what money I had left to purchase a television set, which would cost us ten shillings a week on the 'never-never'. Popea was so worried that we couldn't really afford it, that I agreed we should stop playing Vernons Pools at once and use the cash we saved on those to pay for the television.

Big mistake!

The first week we had the TV was the very first time we didn't play our numbers, and the very week those numbers came up! If we had played as usual, we would have won something in the region of £30,000 – an absolute fortune in those days, especially for a young married couple who were expecting a baby and who were always broke.

I was gutted, but Popea did her best to soothe me down by saying, 'It wasn't meant to be. God didn't mean us to have that kind of money just yet.'

But soothing me down proved to be an uphill task, and I was still bitterly disappointed. From then on, knowing what that wretched television had cost us – and what we could have had if I had not got it – that TV became an even bigger luxury in our life than it had been before.

A couple of weeks after we got back from our dream honeymoon in Paris, we gritted our teeth and went to confront our parents with our secret. Popea's mother was first and, as it turned out, she had already guessed Popea was pregnant.

'Why didn't you tell me before?' she asked gently and compassionately, without the hint of a scold in her voice – and THAT was THAT.

I was just as insecure when it came to telling my parents. I had tremendous respect for them and, knowing how Victorian they were in their values, I didn't want to be a son who upset and disappointed them. All this would probably seem very strange to today's youth. So many couples now live together for years before marriage and many of them have no problem with bearing children without exchanging rings. But it was a tremendous deal for us.

As I said before, parents are much more worldly than you assume them to be and probably knew and kept quiet, knowing the embarrasment it would cause us. In the end, both sets of parents gave us their blessings, and my mother then gave Popea some surprising advice. Having given birth to ten children herself – Olga, Dolly, Tilly, Arthur, Bubbles, Celine, Peggy, Irwin, Pat and me – she said: 'Don't have too many children too soon, dear – maintain a life for yourself.' But I know Mum was proud of and delighted with her ten wonderful children.

I think that was just what Popea needed to hear in order fully to absorb and accept the situation. Somehow, thanks to my mum, she realised that she wasn't giving up anything, she was doing just what she wanted to do. She wanted to have a child and, although she was getting married sooner than expected, she appreciated that she could still be her own person as well as a wife and mother. Having arrived at this point, her other concerns: that people would think she had married me because she had to – or that I had married her out of obligation – fell away.

After a few months spent sleeping on the floor at Jo's place, we were more than ready for an honest-to-goodness bed of our own. Besides, now that we were married, Popea wouldn't be just 'visiting' me any more. So, as husband and wife, Pope and I, along with Gordon and Jo, moved into a flat together in London's very lively Notting Hill Gate.

The four of us had only been there three months, and were barely settled in, when Popea's contractions started and we prepared to add a sixth resident to our flat. Her waters broke when she was doing the washing and ironing and, grabbing hold of a couple of nearby nappies to hold against her, she ran outside looking for me – or Jo or Gordon.

'Is Gerry there? Has anyone seen Gerry?' she kept calling out to all and sundry. 'I need him to get me to the hospital.'

This being her first delivery, I would have expected her to be far more panicked and frantic than she was, but Pope never wanted to be a nuisance to anyone, and has never been one to create a drama. Her sister Mary – whom I call Mary-Moo – told her that women who scream when in hospital giving birth are just doing it for effect, for attention, so Pope was determined from the start that she didn't need attention. All she needed was a ride to the hospital!

She was a real trooper throughout the entire labour and delivery and, although hour upon endless hour passed while she sweated and pushed, our baby came out making far more noise than Popea had throughout the whole procedure. Those cries, though, on 28 July 1964, when we became the proud parents of a baby girl named Louise, were sheer bliss. The so-called 'mistake' that had come about from our joyous reconciliation had turned out to be one of the best things that could ever have happened to us.

Louise, we were told, had been born with a touch of jaundice – and poor Popea immediately became convinced that she had caused this. Late in the pregnancy, she had gone for a picnic with Gordon, Jo, Tom Jones and his wife Linda, and, while there, had lifted up her dress to sun her belly. Now, hearing the doctors say her baby had a hint of this 'yellow' condition, she was filled with the ridiculous image – and she now laughs at this herself – of the sun's rays going right through her bare tummy to tint the baby.

Fortunately, Louise was soon declared fit and well and she remained in the pink until she was six months old when she got a terrible bout of gastroenteritis and was seriously ill. It was a very traumatic time for us and we felt so helpless, as we stood in line at the hospital, waiting for her medical assistance. While I had managed to convince Popea that Louise's jaundice at birth was certainly not her fault, nobody could persuade me that this new – far more life-threatening illness, during which our baby also received Last Rites, was not my fault. I was totally convinced I was to blame for the whole sorry business.

At the time I had purchased a green van for £11 – and although green has always been my favourite colour, I've always found it to be an unlucky one for me. In the normal course of events, I just used the van to transport the band and our instruments to gigs. But, as the Pope and I had just moved into our first solo home together – a minuscule but wonderful flat in Hammersmith – we took the sputtering green van to Leicester one weekend to pick up a hundred-pound lot of used furniture and bits-and-bobs of old carpeting from different people's homes. The pieces were all mismatched, frayed and worn out in a number of places, but Popea sewed the various snippets together and made one big patchwork carpet for our floor.

When we made the trip, to Leicester and back, Louise was in the back of the van. I realised later she should have been up front with us, but I thought she'd be more comfortable in her crib for the long journey. It turned out that there were rust-holes in the back of the van and the fumes from the damaged exhaust entered and got right inside Louise and made her ill. I could have kicked myself for being responsible for her getting gastroenteritis, and I kept praying that God would forgive me for my stupid behaviour

– and make her better. At least I was smart enough to get rid of the van right away.

Luckily, Louise was a strong baby – now an even stronger woman! – and she recovered quite promptly.

While it may sound like a cliché – unbelievable – I have to say that those years living in the flat above the Times Furniture shop in King Street in Hammersmith, in the 'hungry years' – were actually some of our happiest ones to date.

To say our flat was a modest one would be a huge understatement. The overhead light in our living-room was just an exposed bulb hanging on a bare wire – the only lampshade to be seen was across the way in another flat – the windows were naked of curtains, the kitchen was minute and the place had an overall layout that made it feel no bigger than a breadbin. Pope offered to clean the girl next-door's flat in exchange for borrowing her vacuum cleaner at the weekends and, when our neighbour, a young doctor, threw out a large kitchen cabinet for rubbish, I rescued it after my wife had asked whether he minded us taking it. Once I had got it upstairs, I washed it down, polished it up, put a rod across the back to secure it where it had broken apart, and put it in our kitchen. We hung a washline out of the window to dry our clothes, after we had put them through the mangle, and I made a coffee table out of footboard that had come off an old bed. Having completed all this, we used to wander from room to room, looking at our washline and the 'new' cabinet with a broad smile. It was our first home and we were so proud of what we'd accomplished.

During this time the band I'd got together never had any accommodation, so they stayed with us and the whole lot of them slept on the sitting-room floor. It was a horrible sight in the morning to see this hungry lot strewn about the place on bits of carpets that never quite matched. My wife used to feed them big bowls of porridge in the morning and minced meat and mashed potatoes at night. I am not exaggerating any of these hardships, that's how it was for us. Things only changed when our young drummer, fifteen-year-old Eric Dillon, got fed up with the same old food and, suffering from severe hunger-pains, donned a long, blue coat that had very deep pockets and went out to the supermarket. Deft of hand, as all drummers are, he then slipped a steak into each of the pockets and we had a change of menu. Naughty, but nice – delicious in fact!

Soon after this, we decided that the girl on the check-out in the supermarket liked me and, as she knew Eric was sleeping on my floor, she pretended not to notice when he was nicking the pieces of meat and tins of tomatoes. Either that, or she just felt sorry for the skinny, obviously hungry teenager. It must have been one or the other because it would have been impossible for her not to notice that every time he left the stall, his jacket had taken on a misshapen, bulky look that it hadn't had when he first arrived. As we were all really law-abiding and we all knew the steaks were stolen, it was amazing that we were able to digest them so well – but we did!

Whether she liked me or not, the girl at the supermarket was certainly very generous with me. When Popea and I went shopping, she'd undercharge us by quite a lot. I'd have about three pounds to spend and I'd fill the basket with goods to that amount and take it to the check-out. 'Right then,' she would say, avoiding our eyes. 'That will be six shillings, please.'

'But, but . . .'

'I SAID – *six shillings*, please.'

When I finally made it big, Popea brought her a long ponytail of beautiful, real, dark hair to wrap around her own hair and make it into a beehive, just like the ones I styled for Popea. She showed the girl how to attach it and wrap it just so, and how to retain the style for many days by fixing it with knitting needles. Neither Popea nor the girl ever acknowledged that the gift of the hairpiece – and beauty lesson – were gestures of our supreme gratitude for the fact that, for so many years, our pound-notes had not made it into her cash till.

Sometimes as I look back now, I do not know how we survived during those years. The act of hiding the car from the finance company, for example, hadn't ended when I left the sanatorium; that behaviour continued for quite a few years.

Before – and after – Popea and I were married, I would always save a little money here and there from my gigs and then, when there was enough, I would blow it all on the deposit for another car, which I knew I couldn't rightly afford. Invariably, after just a few weeks when I had failed to make the agreed weekly payments, the finance company would come and cart the car away. Each time this happened, I would park the next car further away from where we lived, and cover it with tarpaulin, hoping the finance company wouldn't recognise it. Then, each time I wanted to use it, I would delay my departure for several minutes, while I removed the tarpaulin, bundled it all up and placed it in the boot. When I couldn't afford the road-tax disc, which was all the time then, I used to put something that resembled the disc on the windscreen. The best match, I discovered, was a certain beer-bottle label. I would spend ages peeling this off the bottle without tearing it, then stick it to the windscreen. I then lived in the hope that any policeman passing by would just give it a cursory glance and think it was the real thing! Likewise, I can still remember one occasion when Barry Mason and I were driving around in some old banger of mine, and we only had one pound between the two of us for petrol.

The finance companies were not the only ones who were after me for money in those days. Every Monday morning, just like clockwork, Mr Bland, the tax man, would arrive in his pinstripe suit and bowler hat, and ask me for some money to pay something off the fairly big back-tax bill I had accumulated. But, with a newborn baby to care for – and the TV and the car – I didn't have a pot to piss in. To offset yet another disappointment for Mr Bland, we used to invite him in and offer him a cup of tea. Every week, looking utterly miserable to have to mention it, he'd say: 'You know, I really do have to get this money from you'; and, each week, just by glancing around the place, he could see by the obvious lack of any possessions that we could not pay up. This routine continued for three years. Once or twice, Popea and I hid and pretended to be out when he rang, just to avoid the torment of disappointing him again but, more often than not, we felt it would be mean to leave him standing outside and we let him in! Eventually when I made No. 1 with 'Release Me' in 1967, I gave him the money for all my back taxes. This just happened to coincide with the year Mr Bland told us he was retiring.

'I'm really happy for you,' I replied, thinking he must be thrilled that, very soon, he would not have to deal with the likes of poverty-stricken people like we had been.

'I'm getting married, too,' he said, 'and I may need a part-time job in the future, but just for now I'm going to retire.'

'If there's ever anything I can do to help,' I began, 'I'd be happy to do so.'

His response was tender, flattering, and surprising.

'If there's anybody in this world I'd want to work for, it's you. I really respected your honesty throughout all the years I paid you visits – and I was always grateful for how up-front you were with me about not having the money.'

Can you believe that? After years of tormenting me for money and being tormented in return because we never had any, he liked us!

In truth, though, we always understood he was just doing his job, and we always treated him with great respect. We never once answered the door with: 'Oh, not you again?' and he never once appeared unsympathetic to our situation.

'I'll keep in mind what you said about needing part-time work,' I replied, 'and if I ever need someone, Mr Bland, I will be sure to let you know.'

In those early days of being a father, when baby Louise got colic and cried and doubled up her tiny legs in agony, I used to lift her out of her crib and rock her in my arms to the beat of whatever singer was on the television. When she couldn't sleep, I would tie one end of the string to the cradle in her room, and the other end – more than one room away – to my big toe. Then I would sit watching television and wriggle my toe, rocking her until she fell asleep.

On one occasion, soon after our son Jason was born in 1965 and we had two babies in one room, I gave Popea the fright of her life.

I'd been away on a few gigs, and I came back very late one night, a full day earlier than expected. As my mother-in-law was visiting for the weekend and sharing our bed with Pope and I'd missed my two children so much, I decided to bypass the treat of watching some pre-bed telly and, although I knew they were fast asleep, I tiptoed into their room. Not wanting to wake them, but longing to hold one of my babies, I climbed right into Louise's cot and promptly fell asleep, gazing at her. Of course, my body didn't really fit into the cot, so there I was fast asleep with my head on her mattress and my legs, sticking straight up in the air.

When the Pope came in the next morning to check on the little ones, she was still unaware that I had returned home. When she saw this black-haired, unshaven monster, with far too large a head to be either of her babies, pop up and look right at her, she screamed and nearly peed herself and died of fright.

The moral of this story for anybody else on the road is: always let your gal know when you're coming home!

CHAPTER EIGHT

What my career desperately needed – and had needed for a very long time – was a boost. It was 1965, I was 28 and, although I was still willing to work my socks off to make my dreams true, I knew I couldn't *keep* grovelling around for a few bob at gigs. I would never earn enough money that way to support myself – let alone my family.

So I tried to give my career another boost by experimenting with new sounds and new instruments. During this time, I wrote and recorded a song called 'Stay'. I knew that George Harrison of the Beatles was using the sounds of a sitar – the Ravi Shankar sound of the day – and I wrote a sitar feel into my song.

This is the kind of sound people are obviously enjoying right now on the radio, I thought, so I'll give it my best shot, too.

Gordon Mills was very pleased with the result and thought it was a good song. 'I'll try Decca,' he said.

But when the record-producers heard 'Stay', they just turned up their noses and turned it – and me – down.

'Gerry Dorsey,' one of them exclaimed. 'He's *old* hat.'

I had pinned so many hopes on this record with its slightly different sound and I was very disappointed and I *couldn't believe* what the guy had said. I wasn't even out of my twenties, but being called 'old hat' was very nearly the last straw, enough to make me wonder after all the years of trying whether I was in the right business.

Gordon, however, never a man to accept defeat, knew just what was needed and what to do.

I was in digs in Darlington, in County Durham, when the lady who owned the place came into the lounge where I was having afternoon tea, and said: 'There's a Gordon Mills on the phone for you. He says it's *very* urgent and he must speak to you right away.'

Thinking he must have some good news for me at last, I was instantly excited.

'Hey, Gord,' I said when I picked up the phone, 'what's up?'

'I've got the answer,' he replied, excited and out of breath. 'I've got you a *new* name. And, as it belonged to a man who died in 1921, you won't get into any trouble with this one.'

'Oh,' I said, deflated that he hadn't phoned about something *really* important – a good job. 'What is it?'

We had been thinking for some time that Gerry Dorsey just did *not* have a showbiz ring – and that Arnold George Dorsey was even worse! And, having decided that a change of name might help, we had often sat around trying to figure out what to call me. It was not uncommon for showbiz people to have two names – their real name and a professional one. Anthony Bennedetto, the American singer, who was best known for his UK No. 1 'Stranger in Paradise', and chart entries 'Till' and 'I Left My Heart in San Francisco', for example, shortened his name to the snappier Tony Bennett; and John Wayne, the broad-shouldered actor and star of all those westerns, had shed – who can blame him! – his birth name of Marion Morrison. *Marion!* So, deciding to take on a new name, wasn't so way out.

'You are *now*,' Gordon said, giving me a dramatic stage pause: 'Engelbert Humperdinck.'

'Engawhat?' I exclaimed aghast, almost falling off the stool I was sitting.

'ENG-EL-BERT, HUM-PER-DINCK – got it?'

Not quite!

But I wasn't about to argue with him. At this time Gordon had a nose for success and I was relying on him to give my career the boost it needed. I was still working for peanuts in small clubs and I was willing to be called anything – even *Marion!* – if it meant success. Even so, Gordon had to spell Engelbert Humperdinck three times while I rolled it around my tongue and wrote it down on a piece of paper.

Could it *really* work, I wondered, to have such a complex name that seemed to use up half the letters of the alphabet? But, even though I had my doubts, I went along with it. At least it was an unusual and 'catchy' name, and DJs and comics and people who hosted shows might, if nothing else, find it an interesting topic of conversation.

And it turned out they did!

* * *

The new name was all I'd needed to get the people who mattered to sit up and notice that I'd snuck my foot in the showbiz door. By then, so many years down the line, I was honestly ready to try anything to make a name for myself – and Engelbert Humperdinck was *SOME* name.

With everyone now chatting about this strange name, I began to believe that I was really going to get somewhere at last. I had no problem whatsoever with the notion that the appreciation of my singing was a step behind the appreciation of my tongue-twister name. The rest, I felt sure, would follow and I would get on and become known as the man with the voice as well as the strange handle.

I had already heard of the Azule Music Festival that was to be held in Knokke-le-Zoute in Belgium. This was *the* music festival in Europe at the time, a prestigious one that mattered to each country almost as much as it mattered to the singers that were chosen to take part in it. And I really wanted to represent Great Britain.

Gordon got in touch with one of the executives at Decca, Marcel Stellman, and told him he had a singer that Marcel should definitely take to the contest.

When Marcel asked who it was, Gordon told him that he would send over my picture and a tape so Marcel could listen to me. Marcel had already contacted the venue of the contest and its organiser there to see if it would be possible to include another singer. He was told that it was, but it would mean dropping someone else's song. Marcel also contacted the musical arranger for the British contingent, Arthur Greenslade, and explained what he planned to do.

Once he saw my picture and heard the tape, however, he called Gordon and said, 'But this is Gerry Dorsey.'

'Well, it was,' said Gordon, but he's now Engelbert Humperdinck.

'But why did you decide on this name?' said Marcel. 'Do you know who he was?'

Gordon explained that he'd come across the name in a book and Marcel then told him that Humperdinck had been the composer of an opera called 'Hansel & Gretel' and he thought it might cause some problems.

Gordon pleaded with Marcel to take me to Belgium as part of the British entry and he agreed.

So it was that Marcel, accompanied by his wife Jean and an agent called Colin Berlin, picked me up outside my flat in Hammersmith and we all set off down to Dover to catch the ferry to Calais.

From there, we drove up into Belgium and, along the way, I turned to Marcel and said, 'What chance do we have of winning the competition?' and Marcel said, 'Yes, we've got quite a strong team.'

So I asked, 'Do we get any money?'

Marcel responded, 'Well, I hope so – if we reach the quarter-final stage, you could get around eighty pounds.'

'What about if we reach the semis?' I asked.

'Then you might get one hundred and sixty,' he replied.

'And if we win?'

'Well, keep your fingers crossed. If we win you could get as much as three hundred and twenty pounds.'

Hearing that, I turned to Jean and said, 'If we win, will you come with me and help me buy a bottle of perfume for my wife?' and she said, 'Of course I will.'

The song I sang was 'What Now My Love?' and – unbelievably – the British team won the competition. When the result first came through the speakers, my heart ran a marathon and I was absolutely thrilled. There is no boost quite like a winning boost – and my smile must have been big enough and wide enough to irradiate the whole universe!

Outside the stage door, a crowd of young girls had gathered, calling out 'Autograph? Autograph?' in their lovely French accents and, being so nervous, I turned to Jean Stellman and asked, 'How do I spell Humperdinck?'

Thanks to my success in the competition, on my return home I was offered a contract with Decca, and the first song I recorded for them was 'Dommage, Dommage'. In French, the expression 'C'est dommage,' means 'It's too bad', or 'That's too bad' – and it turned out to be a very *apt* title. 'Dommage, Dommage' was never released in the UK, because it was deemed too European in style, so fame and fortune didn't follow me immediately.

The time between the recording and the release of the record was actually very short, but it felt like forever to me. I was so excited I couldn't sleep. The single of 'Dommage, Dommage' went to No. 1 in Belgium and, when I first heard that I'd got my very first chart entry, I ricocheted off the earth over the moon! A No. 1 for the very first disc I had cut with Decca was *not* bad!

Once the wheels were in motion, the combination of an unusual name, and a new image – a mass of black hair and long sideburns – all came together. It proved to be a hit formula, and gave the longed-for jump-start to my career.

There is no doubt about it, image *is* important. I first realised this when I began to appreciate just how clever the Beatles had been to have the *same* haircut. Success often starts with getting the right image – and I learnt that lesson from the Beatles.

My attitude was: if you're going to steal, then steal from the best.

My father was a little disappointed that I was dropping the family name, but the Pope took it in her stride. Pope was the kind of person who was prepared to go along with anything that I thought I needed to enhance or forward my career. Remember, it it was she, who, in the early days, had said to my father: 'Look, Dad, he's got a mind of his own. He'll do what *he* wants to do – and that's what will make him happy. Just let him stick with his dreams.'

In Germany, however, there really was a problem with my name. When Decca's sister company over there announced that they liked 'Release Me' and wanted to release it, they explained to Marcel Stellman that they couldn't use the name Engelbert Humperdinck.

Marcel asked why not and was told that the family of the original Engelbert Humperdinck was in dispute with the company and wanted them to do a new recording of 'Hansel & Gretel' which the German record company had been refusing to do. But so keen were they to release my record that they gave in to the Humperdinck family, recorded a full-scale version of the opera and then simply released my song under the name of 'Engelbert' only. As 'Release Me' became No. 1 around the world, every country in Europe wanted to release it, and every country – except Germany – released it under 'my' full name, Humperdinck included.

Back in England, the DJs started to play around with my new name: 'Engeldink Humperbump,' they would say, or 'Dinkeldink,' or even 'Pumpernickel. Who?'

In later times, when I had become truly established, the DJ Jimmy Savile, a wonderful man who is now deservedly Sir Jimmy Savile, used to announce my songs on his Sunday afternoon radio programme by saying, 'Last week's No. 2, this week's No. 1: here he is, our very own, *The Hump.*'

So, at last, people in the business were talking about me. What's in a name? *Everything*, it seemed!

All these factors, then, combined with the sure-footed guidance of Gordon Mills, who was already having mega success with Tom Jones, who had just made 'Green, Green Grass of Home' a No. 1 in the UK charts for 22 weeks, really helped me to make it. I became a truly active part of Gordon's new stable, and took my place as one of two horses that were about to become *big* winners. He held the reins and guided me into a world of recognition, big money and fame.

Following the success of 'Dommage, Dommage', Decca released 'Stay' in 1966, but it didn't achieve the success we'd hoped for and we spent the rest of the year looking for the right song with which to build up my new career.

It came first in the form of a melody that Gordon brought to me that I really loved, which was played by the soprano sax player Frank Weir, and when it was married together with some lyrics that had been the basis of an R & B song from the blues singer Esther Phillips and the whole thing arranged by Charles Blackwell, I knew I had my next single.

On 13 January 1967 'Release Me', the record that was to become a No. 1 hit – and retain that position in the charts for an amazing 56 weeks – was launched.

Mind you, it didn't take off overnight – and one huge disappointment nearly caused me to throw in the sponge. At that time, the biggest pop show on TV was *Juke Box Jury*. Records were played on the show and a panel of 'judges', drawn from the pop industry, voted them a 'hit' or 'miss'. The show was hugely influential and if your song was voted a miss, then it was truly destined to be just that. So, when it came to the moment for 'Release Me' to be played, it was a truly nail-chewing time for me – and for the band.

One of the judges, a girl called Lulu – who had made her first chart-topper at the age of fifteen with 'Shout' and who had just had a big hit with 'To Sir with Love' in the US – voted my song a hit. For one moment, bless her, we were all ecstatic, on Cloud Nine, but then we hit the ground with a crash. Everyone else on the panel thought the song was a miss and it was voted down. I was absolutely *choked*.

'Don't vorry, my boy,' Helen Bradley, the woman who owned the house where I was staying in digs, soothed, 'you're watching this in a Jewish home, and you've got mazel. It's going to be a smash hit.'

But I was utterly devastated and deflated and no longer sure of anything any more. I guess I was also exhausted by all the hype that had gone into the recording of the record, not to mention the period of living on my nerves while I awaited the day of its release and the reactions that would follow. As Helen switched off the TV, I turned to my mate, Tony, and said, 'I've *had* it! I think I'm done with all this now. I've given it a go, but it's time for me to get some regular work.'

'Don't be *daft*,' he replied, alarmed. 'Something will happen.'

'I'm not so sure any more,' I said, 'I honestly think I ought to do what my father's always told me to do and get a *proper* job. It might not pay much, but at least it will be regular money coming in.'

I might have won the competition in Belgium and got a contract with Decca, but I was still on my beam end. I could have asked my parents for help, but I was too proud. I wanted to fulfil my dreams without anybody's assistance, even theirs, and do everything myself. Dreadful though things were, I refused to ask for a shilling, even when I was in desperate need of a new pair of shoes. My current pair had enormous holes in their soles and I was too broke even to get them repaired let alone consider purchasing a new pair. Tony, helpful guy that he was, used to trace the outline of the soles of my shoes in pencil on some brown paper bags he picked up at Woolworth, and then cut out the patches for me to slip inside and wear like inserts. He even varnished the bottom of the paper so that the paper soles would more closely match the existing bottom of the shoe.

'Whatever you do, Enge,' he used to warn me, 'be careful how you walk – and do *not* sit with your feet up or people will notice you've got paper soles.'

What a life! How could I leave my mark with *paper* footprints, or climb fame's treacherous ladder in paper-soled shoes? I couldn't have guessed then that, before the 60s were out, I would have enough shoes, with real leather soles, to open several shoe shops!

A few weeks later, still very depressed after the *Juke Box Jury* event on which I had pinned so many hopes and dreams, I was sitting looking gloomily down at my shoes, which were disintegrating more each day and had just developed another hole, when I received a phone call and an offer that would change my life forever.

The singer Dickie Valentine, Britain's No. 1 pre-rock'n'roll 1950s' heart-throb crooner, who was scheduled to appear on Val Parnell's phenomenally successful show, *Sunday Night at the London Palladium*, on the Independent Television Channel, had fallen ill – and they needed someone to fill his shoes. Paper soled or not!

It was THE moment I had been waiting for – and the rush of adrenalin that I experienced following that offer was so momentous, it has never been surpassed!

CHAPTER NINE

Just 24 hours after giving my all, singing 'Release Me', on *Sunday Night at the London Palladium*, my records began flying off the record-shop shelves with such speed that the stores could not get hold of the reprints fast enough to keep up with the demand: 80,000 copies a day for six weeks.

In fact, by the time Popea and I had left the Palladium theatre in the centre of London, where the television extravaganzas were filmed, agent-managers, press and fellow entertainers were already phoning to congratulate me on my performance. The very first call I received was from Dickie Valentine himself, thanking me for stepping in for him at the last minute and saying how impressed he was with my appearance. His call was then followed by one from another of my favourite people in show business, Frankie Vaughan.

Success, when it came, arrived like a meteor, and events happened so fast I could hardly keep up with them. The week of 8 April 1967, when I heard that 'Release Me' had taken roost at the top of the ladder as No. 1 in the charts, curbing the rise of the Beatles' 'Penny Lane', nearly saw me go into shock. It was just too much to process. Top of the charts? *Really? Me?* It was what I had always dreamed of, fantasised about, yet when it arrived, it felt unreal – just like a dream!

When the press first asked if they could come round to our flat to interview me, I was momentarily flustered. We still hadn't got any furniture to speak of. So, in a mad flurry and a panic, we rushed downstairs and borrowed some items from Harry Morrel who ran the Times Furniture shop just beneath our flat. Then, armed with our trophies, we filled our place with all sorts of couches, armchairs and occasional tables.

'Just for twenty-four hours, Harry,' I kept saying, 'then we'll return every piece undamaged, I *promise*.'

Harry was so bemused by the thought of all those journalists buzzing round to our neck of the woods to interview me, of all people, he agreed. Later we dubbed him 'Hot Lips' after we introduced him to some seriously hot, spicy curry that was afloat with chilies.

It was not difficult, I discovered, to give an appearance of an established, well-ordered way of life once we had placed the borrowed furniture in position. I hadn't, however, caught up with this amazing thought just yet and I was still in my habitual mindset of: 'Steady on – you never know what's going to happen tomorrow.'

What did happen next, though, was the offer of a four-month run playing the lead role in *Robinson Crusoe* at the London Palladium. This theatre, which opened in 1910 and was the first metropolitan theatre that had tip-up seats and a royal circle that swept right round almost touching the stage, was *the* theatre that every entertainer dreamed of performing in – and many stars regarded it as the greatest show business stage in the world. In the circumstances, I could not have felt more honoured to be included in the ranks of entertainers who had appeared there, and prancing the boards as Robinson Crusoe was wonderful fun. I was performing with the much-loved actor Arthur Askey, who was well-known for his performances on the radio show *ITMA* (which stood for It's That Man Again) and for his film and television work. He was a real legend and taught me a lot about the craft of acting. With all the evening performances and two matinees a week, and because each show was a sell-out, the production broke all box office records and proved to be the longest-running pantomime that the Palladium had ever hosted. Good for them and great for me! I was so happy and felt truly proud.

Word of my new, meteoric success in Britain must have got around really fast and, in double-quick time, it reached the US. The first I knew of this was when Gordon told me that he had been called by Ed Sullivan from across the Atlantic, and that he wanted to invite me to be a guest on his show. I had never been to the USA and had no idea how huge this guy was; no idea that his show was one of the most important, influential US talk shows and that stars would tumble over each other to appear on it. Perhaps it was just as well I didn't know, I might have passed out awe-struck. As it was, I was totally unruffled by the offer, just thinking: Wow, *fancy* that! A trip to the States!

'Thank you *very* much, Mr Sullivan,' Gordon said to him. 'My artist will be delighted and honoured to appear on your show.'

New fame, then, was a whirlwind, tugging me along all day in its backdraught, then dropping me exhausted – and too over-excited to sleep – into my bed at night. I used to lie there open-eyed, looking at the ceiling, while one show after another, one interview after another, one snatch of a day after another, cascaded like a speeded-up kaleidoscope before my eyes. In the beginning, I had scurried out for the papers first thing in the morning and read all the interviews I had given, but soon I couldn't keep up with the flow.

Life was so hectic that everything became a fast-forward haze, with no time for rewinds and backtracking. For example, I really do *not* remember very much about being on *The Ed Sullivan Show*. All I can say is that it was a momentous event that gave my career a *phenomenal* boost. No talk-show host anywhere else in the world had Ed Sullivan's charisma and his almost magical ability to launch a performer into fame and stardom. He was brilliant! He gave Elvis this kind of liftoff, and the Beatles their US liftoff, and he launched me into international stardom as well. He was such a nice fellow, too, a former columnist for a newspaper in New York, who often made cockups on air and got away with them. After I had appeared for the second time on his show, he was telling a later studio audience how much he hated announcing long names – and how easy it was to mispronounce and get them wrong. He followed this comment by saying, 'Would you believe one of my best friends is named Engelbert Humperdinck!'

I was *very* touched – and so proud that he had called me a best friend!

After my first appearance on Ed's show, I headed to Los Angeles with Gordon for meetings with managers and agents at the Beverly Hills Hotel. At this get-together, all the bigwigs and their backup staff were present, sitting around a very grand-looking conference table. It was the kind of scene and setup that would have induced a dreamlike, 'I'm *not* really here – *not* really sitting with these people' quality into anyone who, like me, was so new to fame and fortune. I had just arrived from New York and I was having trouble adjusting to the whirlwind that had overtaken my life. As a result, exhausted from all the travel and the excitement, I fell asleep, right there in the meeting, while they were having an important discussion about my career – and fulfilling all my dreams. Can you beat *that*? They were all present to discuss my future and move my showbiz dreams along, and there I was in the land of nod, missing out on it all, and having much less interesting dreams. I am not at all sure that I snore as well as I can sing but, luckily for me, I had made a good impression on them *before* I arrived – and, being Americans, they were much too polite at our first meeting to let me know they'd noticed I'd nodded off.

When I did honour them with my presence by jerking awake and nearly falling out of my executive, black leather chair, they were discussing where I should perform in Las Vegas.

'*Las Vegas*,' one of them – politeness-personified – without making any reference to my previous absence or startled awakening, said, cueing me in. 'We were just wondering where you'd like to perform in Las Vegas.'

I stayed awake momentarily, but my eyelids were as plough horses' horseshoes, and I started to droop off again before anybody came to a decision. I was just a hunk of 'too-too solid' jet-lagged flesh that needed a bed and a good 24 hours of nonstop shuteye.

When I arrived on the strip of brilliantly coloured neon lights in the desert that is Las Vegas, I found that the gambling in the casinos and glamorous shows there went on around the clock. In fact, you wouldn't have found a clock anywhere – day just seemed to blend into night, which then blended into day again. Nobody seemed to sleep – *ever*! It was just one long party with the gambling tables crowded with hopeful players, but little did they know that Vegas was built on people like them.

Once there, I met a man called Bill Miller, who was responsible for booking all the major stars in Vegas venues. He took me round the city in his red Cadillac car, showing me all the glitzy hotels in which I might want to perform. I couldn't stop looking at – *fingering* – the white leather interior of that car! It was a mite different from any car I'd ever part-owned!

I visited all the hotels, then I concluded with the kind of suave sophistication I had never had a chance to muster before: 'I *think* . . . I'd like to play at the Riviera.'

Happy with that decision, Bill Miller drove me to the Flamingo Hotel and parked me in a luxury suite with a bottle of Champagne 'on the house'. It was all just wonderful – absolutely great. When he came and picked me up to take me back to the airport the next day, we discussed my decision to target the Riviera, and I expressed my hopes that the audiences there might like me. I could not have known then that, after my first appearance there, I would be re-booked for nine years at the Riviera, and that I would play to capacity crowds every night.

Before the year, 1967, came to a close, I had repeated what I had done with 'Release Me'. My new recording of 'The Last Waltz', was in the charts for 29 weeks, and my recording of 'There Goes My Everything', another No. 1 for me, was in the charts for 27 weeks. Les Reed and Barry Mason were responsible for writing 'The Last Waltz', and little did I know at the time that they would end up being played in every dance hall and club across the country.

During this time, my life in show business had changed beyond all recognition. I once said that I hoped the screaming of ecstatic fans would always be a part of my life on stage, but now I often had to fear whether or not I would manage to get back to my dressing-room with my limbs – and other bits and pieces! – intact. As well as throwing their knickers on the stage, women, in a primordial frenzy, would leap around and succeed in tearing the shirt off my back every night. It would never have surprised me if, cave-woman style, one of them had succeeded in dragging me off by my long, dark hair to her lair! Many would certainly have been happy to have their wicked way with me!

I was now travelling with twenty, sometimes twenty-six, trunks of clothes, and there were occasions when about seventeen of these were lined up in my room at one time. There were also memorable occasions when I travelled with 150 stage shirts and, believe me, this was necessary at the rate the women were tearing them off my back. This was, as they say, an occupational hazard!

To take care of me, I had a hairdresser and a dresser and, since then, I have never been without a dresser. In the early days, I used to say to George Clarke, my dresser, 'I want to wear . . .' and, astonishingly, he would reply, 'Fine. That's in . . . It will only take me a minute to find it.'

'Do you think we can cut down on the number of shirts?' he once asked me. 'I've just counted up to one hundred and forty-seven – and that's a lot to lug around.'

'There's not much we can do about *that*, George,' I replied, 'They rip 'em off me every night – and I can't appear at the next performance in shreds.'

As it turned out, the need for shirts came in handy for the unfortunate times when I had to sack a member of staff. Sending someone back to England to pick up my shirts became a coded message to my management to let them know that that particular person was to be let go.

This ripping lark was also why I never wore expensive leather outfits on stage. Instead, I wore very strong material and, even then, my trousers were so figure-hugging tight they used to split open! I never ever had pockets in my trousers. The trousers I wore were a second skin, the style in those days, and much too tight for pockets. Like the pony-tailed singer, PJ Proby, I was always splitting them.

When I arrived in Las Vegas in 1968 for my first convention performance date, I was picked up at the airport in a big limousine and driven to the hotel. There I was, 32-year-old Arnold George Dorsey from Leicester, getting off my first-class seat in the plane and getting into a squeaky-clean, shiny limo that seemed to be calling out to everybody, 'Look out, everyone! Here comes The Hump!'

The scheduled show – which turned out to be for an all-male convention – and, oh, how the Americans *love* their business conventions – terrified me. I had never sung 'love' songs to a men-only group before, and, although they'd heard the name Engelbert Humperdinck, they didn't know what an Engelbert Humperdinck *was*. At the end of a performance, however, when I had cast all my inhibitions aside and just gone for it, all the men stood up and cheered.

Left Seventeen years old

Below Me in training

Above Eighteen years old in national service, Royal Army Service Corps

Left With Patricia at Les Arch in Jersey in the mid-50s

Below left On *Song Parade*, with the Grenadiers

Below right Gerry Dorsey on Parlophone Records

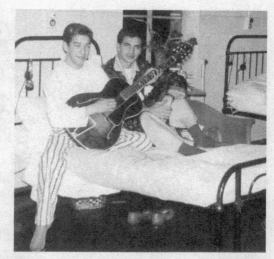

Right In the sanatorium in Groby Road Hospital (note empty bed next to me, where I tied up the nurse)

Below Playing Robinson Crusoe in 1967

Above With Tom Jones and Raquel Welch on my special, ATV Studios, 1970

Left With Dame Shirley Bassey during my ATV series

Right One of my
favourite guests:
Milton Berle

Right With the Queen
Mother at the *Royal
Variety Show*

Left On *The Sonny
and Cher Show*

Left I am lucky to know this man; he's a wonderful person

Below With Ringo Starr and Sonny Bono after my show at the Hilton

Right My first
meeting with Elvis in
1973

Below At The
Osmond Family Show

Above In Dino's Den at The Riviera

Above With Gordon Mills in 1970

'If you can win that audience over, you can win *anybody* over, especially in Las Vegas – they've seen it all,' said one of the promoters.

By the next night, the show was filled to capacity and, by my return performance the following year, I was playing in venues with crowds of up 110,000 people per day. Am American friend of mine, Jack Turner, came to see me perform at the Riviera in 1968. Next door to the Riviera was another hotel called the Thunderbird and Jack said: 'Enge, you must be doing great business. The lines outside are so long around the block – it's making next-door's Thunderbird look busy!'

The Ed Sullivan Show really did kick my career off in the US and, after that, I played so many dates in a row in Las Vegas – and performed in so many venues and stadiums etc., that my life was consumed by work and I couldn't wait for my next visit home to the UK.

I have often thought, since those days, that if I had changed my name earlier from Gerry Dorsey to Engelbert Humperdinck, I would doubtless have arrived much sooner on the showbiz scene, but I have no regrets. My life as a singer who, after 'Release Me', was to become known as 'King of Romance', and who sold 130 million records, had four Grammy nominations, and earned a place in the *Guinness Book of Records*, was – and *still* is – magic.

CHAPTER TEN

One of my idols, Dean Martin, had a television special in the US in those days which lasted an hour and stayed at No. 1 in the ratings week after week. I was absolutely thrilled when Gordon told me I had been invited to make a guest appearance on it.

Very excited, Gordon and I flew out from England to do the show, arriving on a Sunday, even though the live show was not until the following Saturday. Greg Garrison, the show's producer, knowing that we had time on our hands, was very kind. He took us around, showing us the sights, and also set us up with plenty of studio space where we could rehearse. Dean was not there for any of this and, to my great disappointment, we never clapped eyes on the great man himself until it was time to record the programme.

But it didn't really matter because when the time came to do the recording we got on very well indeed. Dean was a superb, natural performer and the banter between us and the duets that we sang together made it seem as if we had been doing this kind of thing together for ever.

Dean was very taken with the whole concept of 'Engelbert Humperdinck', that is with my look as well as my singing, and humorously referred to me as 'Humpy Bumpy Lumpy Dumpy' in that teasing way he had. In fact, we got on so well that I was invited back several times onto his show and he decided to sponsor my appearances at the Riviera, which he partly owned, by changing the billing so it read: 'Dean Martin presents ENGELBERT HUMPERDINCK'. And I would often enjoy a drink with him in Dino's Den, his private room at the hotel, along with Pope when she was with me.

As I came to the end of my appearances at the Riviera, Gordon told me he thought that it was time for me to do a UK tour. After the sheer, overwhelming enormity of the US – even the little I had seen from the sky – I thought we could cover Great Britain in a heartbeat, and I was more than ready to do that!

At the same time, there was also a plan afoot for me to record my third album between live performances on stage in Great

Yarmouth. As it turned out, however, the winding roads and motorways we had to take to and from the recording studio in London took up too much time and interfered too much with my scheduled shows. So we had to abandon that idea and, as there were no recording studios in Yarmouth, and getting to and from the London studios didn't get us back until four in the morning, we had to come up with another idea. No problem! I recorded the album – no kidding – in a toilet in Yarmouth.

How did this come about? Simple. The record label Decca brought a truck over to where we were staying in a rented house in Yarmouth, borrowed a mobile unit that belonged to the Rolling Stones, and sewed the lines all the way up to the upstairs' toilet, because it had such good acoustics! Honestly, we just couldn't find anywhere else in the house that was suitable enough where I could stand with the microphone and sing, so I sat on the toilet seat. Meanwhile, the rest of the band were downstairs, making a racket with balls on a snooker table, and somebody had to keep on calling out: 'Hold your balls down there! We're going for another take!'

I recorded some great hit songs in that loo – and we released Mason and Reed's single 'Les Bicyclettes de Belsize' first. When the entire album was released, it went straight to No. 1 in America, selling about three million copies. At the time, I never mentioned the setting for the recording during any of the press interviews!

After three months in Yarmouth, the band and I approached Gordon and asked where, in the UK, we were headed for next?

'We're going to tour America,' was his reply.

'Are you kidding us?' we said in unison.

He wasn't.

We flew from the seaside town of Yarmouth to London on a Sunday evening, and then left for America the very next day.

Aside from the success of my album in the States, America had also picked up on the TV special I had done in England for Fabergé. By then, I'd appeared in several other television shows in the US including Laugh In, the Mike Douglas Show, Late Night with Johnny Carson and the Merv Griffin Show, but I hadn't a clue how popular I had become over the other side of the Atlantic and I certainly had no idea that my status had become worthy of an attempted kidnapping, or that Tony Cartwright, my road manager, would be held up at gunpoint in Canada when it looked as if I was going to cancel a show.

The Carpenters – the brother-and-sister singing duo, who became superstars themselves – played with us for eight months on that tour, and were with us when we went to play a week in Chicago at the Mill Run Theater. At the end of each of these shows, the band used to play my finale music over and over to allow me time to duck out of the theatre and get to the limousine, where my valet – at that time a lovely man called Georgie – would be waiting with Tony, who had already made sure everything was in order.

One Chicago night, however, Tony noticed that the limousine driver wasn't the same hired man who had dropped us off at the theatre at the beginning of the evening. Having had quite a sharp exchange with him, Tony was not a happy man and he turned to Georgie and said: 'Georgie, get all the gear out of the car – there's something wrong here.'

'No, I am the right guy – the right guy!' the driver kept protesting, as Georgie started to pull all the bags from the boot.

Right then, unaware that there was a problem, I came running out as usual to make good my escape and jumped into the car and Tony pulled me out of the limousine and it shot off with the doors and the boot still hanging open.

Tony had the presence of mind to take down the details of the limo's number plate, but it turned out to be phoney. Kenny Leonard, who became a great friend of mine after he and his family followed me on tour around the country, and who knew the police and dignitaries, tracked down the origin of that number plate, and it came up as belonging to a milk float! Kenny also called the police station to investigate the situation and, from what was said, it turned out that I was a very lucky guy not to have got into that car. What the kidnappers might have done to me is too horrible to contemplate, and who they might have called for the ransom, we luckily never had to find out.

While we were in Chicago on another visit, we found ourselves with a blessed day off and Dick Capri, my opening act comedian, and Alan Warman, my hairdresser and then road manager, called up our limo driver to take us on a drive around the city to seek a little excitement. When we cruised past a movie theater that was playing *Deep Throat*, we turned and looked at each other like naughty schoolboys.

'Have you seen it?' I asked.

'No. Have you?'

'No – and you haven't either, Alan?'

And he stuttered, 'No.'

'Then maybe we should go in and have a look at it?'

'Yes, why not.'

So, knowing I couldn't be the one to go in and buy tickets lest I was recognised, I waited in the limo with the driver while Alan went in and got them. Alan came out and said, 'Enge, you can't go in while the lights are up.' So I then waited for the lights to go dim in the auditorium, then slipped in unnoticed. Just before I did this, Alan told the limo driver what time the film ended, and instructed him to return ten minutes ahead of that time. Alan's idea was that we could then sneak out ten minutes ahead of everybody else, jump in the limo, and make our getaway, unnoticed.

So, there we were in the theatre – and, towards the end of the film, Dick was holding the face of his watch towards the light of the screen trying to read its hands so that we could be on time for our sneaky departure. He need not have bothered. Exactly ten minutes before the film ended, an usher came in with a torch and, shining its beam on the audience as he walked down the aisle, he announced: 'MR ENGELBERT HUMPERDINCK? MR ENGELBERT HUMPERDINCK – YOUR LIMOUSINE IS OUTSIDE WAITING FOR YOU!'

In Buffalo, New York, I stayed at a hotel that belonged to a man called Jim Cosentino and, from the first night I stayed there, we became good friends. While I was there, it just happened to be my birthday and they bought me this big cake. I was *very* mischievous in those days, and I took a big chunk of this gooey cake into the palm of my hand and threw it all the way across the room on to a large, gilt-edged mirror on the wall. When I turned around, who should be walking through the door right at that moment, but the owner of the hotel himself – Jim Cosentino.

'Oh God, Jim,' I stuttered. 'I'm sorry, I . . . I guess things just got a little out of hand.'

As the cake slid down the glass in streaks of cherry-coloured icing, he shrugged and said, 'Sorry about what?' Then he asked, 'Oh, is that your cake? Can I have a piece of that?'

So, having nodded a yes I cut him a dainty piece, while he looked on.

'No, I want a bigger piece than that,' he said, tut-tutting.

So I started to cut him a bigger slice of the stuff.

'Bigger,' he kept indicating, '*bigger*'.

When I finally handed him a huge chunk of the cake on one of his hotel's linen napkins, he paused a moment then he hurled it across the room at the mirror. Obviously, this man knew how to show me he didn't care a monkey's that there was cake spattered on the mirror in one of his suites. We both just laughed.

It was on that trip that I also met Jim's cousin, Frankie, whom everyone just called 'Frankie C'. Whenever I came into town, Frankie C would pick me up at the airport in one of the many Rolls-Royces that Jim owned, and take me to Jim's hotel, which is now renamed The Renaissance. And, every time, he met me, we decided to have a bit of fun with the crowds of fans we knew would be standing around the hotel awaiting my arrival.

When Fankie C arrived at the airport, he would bring the car right on to the runway and, as all the baggage was being taken care of, and each trunk and case was loaded into the Roller, I would say, 'Frankie, get in the back – I'll drive tonight.' So he would hand me the chauffeur's cap, which he wore as a joke, and I'd get in the front seat while he climbed in the back. Then I'd drive us back to the hotel where all the fans would be going crazy and screaming: 'Here's his Rolls! Oh, here he comes! Here he is!' Then, as a member of the hotel staff approached the car and opened the door, Frankie C would step out. It was hilarious. He had such a good sense of humour that his ego was never bruised by the audible sounds of disappointment that arose from the crowd when they saw his face. This moment didn't last long, of course, and, as I exited from the driver's seat, they would all start screaming again. We would then make such a show of our duplicity.

'Here's your hat back,' I'd call out as I tossed it to Frankie C, who would always be laughing.

'Come on now, Enge,' he'd say, leading me safely through the frantic, no-holds-barred crowd, 'let's get you into the hotel.'

In those days, I used to hang out at the 747 Club in that hotel and Jim would put a huge, muscular bodyguard named Big Bob right in front of my table so that nobody would bother me. No one, not anyone, got past this guy. Some years later, though, somebody did creep up on him and he was shot in the back of the head. We all missed him something awful. He was amazing, so unbelievably strong, he could go out into the street, hit a metal street lamp with the back of his hand and dent it but, inside the hotel, he always made you feel safe with a gentle smile and a mere nod of his head.

Jimmy and Frankie C treated me like a brother. My entourage, then, was about 28 people, and every visit Jim refused to charge us for the rooms. 'Jim, that's enough now,' I said on one of our visits. 'If you don't give me a check next time, I won't come back here again.' Every time, his response was always the same: 'OK OK. Next time'. But, of course, the same thing happened time and time again, and this generosity has now been going on for over thirty years.

One night, when Jimmy threw one of his parties, I was dancing with a very pretty girl and, as she gave a twirl, Frankie approached to check up on me and to make sure I was happy. 'Frankie,' I said, 'why don't you dance with this lovely young lady?' Then I added: 'Terry, this is Frankie C. Frankie C, this is Terry.' They danced together all night after that, and, a few years later, they were married.

I truly cherished my visits to them in New York. One winter's night, when I was leaving the club, I complimented Jim on the boots he was wearing.

'Your footwear's not bad,' I said. 'I like those boots you're wearing. Where did you get them?'

'Try them on,' he instructed.

'Hey, Jim,' I said when I did. 'You and I have the same size feet!'

'You like those boots?'

'Yes I do – I'm going to go out and get myself a pair this week. Where did you say you got them?'

'Never mind,' was his reply. 'They're yours. I'll see you tomorrow.'

And out he walked, barefoot, into the New York snow storm.

On one of my earlier visits to New York – before I got to sing in Dean Martin's show at the Riviera, we played The Americana – and what a crazy time that proved to be.

We were on the nineteenth floor, with a security guard perpetually posted outside the door. He was a German fellow called Schultz, who, along with another man, guarded that entire floor, including all the rooms of my entourage, and he always stood with his arms folded across his chest and two feral-looking dogs at his side.

One night, there was a knock on my door. I knew it wasn't Schultz's beat. He had a meaty fist, but he knocked very gingerly when he needed to speak with Tony or get in touch with me. This knocking, however, was more like a banging, and a loud, constant one as if the person on the other side thought that if he hit a door long enough it would open on its own.

'Listen, we're big fans out here, all right?' a voice called out. 'And we want to come in and see Engelbert, all right?'

I had just finished a show, was feeling emotionally drained and, in addition, not feeling very well that night, so I just continued to lie on the bed and asked Tony to go and see what the racket was about, and to explain to Schultz that I was not feeling well enough to greet anyone.

Tony got up from the couch, walked to the door, and stood peering through the peephole for what seemed like an unnecessarily long time. But the reason was that neither Schultz nor his partner was anywhere to be seen. They'd vanished. In their place were these two men, banging repeatedly on the door, asking to be let in.

'Hey, it's the Gallo brothers out here, and we want to come in and say hello to Engelbert,' said another voice.

Tony walked away from the door, grabbed a few of my press photos and brought them over to me. 'Enge,' he said apologetically, 'I think you'd better sign these for the Gallo brothers.'

Realising that they were well connected with the mob, I did, but, apparently, that was not what they wanted. They wanted to come in and say hello to me personally, and they continued to repeat that they were big fans of mine. Tony tried, and eventually succeeded in convincing them that I wasn't going to greet anyone that night, although he did ultimately have to solicit the help of the police in this. In fact, while they were carrying on outside the hotel room door, I had already climbed into bed to try and get some rest before my next show. As I did so, I heard their last shout, 'Oh, yeah? *Not* going to let us in, eh? That's just *fine*, Engelbert, we'll move on to support another singer instead of you like your buddy Tom Jones! How do you like that?'

I didn't like *that* because I respect all my fans and don't ever want to let them down, for any reason. But, in those days, I was playing New York so often that I hoped I could meet the Gallo brothers some day and make up for the fact that I wouldn't see them then.

Later, I found out that, apart from being big fans of mine, they were known for being slightly unusual. This was partly, but not entirely, because Joe Gallo was often seen with his pet, which was not a miniature poodle, or indeed any other kind of small breed dog that was so popular in New York apartments and prevalent in its parks and streets. Joe Gallo's four-legged, domestic pet was a tiger – a full-grown, enormous tiger.

Unfortunately, I never got to meet either of the Gallo brothers. Joe Gallo was shot and killed a few months later, while he was celebrating his birthday with a dinner at Umberto's Clam House in New York's Little Italy. My career has introduced me to all walks of life, and unbeknown to me, some portion of my audiences have been part of the underworld. All I knew was that members of the Mafia loved entertainers, and I was one of them. Their business was their business; entertaining them was mine.

My encounters with members of the Mafia didn't end there.

I met Bill LoSapio when I was playing in Westchester, in New York, when he brought his aunt and his mother backstage to meet me. He told me he owned a restaurant called Gregory's located in White Plains, and invited me to come in next time I was in New York. Three months later I returned, and, remembering his kind invitation, I made my way to the restaurant and ordered the Clams Oreganata, which I now simply call 'The Engelbert Clams'. Bill, whom I now call Billy Boy – and he calls me Dukey – took one look at me that day and commented, 'You look a little down. Are you OK?' I told him I was feeling a little blue, and he suggested I meet him the next day, and he would take me out for a few rounds of golf. The fresh air and new friend were exactly what the doctor ordered.

But it almost got me into trouble. After a day of golf, Big Al, came to me and told me that Paulie Castellano, also well known for his heavy connections and apparently a fan of mine, wanted to meet me. I met Big Al through John Smythe, who was running the Colony Hill Hotel in New York. Big Al ran a lot of the unions and was a force to contend with, despite the fact that everywhere he went, he wore slippers on his feet, I'll never forget that. He was powerful, and always very polite and courteous to me, and always wore thse slippers! I told Big Al I couldn't possibly meet a man of Castellano's stature dressed in casual golf clothing as I was, which Castellano interpreted as a snub. When Big Al told him I couldn't meet him that day, he replied, 'Wow. This kid's got *cojones*!' Which means, in simple language – balls!

Despite those gentlemen's associations, I have only once ever had a problem with someone like that and it wasn't even in the US, but in Mexico.

In 1971, as a thank-you for all their support, I took my band on holiday to Acapulco, where I had rented a mountainside villa. It was a beautiful, sun-drenched setting, with vines and olives and sweet-smelling herbs in the garden but, on the very first night when we were asleep, every member of the band – including me – got robbed. When we woke up, all our rings, watches, and gold chains had been slipped right off our sleeping bodies! The thieves were obviously quite talented, but they were also pranksters. When I awoke in the morning, the Band-Aid that covered a small cut on my left leg had been moved to *exactly* the same spot on my *right* leg! But I was *very* upset about being burgled, so I called the guy who owned the villa.

'Look here,' I said, incensed. 'we've rented a villa, where there is no security, and I and all my people have been *robbed*. Our watches, cufflinks, wallets – all our valuables – have gone. What are we supposed to do now?'

'Wait a minute,' he said, 'I have to make a phone call.'

It wasn't quite the response I'd expected, but I waited by the phone!

When he called back, he said: 'OK. No problem. Everything will be returned.'

'*What*?' I queried, shocked.

'Everything will be returned,' he repeated and, obviously a man of few words, he hung up.

And everything was returned!

It was understood that the man who owned the villa was connected with the underworld, and one call from him must have made those thieves shiver!

Bad shows for me, caused by bad sound, were never a laughing matter. Whenever I felt I hadn't been able to give my best to an audience, I was always very upset – I still am. Before now, I've gone through four soundmen in one week; at one time, I'm sure I was the most hated guy in show business as far as sound people were concerned. I never kept them on for long if I found them to be incapable or incompetent. I hate incompetence. If I can go on and give my show a hundred per cent, I expect them to give their hundred per cent as well. If they don't, it takes away a piece of my thunder, and I just can't stand that because I live for perfection when I'm on stage. I had – and probably still have – the reputation of having worked my way through the most sound men; and that, I am sorry to say, is because of my need for perfection. All I want is for the sound on stage to come across as perfectly as it does when I am in a recording studio. If that happens, then I'm happy.

Once I did a really bad show because the sound and the acoustics were terrible. Deeply frustrated after I came off stage, I hit the metal door of my hotel room, splitting two of my knuckles open and creating a blood-soaked seam down the back of my hand, and I soon realised I had hurt myself quite badly. So, I wrapped my hand up and went to ask some medical people who just happened to be staying in the hotel, if I should go to the hospital and have it dressed or stitched up. When they said the hospital doctors would only wrap it for me anyway, and then confirmed that although the skin was split, the bones of the knuckle were not broken, I decided to tough it out.

But the sound is so crucial. In my early years it came through speakers, then headphones, now we have earpieces – tiny little inserts – that the audience cannot see. So the revolution in sound has come full circle, away from big monitors, back to the ears, and now that we've got reverb in our ears it's much better. It's more like a studio sound. Things are still not perfect, though, and even today soundmen remain the ones among my entourage who suffer the most frequent bollockings.

The band and the entire entourage are such an important backbone to whatever I do on stage, and they are the people who really matter when it's showtime. Lights, sound and music are all essential elements to putting on a great show. It's never just a case of me, a microphone and a handful of hits!

In the early days, John Spooner, Mick Greene, Robbie Mac-Donald, Mike Egan, and Laurie Holloway were the legends in my band. Jeff Sturges has been my conductor and arranger for eleven years, and prior to him there were some great people in my life as far as musicians were concerned. The very first person that came over from England to America with me was Laurie Holloway, who proved to be one of the greatest musicians and musical directors I have ever worked with. After Laurie, there was another gentleman called Arthur Greenslade, whom unfortunately we lost just last year. But I'll never forget what a great musician, great arranger, fabulous conductor, and dear friend he was to me. These are the great people in my life here. When you spend as many hours, days and weeks in a row with the people you work with as I do – it's not like leaving an office at 5 p.m. – it's more than wonderful to find great talent in people that you can also deem great friends.

When Jeff Sturges and I first started working together, working hand in hand on multiple arrangements, we used to get a few bottles of wine from the cellar at the Pink Palace and just collaborate all night. On one occasion, when I was on tour, I was trying to work out some new arrangements over the phone with Jeff, who was at home in Los Angeles. I sang a few parts to him, then sang the backup girls' parts and said, 'Now you do some, Jeff.'

So Jeff began offering arrangements for the various girls' background vocals and then he sang all sorts of other sounds and variations for my approval.

There was a growing silence on my end of the phone.

'Enge, Enge?' he prompted, after about ten minutes of singing and getting excited about the new arrangement.

But there was no response from me.

'Enge? What do you think?' he tried once more.

Doug Ivan, my bodyguard and martial arts teacher, picked up the phone and said, 'Jeff, you'll have to finish this tomorrow.'

'Why?' Jeff asked, puzzled.

Doug replied, 'Because Enge is fast asleep.'

It was true, Jeff had sung me to sleep.

The Bee Gees were touring in the US at the time and their manager, Robert Stigwood, approached Tony Cartwright, saying, 'Barry and Robin have a song for Engelbert to sing. Can they meet you in his room?'

So Barry Gibb came up to the suite and played 'Sweetheart', which ended up being a very big song for me.

We had a lot of fun that afternoon, with Barry playing the guitar while I was singing along. We made plans to record it, but when Gordon Mills heard of these, he was furious: 'How dare he come up and play you songs,' he growled.

I suppose he wanted to be in control and in on everything before anyone else, but I can't be sure.

When Tony got on the phone, he said: 'Just listen, Gordon,' and he held the phone receiver near Barry and me like a microphone. Gordon loved the song and, recently, 'Sweetheart' became part of the 'Greatest Love Songs' album I compiled, and which climbed to No. 4 in the charts.

When we got up to Maple Leaf Gardens, a 20,000-seater venue in Toronto, in Canada, there was a near-riot and Tony was held up at gunpoint.

This came about because, when I checked into the Skyland Hotel at the airport, I decided I would go to bed and have a good rest so that I could handle the huge, sell-out performance that night. While I was resting in the afternoon, the air conditioning kicked on – and dried my throat out, sucked the sound right out of me. When I woke up, I could barely clear my throat, let alone whisper. It was pathetic. I kept croaking, 'Hello, hello, hello' as if

I were in one of those dreams where you keep running and calling for help, but nothing comes out of your mouth. With barely an audible whisper to help me, I phoned my agent Barry Clayman, who was in Canada with me at the time.

'Barry,' I croaked, 'you had better help me – I've lost my voice.'

He said, 'Hang on, I'll come over and help you find it.'

When he arrived, he could tell things were dreadfully serious and that help was needed fast. It really was getting on the late side and my voice was still sounding like I was speaking through a mouthful of wool.

'You'd better get a doctor quick,' I croaked, 'or I really won't be able to sing tonight.'

But he couldn't find a doctor, no matter how hard he tried and, although it was time for me to go to the Maple Leaf Gardens venue, I couldn't sing. My windpipes felt smaller than my little finger, and I couldn't believe they'd allow me the strength of volume, or steady pitch, that I needed for my performance. Finally, a doctor arrived backstage, a real pro called Dr Simon McGrail, who began treating me immediately. Dr McGrail, an Englishman and a brilliant ears, nose and throat specialist, who put voice boxes into cancer patients, kept spraying my throat while Alan Drake, the warm-up comedian, who was with me, went out to open the show.

Alan was aware of my situation, and I'm sure his nerves were responsible for what was about to happen next on stage. He spent thirty minutes working the crowd, getting the audience warmed up, then The Carpenters went out and did their bit for half an hour, but I still wasn't ready to go on. That, actually, is an understatement – at that point I was throwing up, I was so nervous that I wouldn't get my voice back.

'This situation is just the absolute worst,' I thought.

As it turned out, however, Alan was facing a near-riot on stage and Tony was facing an even worse situation. He was being held up, backstage, by two guys who had pressed their guns to both sides of his throat.

'Get him on stage or you're a dead man,' was the hushed warning.

To Tony's credit, when he came to check on my progress, which entailed Dr McGrail trying to soothe my throat in between my frequent trips to the toilet, he never let on that either of us were in grave danger.

'I will go out there and try to perform, and see what happens,' I said.

I imagine Tony was standing there trying to visualise exactly where the exits were in case we needed to flee. The two men who had threatened Tony asked him once again to get me on stage and so I went out.

I managed to get through four numbers in a monotone, 'Johnny one-note'. And I really couldn't sing any of my hit songs. It was just a case of 'Every day I wake up, then I start to break up, lonely is a man without a voice . . .' all in the *same* tone. It was *dreadful – no good at all*. I had this big orchestra behind me and I had to turn and say, 'Hold it – *hold it* . . .' Then, addressing the audience in a hoarse whisper, I said, 'Ladies and gentlemen, you know I don't really sing the way I have tonight. When I arrived in your country today, I was ready to do a big show for all 20,000 here tonight. But this is what happened: I got into my room and had a little sleep and the air conditioning kicked on and took my voice away, but I'm not going to ask you to go away and come back tomorrow because I know you can't do that. And neither can I because I have to be in another place tomorrow evening. So I can only ask you to bear with me. Maybe my voice will come back, maybe it won't, the doctor backstage has promised me it would.

Luckily on the fifth song my voice returned and I sang for an hour and a half. I wanted to give these people what they came to hear – my hit songs and good entertainment.

As a result of the extra-long performance, everybody had missed their buses and trains, and every other kind of ride they had previously arranged. They must also have known they were in for total gridlock – and a real battle when they tried to hail cabs after midnight. Nevertheless, they all stood up and gave me an ovation, thanking me by cheering and applauding for being such a trooper and making such an heroic attempt right in front of their eyes.

It was a marvellous performance, somehow made even better by the fact that I had to struggle in front of them before I could pull through and become the performer they knew with the voice they'd heard before on records.

The encore cries were wonderful – music to my ears – and I remember repeating, 'Thank you for bearing with me,' as I bowed.

Somewhere backstage, Tony was thankful for being able to walk out of the building in one piece.

Who were the guys who threatened him that night? Sorry, I'd rather *not* tempt fate and name names!

CHAPTER ELEVEN

Dear old Dean was very good to me when I went to Las Vegas. Although I was still teetering on the verge of becoming an internationally successful singing star, Dean had taken a shine to me and he made sure that my Vegas deals were up to par, telling his lawyers that they should negotiate the same rates for me that he was paid.

'If he's gonna do my kind of business,' Dean said, 'he should get my kind of money.'

That really was generous of him!

Luckily, my shows were becoming a sell-out within a couple of days and I was becoming 'red hot'.

Dean, who invited me to be part of 'Dino's Den', always treated me very well and seemed to enjoy my company. Nobody was allowed to cross the threshold of Dino's Den without an invitation, so there were no strangers in there, only friends. I was the only British performer he really took a personal liking to, and put his name behind.

'Set him up with whatever he needs,' he told his lawyers, 'house, car – *anything*.'

I was thrilled. If you had Dean Martin on your side in Vegas, you were all set for decades to come.

On my opening night at the Riviera, it was jam packed. You couldn't get to the coffee shop for a sandwich. Dean Martin came in with Frank Sinatra, Juliet Prowse, Sammy Davis Jr and a whole host of other big stars. In those days, it was customary to acknowledge the stars in the audience and announce their presence to everyone else, making sure you gave each of them the same prominence. And they were all first class. Choosing the first to do, the woman, obviously, I went on to announce Dean last because his name was on the marquee (the awning over the hotel entrance) and because he had 'a piece in the hotel' at that time, but as I used to say in my monologue, every time I went to the hotel and looked around, I couldn't find her!

The surprise of having these massive show business names come into the hotel became an everyday occurrence. Sonny Liston, the former heavyweight champion of the world, was a frequent visitor, as were Telly Savalas and Cary Grant, who took one look at me backstage and said: 'My you are a handsome boy. If I was twenty years younger, I'd marry you!'.

The news of my performance and stature went all around America. 'DEAN GETS THE HUMP,' read the headlines. It was the most outrageous thing that had ever been said, and many folks still didn't know what 'getting the hump' actually meant. Ultimately, of course, the public figured it out, but by the second show – whether people knew what a Hump was or not – I sold out for the rest of the month, and then sold out for a further five years. Part of the success, I think, was due to Las Vegas being a 'cab' town, where people would hop into taxis and ask, 'Where's the hottest place in town? If we really want to do Vegas right, where should we go?' And cabbies always responded, 'Well that would be where Dean Martin, Frank Sinatra, Juliet Prowse and everybody else hangs out.'

'Where's that?' came the question, of course.

And thus everyone, absolutely everyone, was dropped off at the Riviera. That was the power of Dean Martin.

One of the most exciting early moments for me in the US was when I saw Dean at one of my shows with the legendary film star Betty Grable. They were lovely to Popea. Having noticed that she was feeling out on a limb and nervous – and trying so hard to be grown up – Dean went over to her and said: 'Come and sit with us and have a photograph taken.'

We still have that photograph today.

Another key moment in those days was when I saw Doris Day, whom I had always adored on the big screen, and went up to her and shook her hand and asked for her autograph, which I still have.

Those really were wonderful years and I had so much fun meeting the stars who crossed my path. They often amused me with their funny remarks as when the actor Stewart Grainger and I appeared in the spectacular, *Night of a Thousand Stars*. Stewart turned to me and said, 'I know we're the stars, but who the fuck are these other people?'

When I eventually got round to buying my own home in Vegas around 1970, I rented it out to everybody. Rich Little, an impersonator who was big in the US and well known for his impressions of presidents and celebrities – like me – used to leave his pictures – his 8x10s – underneath the toilet seat and all over the place. Everywhere you went around the house, there was a Rich Little print. The singers Diana Ross and Barry Manilow and the actress Shirley MacLaine, all used to stay there. Shirley always slept with the doors wide open and a bodyguard sitting by the pool. Dean also used to hire it quite a lot because it was a single-level house and he didn't like heights. He hated going to places that required an escalator or elevator or lift to get to where he needed to be. He used to leave cigarette burns on one of our bedside tables.

I went out to dinner many times with Dean and my agent from ICM, Mort Viner, who sadly died last year, and it was always the same routine. He would sit at his favourite table at La Famiglia, and the owner would come over and ask, 'What would you like, Dean?'

'What are you serving tonight?' Dean would reply. 'Show me the menu, please.'

It was all a big act. Every evening, having gone through this routine with the Maitre d' for what seemed like a two-hour session, Dean would order exactly the same meal – a meat-and-potatoes dish – that he had had the night before and the night before that.

It was hard to stop laughing around him, and quite common for one's ribs to ache. One night, after we'd all been drinking gallons of wine at La Famiglia, someone turned to Dean and asked, 'Hey Duke, are you driving home?'

'Well, of course, I am,' he replied. 'I'm too damn drunk to walk.'

After making my first couple of trips to Las Vegas, I embarked on my first major UK tour – 36 dates in England, Ireland, Scotland and Wales – and I was really looking forward to this.

On the bill with me was the singer Cat Stevens, who later changed his name to Yusuf Islam when he converted to the Islamic faith. In the 60s, when we were together, he'd been in the UK charts with songs, such as 'I Love My Dog', 'Matthew and Son' and 'I'm Gonna Get Me a Gun'. Later on in the 70s, he became one of the world's biggest album sellers with his No. 1 'Lady D'Arbanville' and his much-loved record, 'Morning Has Broken'.

When his record company was trying to break Jimi Hendrix into the British market, it had to team him with a well-known performer, so he also came on tour with me. He was an ace rock-'n'roller guitarist, wildly energetic, and he played his guitar with his teeth and sometimes ended his set by thrashing his guitar to pieces on the stage or by setting the thing on fire. *Unbelievable*! It was very exciting to be involved with someone like that who had had hits in the UK 60s' charts with songs which included 'Hey Joe', 'Purple Haze' and 'The Wind Cries Mary'. One night, on that tour, he was a real trouper who came through for me – and saved my bacon.

When one of my guitar players fell ill at the very last minute, and couldn't go on stage, I wasn't at all sure how I'd be able to go on either that night, but Jimi had the answer. Stars, as proved by Dean Martin, can be among the most generous, non-egotistical people in the world.

'Don't *worry*, man,' he said, as if it were no big deal, 'I'll play for you.'

'You *can't* do that,' I responded. 'You're too big a star. You *can't* just walk out there with me, you know?'

'OK,' he said, 'I'll hide in the curtains and nobody will ever know who's playing.'

By now I'd performed with quite a few top musicians, even though at the time none of us knew they'd go on to be such big stars. On my 'Release Me' album, for example, I had Elton John on piano, Jimmy Paige playing guitar and John Paul Jones strumming the bass, while Big Jim Sullivan performed on a few of the tracks. When Jimi played behind the curtains for me, it sounded like three guitars instead of one.

That tour really was a massive success and, on a couple of occasions, things very nearly got out of hand and we were in serious danger of being mobbed. It really was frightening. After a few scares, we had to take extra precautions. Having driven to a city, we would have to sit outside it – sometimes for a couple of hours – while the various authorities got control of the crowd. I am not at all sure anyone would attempt the kind of performances we did in Glasgow, Manchester, Liverpool and London today in quite the same way. Mob rule really is scary! I was still too excited, though, to be put off by any of this and give into fear – I really didn't mind having to wait outside the city walls before driving in just in time for the show. I had waited too long for success to mind any of it! It was like a game of hit-and-run: getting into the theatre, taking the stage right on time, then getting out of whatever city we were in as fast as we could.

Jimi and I got on very well after he stood in for my guitarist and became good friends who shared backstage drinks; and I never blamed him when, a bit further on down the line, a couple of members of my band left the tour and me to go with Jimi to America. I completely understood that they wanted to make a name for themselves in the US, and Jimi was such a nice guy that I *honestly* didn't mind him stealing them.

Jimi used to collect army uniforms and, one day, generous person that he was, he said he would give one to me and one to Tony.

Soon after this, when Tony was wearing Jimi's gift of an army jacket, we were playing in Liverpool, which was a really crazy city in those days – one you could hardly get into because it was so overcrowded with people. One afternoon while we were there, we decided to go to this private club, where they wouldn't let the crowds in, so that Jimi, Tony and I could escape the attention of our fans and enjoy a quiet pint of bitter. When Tony went up to the bar to order our drinks, a guy, who turned out to be an ex-army colonel, spied him and was obviously pissed off to see him wearing an army jacket as a fashion statement, rather than for Queen and country.

'Excuse me young man,' he said, 'was your father in that regiment?'

'What regiment?' Jimi, who was standing next to Tony, asked, but, oh boy, did he back off when he saw the expression on the colonel's face and realised that the man was very serious and we were in trouble.

'The regiment you've got right *there*, represented on that badge on *your* jacket,' the colonel continued. 'I repeat: did your father belong to that regiment?'

Tony's still-blank expression was really winding this man up and, with no more ado, he began to give him a bollocking.

'No man should be walking around in such a uniform if they haven't earned it,' he said, ramming his face closer and closer to Tony's. 'It's disrespectful – offensive – and downright wrong, young man.'

He was now so in Tony's face that Tony was going cross-eyed and breaking out in a sweat.

When we hurriedly backed off and succeeded in getting out of there, with Tony unharmed, I said: 'Thank God I wasn't wearing one of those jackets, too.' I told Jimi, who couldn't stop laughing, that I wasn't at all sure I wanted mine any more.

'Oh Tony, man,' he said, 'I nearly crapped myself back there. I was crying for you, man, watching you have to stay so polite and so respectful and take all that shit from some guy who was so in your face.'

That same night we were playing De Montfort Hall in my hometown of Leicester, and my parents were very much on my mind. Gordon and I took Jimi out to experience some real English food – roast beef and Yorkshire pudding. Then, having dropped him off at the auditorium, I asked Gordon if we could have a private chat before the show. 'I want to buy my mum and dad a house, Gordon,' I said, once he had parked his car, 'and I've been having a look around.'

'Enge,' he said, 'why don't you wait until you've made some more money and maybe buy yourself a house first, then one for your mother and father?'

'No, Gordon,' I replied, 'my mum and dad come first. I might never have another hit record as long as I live. You never know what's going to happen in this business.'

'My point precisely,' he said.

But I was determined. I had dreamed of being in a position to buy my parents a house for years, and I wasn't going to give up on it now. While Gordon took some persuading and coercing, Popea had agreed wholeheartedly to my suggestion and we'd already been house-hunting together for several days. We continued the search even on the day of my performance in Leicester and we found exactly what we'd been looking for, what we thought would be right for my mum and dad. They agreed, and Mum, with tears glistening in her eyes, called it 'a *lovely* home, a really *lovely* home'.

It was such a great feeling to be able to do that for them and pay cash! Before I went on stage that night at De Montfort Hall, I had made all the necessary arrangements to buy the house and signed on the dotted line. It felt wonderful, and was honestly one of the best moments of my life.

Thus it was that Popea and I remained in our humble, but much-loved Hammersmith flat for a further eighteen months after I found success, and everyone, it seemed, had something to say about that. There were cartoon drawings in the papers of Popea living in a little tent, with me riding around on an old bicycle; and the grapevine quoted Barry Gibb as saying, 'He lives in a very ordinary pad when he could afford a mansion. It's his choice, but it seems very odd to me. I think top stars should live luxuriously because that's what's expected of them. My own attitude is: if you're in the money, you should spend freely, but make sure you have some left over.'

Looking back, maybe I was a little too concerned about having 'some left over', but I was also extremely busy, and Popea and I were never unhappy in that little flat. Barry was right in the sense that, if I'd spent more then, there would have been less for the 'thieves', such as future management figures, to steal later.

At that time, while we were staying put, little Louise, who was by now about three years old, was on the move, without us! One day she managed to creep out of the flat door without us noticing and took her dolly down three flights of stairs and out of the front door. By some miracle, I happened to look out of the living-room window and there she was, standing by the edge of the busy road with her doll clutched in her hands. I went hot, cold and weak at the knees.

'*Oh, God, no,*' I said as I hurled myself out of the flat and slithered and jumped down the stairs six at a time. '*Oh, God, no! Please, God, don't let anything happen to her. Please God keep her safe.*'

I still shudder even now when I think what could have happened to her if I hadn't looked out the window just at that moment and if I hadn't reached her side just as she was about to step off the kerb into the road. When at last I managed to grab hold of her and lift her up into my arms, I was so thankful, but she was totally unafraid, unfazed by all the fast-moving traffic and the racket that it was making as it zoomed by. One step off that kerb into the road and she would have been killed for sure. After that, I could hardly bear to take my eyes off her.

She was my little princess and such a joy! After I'd made a name for myself, members of the press sometimes – or a few fans who had discovered where I lived – would come and knock on our door. Louise would often open it and announce: 'My daddy's Engelbert Humperdinck,' and let them right in. Sometimes, too, when we were out shopping, I would dart into a store to pick up something, while Popea waited outside with Louise. On these occasions my feisty little girl would call out to passers-by, 'My daddy's Engelbert Humperdinck – and Engelbert Humperdinck's in there!'

Having had such a wonderful, first experience of fatherhood with Louise, I'd been absolutely thrilled when Popea told me she was pregnant again this time with Jason, our first son, who weighed in at 10 lb at birth. During her pregnancy with Louise she had hardly shown, and with Jason she seemed a little bigger, but, when she was pregnant with Scott, everything was very different. She was absolutely enormous when expecting him. The doctor said he had never seen anyone with a bump the size of the one she had. She used to have to lift her huge tummy up over the sink in order to peel the potatoes for supper.

On one of her visits to the surgery, Pope noticed that the doctor was looking very grim and her heart went into overdrive.

'I'm sorry,' the doctor said, 'but I'm worried that something might be seriously wrong with your baby. The placenta is pressing on the baby's head, and the child may not be – in fact it is very unlikely to be normal.'

He then wrote down the name and address of a clinic and gave it to Popea with the suggestion that she should go home, pack a toilet bag, and have the baby aborted.

Popea was horrified – and refused at once to do this.

'No, I won't do that,' she said. 'If anything is wrong with the baby, we'll deal with it then.'

Thank heavens she stuck to her guns. When baby Scott entered the world there was nothing wrong with him. He was absolutely *perfect* and we just could not stop grinning from ear to ear.

While Popea was in hospital, her mum showed up, appearing in the maternity ward like it had all been pre-planned, but it hadn't. It has to be understood that she *never* travelled anywhere on her own – and was *never* one to get up and figure out how to get from A to B herself. Yet, there she was, walking down the hospital corridor to her daughter's room. Patricia could *not* believe her eyes.

'How on earth did you get here, Mum?' she asked.

'I can catch a train!' her mother replied with a toss of her head.

Apparently she had asked a lady, a complete stranger whom she passed working in her garden, where the hospital was, and then made her way there. We couldn't believe she had been that daring! After the visit, having been allowed to hold her new grandchild, she decided to go back and look after the flat for us. On her way there, she passed the same lady who was still working in her garden.

'Come in and have a cuppa and tell me all about the new baby,' the woman said – and she did.

Only somebody who has been warned to expect an imperfect child and then gets a perfect one can truly understand how we felt when Scott was born. He would have been a very special baby in whatever shape he came, but we were so glad that he was all right.

We were so lucky – and we have never ever taken any of our children for granted.

I also wrote a poem about Scott's birth:

Naked soil covered in autumn confetti
Colourful as the peacock's comb
Effervescent too the gushing fountain
Leaping in ecstasy from its earthy womb

Tears proudly disguised as dew
Flowing in anguish into a sea of sadness
The pine the birch the weeping willow
Standing in ancient fear of a lumber's axe

Only to find it all a dream
Only to be rewarded by the rising of the sun
Bringing a new day
A new dawn a new life

But also bringing tired smiles to the young mother
Sliding from her tender loins as she lays in sexual poise
A baby cries, a mother sighs, in harmonious rapture
It's a Boy!

Delicate, and then a man
To work and survive
To feed the mouth that is not only for eating
But to continue to age a craft
Of speaking the language of love.

When Bradley, our youngest was born, I took a picture of my lovely wife, Popea, breastfeeding him, and then commissioned an artist to do a painting of it. I have always loved that painting so much, and it is still with us now, hanging over the fireplace in our home in Leicester.

Just as the 60s were drawing to an end and we were staying at the Hawaiian Village Hotel in Honolulu, I couldn't resist playing a great joke on Tony, my road manager. I was standing on the balcony of my fifth-floor suite, looking down at the pool area, when I saw a really beautiful woman, with a baby in her arms, walking back towards the hotel.

'Hey, Tony,' I called out. 'Go and bring that girl up here.'

Coming out to join me on the balcony, Tony took one look at the woman and, tapping his chest – as he always does when he's anxious – he replied: 'Come off it, Enge, she's got a little baby in her arms . . .'

'So? That's OK – just bring her up. We can give the baby some milk.'

'But Enge,' he pleaded, puzzled by my mood and completely misconstruing my intentions. 'She's got a little baby in her arms. And we'll get into trouble!'

'For heaven's sake,' I muttered in a mock growl. '*Go and get her*!'

So, looking very dejected and obviously deeply concerned, he set off to the foyer to cut the woman off as she entered the hotel from the pool area.

The next moment, positively flinging myself down the stairs, I managed to catch up with him just as he had started to talk to this lovely girl. When I tapped him on the shoulder, he turned round and, very red in the face, he stuttered: 'Oh, Enge! I gather you know Priscilla – *Elvis's wife.*'

Of course I knew her. That's *why* I had put him up to it and, for fun, intentionally embarrassed the hell out of him.

When, years later, I reminded Priscilla about what happened, she was very amused, couldn't stop smiling.

Elvis Presley turned up in my audience to watch me perform at the Riviera in 1973. When I introduced him – oh, it was grand. He stood on his chair and opened his gorgeous red velvet cape for the crowd, and it took what seemed like forever – though probably only ten minutes – to calm the audience down. They went absolutely mad.

So I pulled out my big gun, one of my biggest songs, to capture the audience again.

And it worked.

I'll tell you a story – this story is a true story – about the second time I played Vegas. We got a phone call from Colonel Parker, who managed Elvis, asking, 'Elvis is going to come in and watch the show; can we have that centre booth?' 'Of course, of course,' we said, 'No problem.' Tony made the arrangements, and I remember him telling Colonel Parker, 'Bring him in when the lights are down, so it doesn't attract any attention to him, and he can sneak in and watch the show in peace. Not that Elvis could sneak in anywhere. Anyway, they followed the rules per my suggestion, but the buzz was on that Elvis was in the building. Respectfully, they stayed quiet, all the way through – until I introduced him.

Afterwards Elvis came backstage and asked, 'Engelbert, do you like my jacket? Priscilla got it for me. It's real velvet. Feel it.' That's how this man was, he was so down to earth, just like you and I – even though he was this giant of a man. He was excited by the mere fact that he was wearing a velvet jacket. While we talked about Vegas and the scene and how we were getting on – me talking about various Vegas venues, him telling me he was about to go on the road and then would return for a run at The Hilton – Tony and Colonel Parker were off to the side talking quietly to one another. And then I heard Tony raising his voice a little while taking on a stern tone.

'Listen, we're just starting a world tour. We've got an eighteen-month tour coming up and there's no way Elvis can take these fellas from Engelbert.'

I had no idea what they were on about, but Elvis looked a little sorry. Apparently he told Colonel Parker – who told Tony – that he'd like to take my guitar player and my bass player on tour with him and asked that this 'transfer' be handled after the show.

'We need them; there's no way you can take any of his musicians, Colonel,' Tony continued.

'Hey, I'm real sorry Tony,' he replied. 'I thought they were just casual staff, you know.'

Elvis was apologetic as well, and from that point on he seemed to make an extra effort to drop any special requests for grand entrances or suggestions that he be entitled to anything but my friendship, and we became true friends. He shed all pretences and really relaxed around me, which was wonderful, but later, on one occasion he seemed to relax a little too much. Or he tried to, anyway, and his pants just weren't interested in following along.

He came up to my suite for a drink after the show, after I'd said all my 'hellos' and 'thank-yous' to various guests backstage and was ready to relax. He entered, commented on my sideburns for a second time, introduced his valet, Fred West, and then went off to the toilet.

Suddenly we heard him calling, 'Fred! Fred! Come in here! I've split my pants, and I need you to come help my ass!' I think he was kidding about the last part, but he certainly had split those trousers open wide at the seam. Fred kept knocking lightly on the other side of the door, trying to be heard over 'Help get my pants up! Fred! Help me get these pants up!'

'It's me, it's Fred – can I come in? I'm coming in, OK?'

None of us knew which way to look when Fred opened the door to check on the situation. Elvis emerged in his underpants, with his studded leather trousers in Fred's hands. Georgie, my valet – who was by then quite used to stitching my own trousers

– took them from Fred, silently, and went off with a needle and thread to fix them up.

I'll also never forget the night I took Patricia and Jeff Sturges and his wife Sherry to see Elvis at The Hilton. It was 1975, the year Johnny Spence recommended Jeff become my music director, and the year Elvis really started to show signs that he wasn't getting on very well any more. (Two years later, Johnny Spence and Elvis died on the same day, at the same age.)

Anyway, Elvis and I had become quite close by '75, so when I took my guests to see his show they were treated like royalty and given a special VIP booth and everything. During the show, Elvis introduced me and the audience went crazy, and then afterwards we all went back stage and we waited, and waited, and waited – waited quite an unusually long time for Elvis to come out of his private dressing-room into the greeting area of the green room. When he was finally due, they opened the door for Elvis to come out of his private room, and it was one of those double doors between rooms – and Elvis walked straight into the door and hit his head, hard, right on the door.

'I never could figure out how to get out that door,' joked Elvis, trying to make light of such an uncomfortable and obvious blunder. But it was really sad, and not a joke by any means, because he was so sick. He looked like a person that has been in hospital a long time, drained of energy and enthusiasm and general health. He had really pale white skin and, what's worse, he was really disoriented. When he saw me and Patricia, and Jeff and his wife, he came over and said to me, 'Was the introduction OK? During the show, when I introduced you to the audience was that all right?'

Of course it was. 'The introduction was just fine,' I assured him. It was Elvis himself that I was really worried about.

The 60s was a truly *amazing* decade for so many reasons, not least for becoming dubbed as the 'permissive years', for the hippies – 'flower children' – partying for peace at Woodstock, for launching Neil Armstrong (whom I had the pleasure of meeting later on at Doug Sander's golf tournament) as the first man to walk on the moon. And, for me, there are so many reasons why that decade was memorable. After all those years when my career had been rather stop-started, gone into the doldrums and ground to a halt in so many showbiz cul-de-sacs, I had made a meteoric break-through and comeback; and, as the decade ended, far from being reduced to wearing brown paper-bag patches in my shoes to cover the holes in the soles – and trying to support a wife and young family while doing low-paid gigs and living on the dole, I was now travelling to and from the US and enjoying the glittering lifestyle of the Hollywood in-crowd.

CHAPTER TWELVE

'What a difference a day makes' goes the popular song. But, in my life, it was a case of what a difference a couple of years can make! When we finally moved home in 1969, we went from the flat in Hammersmith to an absolute mansion with six bedrooms in the gated Green Belt area of Weybridge. Various television stars were already living there, and now Pope and I and Louise and Scott joined John, Paul, George and Ringo, along with Cliff Richard and Tom Jones. In fact, time was, when anybody who was famous seemed to be living behind one or other of those huge, wrought-iron security gates.

We inherited Mr Speed, the gardener on our property, who stayed on in the gardener's cottage. Every morning, he cleaned and polished my Rolls-Royce, making it shine like it was brand new. Gone were the days of tarpaulin – and finance companies' tow-aways. Thank God!

Popea, however, was not altogether comfortable with some of the changes in our lifestyle. She was intimidated by the size of the mansion and by Mr Speed.

'If only we'd moved from the flat to a semi-detached and then worked our way up, it would have been a much easier transition,' she used to say.

As it was, on the days when the cleaning lady would come in, my nervous wife used to scrub the place from top to bottom before her arrival! For me, however, having spent my boyhood in Madras with fifteen servants waiting on me hand and foot, it was not a tough adjustment. I just thought it was very nice to have people looking after us!

'Mr Speed,' I would say, 'I'm going out, could you just make sure the gates are open?' or 'Mr Speed, thank you for cleaning the car so nicely.'

I have always been this polite to anybody who works for me, and always thanked them. To this day, I still thank my band, saying: 'Thank you for the rehearsal – thank you very much everybody.' I never take anything or anyone for granted. One day, however, when Mr Speed bestowed a compliment upon Patricia, saying, 'Don't ever cut your hair, it's so beautiful,' she regressed to a ten-year-old.

'Oh no, I won't, Mr Speed,' she said, overcome, eyes down.

Once, when her sister, June, was visiting, and Pope left the room for ages when she went to fetch a pot of tea, June thought, Where the hell is she? Pope had gone missing for at least half an hour and, when June found her, she discovered that her sister had painted the entire floor of the utility room. The paint had been flaking off in there, and the week before Pope had been on her hands and knees with wire wool. On the day June arrived, the new paint also arrived. As Pope went to put the kettle on, she figured she would just start painting a small patch while the kettle was boiling and, before she knew it, she had painted the entire room.

Our neighbours, John and Carol Darley, used to joke that Pope polished the drain pipes, and I'm not so sure this wasn't true.

Apparently, one day John saw Patricia driving and said to Carol, 'I've just seen this gorgeous blonde girl in a brown cap driving a white, topless Mercedes.'

When Carol phoned and invited us round to their place for dinner, Pope's sister urged her to accept. 'That's just what you need, Pat, a girlfriend,' she said.

Carol and Patricia became close girlfriends that very first night. 'We're going to Barbados tomorrow,' we said during the dinner. 'Do you want to come?'

'Yes,' they replied without a pause and they managed to get on the same flight with us. Our friendship was meant to be.

Barbados, that dazzling jewel of an island in the Caribbean, became one of my all-time favourite places to go and, after our first visit, we went there regularly as a family, every summer, for six weeks, for about fifteen years.

The year that John and Carol joined us, we all learned to water-ski. When I was learning, I hired an instructor named Andre, who had a wonderful physique and was a very good skier. After I'd been out with him a couple of times, I was already able to ski on two skis, even though I kept falling on to my arse. All the other people on the beach, having recognised me, were all looking at me, but I decided that was OK. I didn't mind the embarrassment. I was, after all, a novice who was learning how to ski, and I wanted to excel at it.

One day we decided to go on 'The Jolly Roger', a boat which offered day cruises on the azure-blue ocean. While on board, we were drinking rum punches and ended up getting pretty merry. Slightly bored, I said to the captain, 'Could you, please, call the shore and ask for Andre to come and pick me up, and give me a ride back?'

We were only a couple of miles out and, sure enough, Andre came out to fetch me.

'Why don't you ski back?' he suggested.

'Can I ski back, too?' asked a blonde lady who was sitting next to me.

'Sure,' I replied, 'why not?'

'Oh good,' she answered, 'because I don't want to stay out here any more. Now, how do you ski? Are you a slalom skier?'

'No – I can only ski on two skis,' I owned up.

'Oh! How boring!'

Boy, did she make me feel small and, opting out of the on-skis return, I said: 'I'll tell you what – why don't you ski back and I'll just sit here and relax in the boat.'

So, off she went, slalom-skiing, cutting the water with great flair. Then, as we came into shore, she slipped out of the skis, and pushed them towards the boat just as I jumped off into the shallow, see-through water. 'Thank you very much,' she waved and, as she turned to walk away, her nose was so high in the air, it seemed to hover above the top of her dyed blonde head.

'Andre,' I said, really pissed off, 'I'd like to have a lesson with you every day next week, and I want you to pick me up early in the morning, so I can ski for about four hours. I want you to get me on one ski, and I want to be able to do a beach start, from here, right where we are standing on this beach. OK?'

And, although my arms were dropping off by the end of it all, I skied every morning, way out of sight of the beach where the blonde usually sunbathed. After all this activity, I was so exhausted I had to go to bed at seven. Nevertheless, I persevered and, when Andre finally got me on to one ski, I skied rather well. So far, so good.

'Now that I can ski reasonably well,' I said to Andre, 'I'd like to learn how to do a beach start.' And we started to practise that, which meant taking off from shore without having to go far out into the water before starting to ski. This was the moment when people on the beach started to recognise me – I guess the sideburns were a giveaway! – and a crowd gathered. Nevertheless, I just kept tumbling and falling as the crowd got bigger and bigger. On one occasion, as I came out with my ski in my hand to get back on again, I looked at them and said: 'You people think show business is easy, huh?' and they all laughed good-naturedly. Finally, after endless attempts, I discovered I could do the beach start and I was able to take off on one ski. We practised that for another couple of days and, by then, I was leaning so far down, my shoulder was touching the water. I really had become quite a good water-skier.

'Andre,' I said at the end of another practice session, 'the time is NOW.'

'What do you mean, Engelbert?' he asked, puzzled.

'I want you to pick me up right here tomorrow at two. Just throw me a ski and I will be ready to go out and ski on the other beach – our beach – Settler's. OK?'

'OK,' he replied.

So, the next day, out I came, dressed to kill in long, white trousers, white T-shirt, sunglasses, a white hat, and white leather loafers. Spying Andre coming in on the boat, I walked around the beach to double-check that the blonde girl was still lying on her lounger. I slipped off my shoes and called, 'Hi, Andre, throw me a ski, please.' Then, as the boat came towards me in the water, I rolled my trousers up to my shins, shoved my ski on and took three coils of rope into my left hand.

'Andre, take it away!' I said.

I stepped onto the water and off I went. Once I was out on the water, I really let rip and started yodeling and yahooing just to make *sure* she kept looking at me.

The fully briefed Andre knew *exactly* how long to keep me out there before taking me in a long curve to swing in back to the shore. That way, I could step out of my ski – right on to shore – without getting wet. The first moment that the blonde sat up to watch me was *so* satisfying. She simply couldn't believe I had the audacity to waterski fully clothed. And the bonus arrived when Andre brought me into shore – and I stepped out of the ski, and rolled down my trousers and put my loafers back on.

'I'll see you tomorrow, Andre,' I said casually, as if my display had taken no effort whatsoever. In truth, that performance had given me one of the best and most satisfactory feelings I've ever had in my life.

'You stubborn bastard,' the toffee-nosed blonde said, smiling, as she caught on to what I had been up to. With a flirtatious smile, she asked 'Can I come and have a drink with you?'

And, I said 'No,' and simply walked away.'

Popea and the kids also learned how to slalom ski with Andre as well. It really was a wonderful thing to learn. My shoulder used to hit the water, but I would still come back dry because there was a minimum of splashing and, with such a hot sun burning overhead, everything just dried right on me.

Every year we used to leave for Barbados as soon as the children broke up for their summer holidays. We also took our mums and my dad, and Arthur, Popea's mother's boyfriend. I really miss not being able to do that any more. It's certainly true that we don't know what we've got until we lose it. I *so* loved having our parents on holiday with us and I miss them all *so* much. Those were golden days with our darling parents.

At the end of that holiday, when we returned to Weybridge, I decided (along with Gordon Mills and Tom Jones) to buy a Rolls-Royce Phantom VI.

This Roller was the biggest limousine ever made and, owning one of these was a joy I shared with other stars, such as John Lennon, who also lived in the peaceful, leafy, greenbelt lanes of St George's Hills, in Weybridge. The car was *the* symbol of our success, and among the owners of the first four ever made was the Queen. Mine had a television, a minibar and all the luxurious trimmings you would never normally see inside a car, and I took proud possession of it soon after I'd been told I was becoming one of the 60s' biggest-earning performers.

I could not have known when it arrived that this sleek beauty was going to provide me with one of the most embarrassing moments of my life.

On the day of this event Tony had driven me to a meeting at MAM, my agent's office, in town. But when we got there, we could not, try as we did, get out of the car. We were trapped! The doors just would not open! Everything in the car was electrically operated and, when Tony brought it to a halt by the kerbside, everything had seized up and the car's engine would not start again.

Almost immediately, a crowd of curious onlookers had gathered around the Phantom, which had such dark-tinted windows, nobody could ever tell if the Queen or somebody less interesting, like me, was inside.

'Who is it?' 'Is it the Queen?' 'Is it the Beatles?' I could hear people saying.

Fortunately, there were manual winders for the windows and, Tony having given up trying to prompt the recalcitrant electrics into life, resorted to those and then had to heave his body through the now open window. It was so embarrassing with members of the public all standing round, and quite a humbling experience to be sitting in such a spectacular car unable to exit. Having made his bid for freedom, Tony ran into a nearby hotel to ring up Rolls-Royce.

'We'll have somebody there within an hour,' was the well-spoken reply.

'But we have an important meeting in five minutes,' Tony said in despair.

'We'll do our very best, Sir.'

There was nothing for it; I had to climb out as well. Praying that my trousers would take the strain – and not end my career just as it had started – I wriggled and squirmed my way to freedom! Stunned by the one standing ovation I could have done without, I smiled wanly at the waiting members of the public and crept into MAM's offices.

I did see the funny side of it!

Climbing out of windows, however, was really nothing new! There had been a time in the earlier years when this had been a fairly regular routine for me. It had, for example, happened quite often when I was performing in the provinces and needed to escape a venue to catch the milk train home. It also happened when the band and I were staying in digs. There were a number of occasions when, not having enough money to put us all up in rooms, Tony would go to the owner, pay the £5 for a room and then open the window and let the rest of us pile in. Of course, come morning, we would all have to exit the same way. It was while we were on one of these sneak-in, sneak-out occasions in Bristol, that we met a major movie star.

The Phantom VI was not the only newcomer to Weybridge's greenbelt area that got me into trouble. On a fairly regular basis, our dog, Cheb, originally named Cherub, but shortened to Cheb when the kids couldn't pronounce it, used to run off around the neighbourhood. Without fail, he always ended up on John Lennon's property and, once there, he would cock his leg and pee on the oversized shoe that John kept in his garden for a time after it was featured in the *Beatles' Magical Mystery Tour*.

John did eventually get rid of the shoe, but this was not on account of Cheb's habits. It turned out to be a much too obvious marker of which home was his, and when John began to break up with his Mrs, he didn't want to risk attracting any more attention than he was already receiving from the paparazzi and the public.

One day, when Cheb had gone walk-and-pee-about as usual, Tony went off to search for him. This time, he found the culprit frolicking at John's feet.

'I swear to God, Tony,' John said, 'that this dog is more often on my property than he is on Engelbert's.'

What could I say! Shoe trouble of one kind or another seemed to be my lot in life.

All this was followed by a period when local teenagers became aware of Cheb's wandering behaviour patterns and realised they were on to a good thing. Lying in wait, they started to dognap him for ransom money. There is a wonderful photograph of me in our family album, with Cheb standing on his hind legs to witness me paying a policeman who is signing the release papers for the kids' latest dognap.

I had to bail that dog out on more than one occasion, but he did try to earn his keep. Every Monday, he used to sneak off and steal a loaf of bread and a carton of cream from somewhere. Then he'd trot back home, carrying both items in his mouth. We never learned where he was committing this dastardly deed, and we never tried very hard to find out, either!

CHAPTER THIRTEEN

Life's wake-up calls come in many shapes and sizes, and, curiously, the first time I ever felt *really* famous was not, as people would suppose, when I was on stage singing my heart out, or being mobbed by screaming fans, or chased for my autograph. It was when Alan Warman, a bright lad of nineteen, whom Gordon had chosen to be my hairdresser stood confronting me for the first time in my house in Weybridge. He made me feel *really* famous because he was so incredibly *nervous*! It was a strange moment in which I couldn't remember ever having had quite that effect on anyone before, and I just thought, '*Good Lord! He's scared of me because I'm a famous somebody now!*'

Alan came from a hairdressing shop in Ashford, in Middlesex, and, a true pro, he had spent some time studying photographs of me before he came to the house. He wanted to get my 'look' right and fixed in his head before approaching me with his scissors and blow-dryer.

After his first visit, he started doing my hair for photo shoots and public appearances and then for thirteen consecutive weeks when I was doing some BBC specials, a series in which, among others, the Four Tops, Ray Charles, Tony Bennett, Gina Lollobrigida, Elke Sommer, Connie Stevens, Phil Silvers, Liberace, Jerry Lewis and Jack Benny made guest appearances.

The strangest thing, about Alan, however, was that he never really wanted to change my hair – never wanted to take too many hairs off my head or touch my sideboards. Basically, he just twiddled around, snipping six hairs off here and there, then whooshed a blow-dryer around to fluff up the remainder. Once, when I thanked him for this approach, he replied, 'Well, I'm no *cowboy* hairdresser – and I wasn't going to start hacking off *your* locks. I'd have been in *big* trouble with your fans if I'd done that, wouldn't I?'

I enjoyed going to pubs with Alan for a game of darts and I became quite an expert at this and, even now, I have a dartboard in my home in Leicester for any guest who fancies – *dares* –

challenge me at a few throws. Alan used to say he liked the game, but he eventually admitted he liked making our entrance even more. I never noticed it, but he always said that when we walked into a pub and the other patrons spotted me, you could hear a pin drop. It was a nice compliment and, perhaps not noticeable to me, but I found the attention hard to acknowledge. I was still so shy offstage and I was never really comfortable.

Once, Alan, Gordon, Barry Mason and I went for a game of darts at the Flint Gate pub in Weybridge, and when a couple of women let out a scream when they saw me enter, Barry looked at my face and doubled up with laughter.

'Sometimes,' he said, 'you look absolutely shit-scared when girls do that!'

Another time when we were staying at a pub-come-hotel in Wales, it turned out there was more than screams to freeze me in my tracks! There was a *bomb* threat. Later, I found out this was targeted at these premises on account of my presence there but, while the drama was unfolding, I never knew that, never caught a whiff of it. Would you believe it, the hotel staff had evacuated the place, but forgotten to include Alan and me! So, there we were just lounging around, reading the papers in my room when the police cars, their lights flashing and sirens blazing, started to arrive – and the rest of the guests were standing, shivering, on the street, scared. Maybe I would have been scared, too, had I known what was going on but, afterwards, when we were told it had proved to be a hoax-call, a false alarm, we were glad we'd been overlooked and found it all hysterically funny.

There then came a time when Alan, who was usually so good and efficient, deserved a real bollocking. This was in Las Vegas, when he came to pick me up from the house in a MAM limousine, that had the number plate GET3 – for Gordon, Engelbert and Tom – to take me to the Riviera Hotel. He arrived a bit early, just as I'd finished playing tennis with the television star, David Janssen, and I was still in my tennis whites and not quite ready to leave.

'Alan, I've just come up from the tennis courts,' I explained, after he had knocked on the door and the security man had quietened the guard dog. 'But, you know what, I think I'll just collect a few things and go to the Riv like this. I can change there.'

I've never really been sure what Alan thought he heard me say, but when I came out there was no limo – he had driven off without me.

That wasn't the only 'driver' mishap to befall me. Tony used to drive me to and fro from Elstree Studios and I would sit in the back of the limo, working on my songs and performance sketches. On one particular morning when I was running late, Tony, who was driving me in my red Phantom VI, got pulled over by the police. When the policeman walked up to the car and tapped on the window, Tony pressed the button to open the window just in time to hear the grim-faced officer ask sarcastically, 'Where's the fire?'

'In *your* eyes, you *gorgeous* beast,' Tony made the mistake of replying.

On hearing that, of course, the copper asked him to step out of the car, and I really had to talk us out of trouble. The situation was eventually resolved by my offering a signed autograph and a cassette of one of my albums for his wife. I am not sure what would have happened if she had not been a fan!

Late in 1969, we set off on a grand tour of South Africa. At this time Nelson Mandela was spending yet another year incarcerated in prison – and one of the tour-promoters' conditions was: 'We want you to play to black as well as white people.' This was a very risky suggestion during the apartheid years when very few people would feel safe playing to both black and white audiences, but I was happy to be one of the first during my three-week tour.

When we were coming into land at the airport in Johannesburg, we could see around five hundred Zulu warriors waiting to greet me and perform a ceremonial dance and, looking over my shoulder, I thought, 'There must be somebody really important on board this plane. I wonder who it is.'

On landing I descended the steps of the airplane and was greeted by the chief of the Zulu tribe who then ordered a ritual dance in honour of my visit. There were so many dancing that the pounding of their feet was literally causing the tarmac to shake. The chief presented me with a shield and a spear and I ended up dancing with them.

The Zulu dance that was performed to mark my arrival was truly *amazing* – unbelievably moving and impressive – and I had never seen anything quite like that before.

On the first night we opened the tour by playing to white people at the Presidential Theatre; then we jumped into a car and drove the few miles to Soweto to play at a theatre called The Look Shirama. There, it was an all-black audience, of course, and they were all so overexcited that their sheer body weight accidentally turned over some of our cars, which were, fortunately, empty. It really was the first time a British performer had dared to perform to both white and black audiences. Before then, the British Embassy in South Africa had dismissed any such idea and we were certainly made aware of a lot of hostility towards us throughout that tour.

'We're only here to *entertain* people,' I kept repeating when we were heckled, but some still believed we were interfering in the politics of the country and the ill-will continued throughout. Nevertheless, we played all across that beautiful country that's so rich in wildlife, it's like watching wall-to-wall natural history programmes on televsion. The places we went to included Johannesburg, Cape Town and Port Elizabeth as well as lots of others.

One night, oblivious of local customs and problems, I made a mistake that cost a man, who was cooking for me in my suite at the hotel, a beating. Having given him a £10 tip, he whispered to me the next day, 'Please *don't* give me any more tips, because the others will give me a *really* hard time when they take the tip off me.'

I could hardly believe what he was saying, but I could tell from his distress that he was serious.

'Well, look,' I said, 'is there anything I can do to make up for this?'

'Would you,' he asked tentatively, his gentle smile reaching from ear to ear, 'like to come and have dinner at my house in the village on Sunday?'

Although *that* was our only day off and I had no idea how far away he lived, I said: 'Sure – I'd like to do that.'

It proved, however, to be a nightmarish journey. There were only Tony and me, plus a very nervous driver in the limousine, and the area, which was swarming with people, was not controlled. The people were tramping around, looking and sounding terrifyingly overexcited. We did finally get to the cook's house, which was the shape of a thimble and not much bigger, and we sat down to eat the special curry he had made for us. It was an amazing experience. We were the first white people ever to visit that particular area. It was absolute mayhem while we were eating the curry and there were moments when I thought that his house was going to collapse and cave in!

I've had a number of similar greetings since then. For example, when I was on tour in New Zealand, I was met by a welcoming committee of Maoris who did their ceremonial dance for me. I found it very funny when they kept making staring eyes and sticking their tongues out at me, but I had been warned not to smile and to remain unsmiling throughout the dance because the greeting was a very serious matter for them.

Afterwards, the Maoris presented me with a good-luck charm, carved out of bone, and hung on a leather cord. When it was placed around my neck, I felt *truly* honoured.

My *worst*-ever greeting took place in South America in Caracas, in Venezuela. I was arrested and handcuffed as I stepped off the plane.

I had been there before and I hadn't had any problems when I was performing at the Hotel Tamanaco, but this particular visit, when I took my whole band on vacation with me, turned out to be a very different story. At the time I was in tax exile from the UK because the British government was taking a large percentage of earnings from those in the supertax bracket. So, for business reasons, and to be able to keep some of the money I was earning, I exiled myself to avoid exceeding the number of days a year that I was allowed back in Great Britain and America, without being financially penalised. Every now and again, I would have to get up and go, and I'd either go to Bermuda or Barbados, or take the band on holiday somewhere nice.

At the time we went to Caracas, although I was on holiday, I had taken something like ten trunks along with me, which was quite a lot of luggage, and this was one reason why it took my travelling companions so long to realise I had gone missing! While they were in Arrivals, taking all these trunks off the conveyor belt, I was being arrested. Customs, I discovered, wanted to look in my hand luggage, a mini leather case, for any illicit drugs I might be carrying. As luck would have it, I was carrying lots of little boxes containing antihistamine and other kinds of medication – not just for me, but for the whole band, just in case one of us fell ill. So, although the drugs in my case were *not* illegal and were ones that any UK chemist would have sold over the counter without a prescription, the Caracas customs' people were not so sure about that and were very suspicious of my pills and potions! Ignoring my protests, they dragged me off with my company manager, Rick Piccone, who was a kind of general manager for us at the time and actually on his honeymoon. By then, Alan had already gone through the customs' checkout with everybody else, while I was being held on suspicion of possessing drugs and being taken, along with Rick Piccone, to a small, grimy, windowless interview room. Meanwhile, Alan continued trying to take the luggage off the conveyor belt, while the airport staff, who had obviously been tipped off that I was in trouble, just kept putting it back on again.

When Alan finally caught on and realised it had been an absolute eternity since he had last seen me, he went off to have a look round and ended up getting arrested, too.

At first, I wasn't too worried. I was just sitting there, finding the events interesting and thinking that it would only be a short time before I was reunited with my companions and the holiday would begin. Soon, however, I realised that things were rather more serious than that and could become really sinister.

'Bloody hell,' I thought at this moment. 'They could plant anything on me just to justify my arrest and I wouldn't be able to do a thing about it.'

By then, the man from Interpol was asking me all sorts of questions, and it was clear he wasn't going to allow me an interpreter. In fact, he made it abundantly clear he wouldn't allow *anybody* else in the room, which really was intimidating – nerve-wracking, to say the least – considering he had placed his gun on the table between us and stationed one of his gun-toting companions to stand, gun cocked, behind me.

It was not until I got arrested in Caracas that I knew what heroin and marijuana looked like. When the interrogator was searching through everything in my briefcase, he took out a capsule that contained ammonia capsules, more commonly known as smelling salts.

'When you faint,' I said at once, trying to explain, 'you break that capsule and put it under your nose like this.' I was miming all the actions because I honestly didn't think he spoke any English. 'Like this,' I repeated, 'and it brings you round, see. Look, let me show you, and I pretended to faint, then broke the capsule, and shoved it under his nose.

Big mistake.

'Jesus Christ,' he exclaimed, reeling back, as the smell penetrated his nostrils.

'It's OK,' I cried out. 'It's supposed to do that – bring you round, see.'

I was also thinking: 'You sneaky sod. You *do* speak English after all.'

From the glare in his eyes, I realised this could be my last moment on earth, but it wasn't.

When they finally decided to take me downstairs, I learned that all the band had been arrested because of me. Outside the building, they had three cars lined up to drive us to another place, God knows where, downtown. So, with guns, rifles and machine guns at the ready, they shoved everybody into the cars. Except me! As the three cars started to pull away, I was left standing there, forgotten. What's that saying? 'More haste less speed'!

'HEY,' I yelled, 'it was me you arrested, right?'

All three of the cars jolted to a stop, reversed and screeched to a halt beside me; a guy leaped out bundled me into the back of the car and off we all went!

It was like a bad 'B' movie – or a comic moment in a slapstick film.

On our arrival downtown, the band was led into one room and I was taken to a dingy little cell with no window and placed behind bars. By this time, the paparazzi had arrived and there were about sixty of them milling around outside my cell. They were all crawling over each other, snapping pictures, while I stood there, playing to camera and holding the bars, singing – I am *not* kidding – 'Please release me, let me go . . .'

To calm my nerves, I was trying to make a joke out of it, but the guys in charge of me didn't think it was so funny. I was kept in that cell, at the mercy of the paparazzi, for six hours. After this, I was taken to a little room that had a slowly churning ceiling fan, just like the one in the classic Humphrey Bogart and Ingrid Bergman film, *Casablanca*. Once there, I was made to sit on a little wooden chair at a wooden table opposite one man – my chief interrogator, who had once again placed his gun on the table between us – while the other guy once again stood behind me with his automatic weapon cocked in his hand.

'Open your case,' my interrogator said, putting it on the table.

Having done this, I passed it back and he started to go through all the pills, tubes, capsules and bottles of antibiotics, et cetera, all over again. While he was doing this, the guy behind me kept tapping the barrel of his machine-gun between my shoulder blades, his finger still on the trigger.

'You *don't* have to do that,' I said, 'and you shouldn't put your finger on the trigger. I'm *not* going anywhere, am I, and you're *not* supposed to put your finger on the trigger like that. It might go off by accident!'

When he ignored me, I tried to calm my nerves by reaching into my breast pocket and taking out one of my Havana cigars.

'You like smoke?' he said, a triumphant note in his voice.

'Yes, I *like* smoke,' I replied, cautiously.

Reaching into a table drawer, he brought out a piece of paper with a mountain of something that looked like tobacco piled six inches high on it. 'You *like* this?' he said, thrusting it under my nose. 'You know what this is, right?'

'Yes – tobacco,' I said.

'No, *marijuana*,' he replied. 'You *like* it?

'No,' I said, firmly. 'I *like* Havana cigars.'

Having crossed the room, he returned with another paper. 'You *like* this?' he began again.

'I don't know what it is.'

'*Cocaine*. You *like* cocaine?'

'I don't even know what it looks like,' I replied, as he showed me a white substance. 'This is the first time I've ever seen it.'

The narcotics agent jabbed his gun into my back and, every time I tried to say something, he kept jabbing it in deeper.

I knew, of course, that he was trying to provoke me, that he wanted me to lose my temper, but I didn't oblige. I just played it very cool, puffing on my Havana, while he and his boss continued to examine everything in minute detail. Having done this by pulling everything apart without finding anything suspicious, the interrogator said: 'OK, everything is good. You can go now.' And, without a single word of apology for their behaviour, they led me out of the room and threw me to the wolves – the paparazzi who then chased me all the way back to the hotel, where I learned the rest of the band had already arrived.

When I eventually got into my room the paparazzi continued to camp outside all night.

'Rick,' I said, when he came in to see me, 'I know we're supposed to stay here for four days, but book us a flight out of here. We'll leave tomorrow and go back to the States.'

He was relieved. It hadn't been much of a honeymoon for him so far, as he had spent most of the hours since our arrival separated from Frankie, his new wife.

I didn't get a wink of sleep all night. The drive from the hotel to the airport in the morning was a complete shambles and an utter nightmare. It was a truly *hair-raising* ride, to say the least, and it must have been very similar to the one that Princess Diana and Dodi Fayed endured on the night of their fatal car crash in the Paris subway. We were racing along the road – almost flying – at about ninety miles an hour, and the paparazzi were along for the ride, hanging out of their car windows taking pictures of me. When we hit some dirt roads, the limousine's wheels began to spin around out of control and, several times, the car spun round to face oncoming cars. By now, we were traversing mountaintop roads with death-defying, hairpin turns and bends; and, still trying to stop the paparazzi from closing the distance between our car and theirs, we were taking all the twists and turns at breakneck speeds. In fact, our journey to the airport was so beset with flashing bulbs and the hue and cry of the paparazzi, that I remember wondering if we were going to survive and actually arrive there in one piece. Meanwhile, giddy, cavernous drops continued to beckon us to a giant leapfrog over the edge at every bend. It was *terrifying*.

When we finally got to the airport, the guy who had arrested me was there on the tarmac but, this time, he just ignored us and we boarded with no further ado. We had still not received any apology for their mistake.

Later, as well as getting the band and me riled up with their daft, exaggerated reports, the paparazzi were successful in riling the public as well. One newspaper claimed there were guns and shootings involved in my incarceration, and another even reported I had been shot and killed. Considering I had only been arrested for carrying aspirins, antihistamine and antacid, the journos certainly made facts fiction. But, then, when did truth have anything to do with selling newspapers!

Perhaps not surprisingly in the circumstances, from the early 70s, Hawaii became – and remained – one of my favourite getaways. I used to take the whole family to Colony Surf Condos in Waikiki, on Oahu, where we loved to celebrate Louise's birthday on 28 July. While we were there, we would often see the glamorous actress, Lana Turner, who got into the habit of sitting with us on Sans Souci Beach. It was Pope who first recognised her and, by the time I turned round to have a look, Lana was on her way over to our loungers to introduce herself. From that day forward, she would sit with us most days and share our picnic lunches. When she died from cancer in June 1995, her daughter, Cheryl, brought her mum's ashes back to Oahu, so she could rest in peace in the same location she had experienced peace when she was alive.

We liked Lana very much and were honoured to have her company. I think she enjoyed spending time with us because we were all so normal, so relaxed with her, and we never tried to pry into her personal life, or asked if we could take any souvenir photographs. It was obviously a very refreshing break for her *not* to have people trying to take advantage of her and asking what '*really* happened' the night Cheryl, then aged fourteen, stabbed and killed Johnny Stompanato, the man Lana was dating at the time. Nor did we ask about her relationship with Frank Sinatra, although it was common knowledge that she and Frank often hid out behind closed doors within the Colony Surf.

I was a great fan of Frank's. I knew that film business had originally called him to the Gold Coast to star in the early 50s' film *From Here to Eternity*, and again in 1965 when he had directed and starred in *None But the Brave*. Ol' Blue Eyes, a truly legendary performer, was even filmed for a guest spot on the Oahu-based television show, *Magnum, P.I.*, where he shared a few scenes with the leading actor, Tom Selleck, who played Magnum. One summer, Mr Magnum seemed to have a few things of his own he wanted to share with our teenage daughter!

'I'm going to have to tell him to shove off,' Popea said to me. 'Louise may be seventeen, but she's not a worldly seventeen. She's still a little girl at heart!'

Pope was very preoccupied with this possible 'romance' and determined to keep her first-born, only daughter, safe from the intentions of the older man on whom she had a crush. We were convinced she *did* have a crush on Tom because she was *so* dreamy. Pope was *so* distracted that one day, when we went out on an all-day boat trip, she turned the tap on to do her hand washing and plum forgot to turn it off again. When we returned, there was chaos. The water had soaked all the way through the floor of our condo and gone through the ceiling of a family's rented unit below. While Pope went looking for the other tenants to offer our sincere apologies, I had to deal with the owner-manager and general muscle of Colony Surf Condos, and incorporate my wallet into the apologies.

It was with great relief, then, that we heard Tom was about to head off to London to make a romantic adventure movie; and an even greater relief, when we, too, had to end our holiday on the island a few days earlier than we'd originally planned. When Louise realised she wasn't going to have a chance to see Tom again and say goodbye in person, she penned him some lines of heartfelt apology for her impending disappearing act: *I have to go, we're on our way early, and I'm so sorry that I have to let you down* . . . Having written this, she scampered off down the beach and slipped the note under his door at the Outrigger Hotel, which was situated right next to our condo on Sans Beach. The proximity of our lodgings on that holiday, which may have been considered very lucky by Louise, was certainly worrying for her parents.

When Louise returned to where the rest of the family were loading bags and cases into the car headed for Honolulu International, we could tell that she was truly upset to be leaving Tom. Listening to her talking to her mum, I realised she really was growing up fast – all our children were – and it had been wonderful to spend every day for six weeks, watching them become teenagers and young adults, and less like children. In those last minutes, however, as we put the final case into the car and ended our holiday, I felt a pang, knowing that I would soon be back on tour and missing such family moments, like Louise and her first crush. Maybe it wasn't her *first* crush, maybe it was just the first one I had witnessed, and maybe it had been quite some time since she could *really* be called my 'little girl'. But, no matter what, Louise would always be – and will always be – my princess.

The king of the Big Island on Hawaii was Don Ho. There is no doubt in my mind that he's there right now, making people laugh as he sings a song, or plays a number on the black and white stripes of a keyboard that's flanked by hula girls wearing giant hibiscus flowers behind their ears. He has held the entertainment throne over there as long as I can remember, and he deserves it. I used to love paying my respects to him and watching him perform, even though I knew it meant he would put me to work right away. Don always made sure my family had the best seats in the house, but he also made sure I earned them! He was a smart fella, who never believed in working too hard himself, yet managed to get everyone else to work very hard while he still looked the consummate entertainer he really was.

'Ladies and gentlemen! We have a superstar here and I want you to meet him,' he would say, seeking help from the audience in coaxing whichever visiting celebrity was present to go on stage while he went to the piano to start the accompaniment. No one ever really stood a chance of escaping his clutches – it worked every time.

'Engelbert, Engelbert, come on up here and give us a song!' he would bellow.

'But I came here to watch your show,' I would reply, smiling hopefully.

'Come on, man, you can sing for us! What key do you want me to play? Just give me a key . . .'

'No-no,' I would try to protest once more.

'NO? Ladies and gentlemen, don't you want him to sing for you?' he would ask, turning to face the room.

'*YEAH*!' they would yell, clapping and cheering in unison.

'Oh, you do? You do want him to sing for you?'

'*YEAH*!'

'What key do you want to start singing us a song then, Engelbert?'

That's what he was like – he'd play a little, sing 'Tiny Bubbles', then venture into the audience to talk to people and have his picture taken with them. He used to ask for the chewing gum right out of girls' mouths! Then, when they gave it to him, he would pop it into his own mouth before moving on to talk to guests at the next table. One hell of a character, he would always say to me: 'If there's anything you want on this island – a boat, a woman, whatever, call me and I will take care of it,' and I knew he could, too. He really did rule the place.

On that same trip, as the family and I moved through a bar-cum-restaurant to find seats and order ourselves something to eat, we noticed an Hawaiian man performing a little karaoke number on a small stage. Wouldn't you just know it, the song he was singing so earnestly and giving his all to was 'After the Lovin'' – one of my No. 1 hits. As the audience watched and took part in the joke, I crept up behind him, let him finish his rendition, then tapped him on the shoulder.

'Hey, that was *pretty* good,' I said, smiling.

'Oh, thank you,' he began, before realising who it was bestowing the compliment on him. Then, doing an enormous double-take, he threw up his arms up and smiled with such glee, it absolutely brought the house down.

Pope and I were planning a return visit to Hawaii and to Don Ho last Christmas but, at the last minute, we changed our minds and decided we'd prefer to have the whole family come and spend the Christmas holidays with us in Los Angeles, which we hadn't done in many moons – not since we moved from the Pink Palace and the children became adults. It was definitely the right decision; the whole family had wonderful fun getting together and arranging decorative lights on the plants and trees outside of our home.

From time to time, we would just all burst out laughing at what we were doing – putting Christmas lights around trees that seemed far too tropical for the season. Once the cacti were appropriately dressed in ornaments and the purple bougainvillaea was full of more lights than flowers, we returned inside the house and Pope gave Louise, Scott, Jason and Bradley the gifts she'd been making for them for quite a few years. Each child got his or her own beautiful scrapbook, full of everything from their baby pictures to a copy of the photograph we had had taken when the family came along on one of my US tours. On that occasion, we stopped in a Wild West saloon in Virginia City in West Virginia and put on gunslinger clothes, or barmaid costumes, and had one of those antique-looking portraits taken. It was another of those wake-up calls; *where had all those years gone?* It was just amazing sitting there, going down memory lane, flipping through all those pages, looking at our past, our family life, and appreciating anew the glue that binds us all together.

CHAPTER FOURTEEN

What a shock – *literally* what a shock – a near-electrocution! As the year 1971 came in, we very nearly suffered a family tragedy – and Pope and I were left counting our lucky stars in a state of quiver. Scott, as children will for no reason other than that they're curious about everything in the universe, stuck a hairpin into an electric socket. The resulting shock blew him backwards, clean off his feet, with such a force that his legs turned black. The fact that his legs had turned this colour meant that the current had passed right through his body before it exited, and we honestly thought he was going to die. Having put him in the car, we drove hell for leather to our local hospital. Although we very nearly lost him, he survived.

'Who'd be a parent?' I kept groaning, as I tried to recover from the shock. It had been almost a repeat of that terrifying day when Louise had teetered on the verge of death at the kerbside. As parents of children endowed with an adventurous spirit, we had now had two *very* lucky escapes.

Once Scott was out of danger, and we had him safely back home with us, tragedy, as it so often does, turned to mirth.

'He's had a *shocking* experience in his life,' Popea and I kept joking, before doubling up with stress- and tension-releasing laughter!

But such events, awful and frightening as they are, always make one pause, take stock and get one's priorities in perspective – reinstated. Between tours, I used to sit and look at my little son when he was sleeping and think: 'Nothing could have made me truly happy ever again if you had died'.

Coincidentally, there was a strange, somewhat ghoulish story about this time that *I* had died!

Apparently, just before I arrived at the theatre in Coventry that night, the backstage people there heard that I had been killed in a car crash. There had been a fatal accident, a head-on collision, in which one of the cars involved was the same make, year and colour as the one I was driving. The victim of the road-traffic accident also bore a close resemblance to me – and news of my death had spread like wildfire. When I walked through the stage door, I was greeted with a series of shocked gasps. Everybody thought they were looking at a ghost!

'We thought you were dead!' they kept saying. 'It was even on the News that you had been killed in a car accident.'

'Well, it's news to me,' I quipped, adding more seriously, 'No – I'm fine. This is really me – I'm alive, well and ready to go on.'

Although we managed to get in touch with members of our families to reassure them that everything was all right, the phone still kept ringing all evening.

People are always fascinated by money – always trying to guess what this or that person is worth! All I am prepared to say is that, during my first US tour in 1971, I did make – and continued to make thereafter – an awful lot of money. Most days in the US, for example, I was doing two shows a night. I am not going to mention figures, though, because if I do, everybody will think I am even richer than I am, without appreciating how much money I have lost to thieves – future management figures – whom I met along the way. But there are also a lot of overheads to consider, including travelling expenses and wages for bands, plus the cost of hotel rooms, tour buses and petrol for the tour buses. When you're on tour, playing all those big cities, it's pay-out time, big time.

I should be worth a lot more money today than I am, but my current manager, Alan Margulies, is the first manager who has been absolutely straight with me. He's my rock. He didn't even want a formal contract.

'Your hand is as good as your word,' he said, 'and, if you don't think I'm good, we'll part as friends.'

For me that was one of the best things I had ever heard – and we started working together there and then.

Such was the economic climate in Britain at that time that the rates of income tax imposed on high earners such as I were absolutely swingeing. I had to keep going into exile because, before I became a US resident and got my green card, I was only allowed to stay for 180 days in America at any one time; and, as the members of my band were all British musicians who couldn't stay longer either, I liked being benevolent and taking them away with me to holiday resorts outside the country.

Members of the press in England were aware that I was living in the US for tax reasons, but they kept suggesting that I was a rat who had left a sinking ship. One journalist, in particular, who kept shoving this down my throat, suggested that I had made the decision to leave my homeland because I wanted to become an even wealthier man than I was already. But that was not the reason why I left England. It was true I didn't want to keep paying the horrendous ninety-eight per cent tax on a large part of my earnings, but the actual decision to go and live in America, was a management decision. Gordon wanted us to make the US the hub of our activities, so that I could become an international star and we could travel about more easily. Los Angeles was very well placed for jetting around the world. You could go anywhere from there, from Asia to Europe, and that is exactly what I did. Life really was hectic in those days.

There were compensations, other than money, though. I have a lot of fun in my life and met some truly remarkable, talented people. I was a guest on great shows, hosted by people like Dean Martin, Bing Crosby and Bob Hope, among others. I remember appearing on *Rowan & Martin's Laugh-In*, where I met the vivacious Goldie Hawn, who totally bowled me over and whom I found extremely attractive. And so did Pope!

I also had some amazing guests on my shows in England, as I have already mentioned, and, of course, one of my favourites was Jerry Lewis. It was during one of my shows that Jerry said, while we were doing a comedy sketch together, 'Don't give up your day job – you'll never make an actor.' What a guy!

Parties are supposed to be fun, but back home in England in 1972 this proved not to be the case. One evening, one of the guests had a close encounter with a hairy paw, just like Fay Wray, the heroine of *King Kong*.

We were at Gordon's house for a Roman Empire-themed party, and everyone was dressed in white togas, with sprigs of this-and-that, made up in circular headdresses, attached to their hair.

Soon after midnight, too early for any of us to be feeling any pain(!), Barry Mason and his then-wife, Sylvan, and Tom Jones, Bobby Darin and various other superstars all decided that we were going to look at Ollie, the gorilla. One of the biggest gorillas you could ever see, Ollie ruled Gordon's private zoo in his five-acre garden, where, in addition to Ollie, there were also tigers, monkeys and orang-utans. Given his size, Ollie's cage was enormous, just like those in public zoos where the keepers can enter to have a closer look and feed the animal or have a good clean-out.

So, there we all were in our togas standing in a narrow, leafy corridor, looking at Ollie in his cage, when suddenly the gorilla made a dive forward, thrust his hand through a little letterbox opening, and grabbed Mason's wife's leg. Pulling her King Kong-style towards the cage, he really could have ripped her calf off but, instead, he ended up in a life-and-death tug-of-war with Barry.

For a few moments, time seemed to stand still as Sylvan was suspended in midair with Barry desperately trying to hang on and get a firmer grip under her arms. It was such a horrifying scene, punctuated by so many blood-curdling screams and shouts, that Tom Jones and I – and everybody else – just stood there mesmerised.

Moments later, there was a terrible rending sound of cloth tearing and Sylvan's toga split apart, and she tumbled backwards out of it into Barry's waiting arms.

It seemed Ollie was capable of sticking one finger out of that cage and ripping anybody's clothes off with one swipe. I had no idea Ollie had been taking lessons from me! Just kidding, although I always have had animal instincts, you know!

Although she was now naked, Sylvan knew she was safe from Ollie's gigantic paws and, some time later when she had recovered from her terrible ordeal, we were all able to have a good laugh.

'I've heard of trying to draw attention to yourself,' Barry said, 'but that was ridiculous.'

As for Ollie, he seemed just as surprised as we were by his behaviour, which was completely out of character, and he went to sit down in the corner. What he was thinking, nobody really knew. But, perhaps, he was reminiscing about Barry's wife and thinking, 'Nice gams'!

I first started playing golf when I was living in Weybridge and, in those days, I had lessons with a pro named Jack Hawkins – *not* the actor! Jack always wore plus-fours when he came to teach me in my garden. In my army days it was all cricket, soccer and fencing, but now all my friends were playing golf and I, too, made Pope a 'golf widow' when I started to live and breathe the game! For the teaching practice in my back garden – it was quite an acreage – I had a net, a chipping place, track, bunker and putting green installed. And, with an average of three lessons a week with Jack whenever I had time off from concerts or recording, I learned how to do a great number of things at home before I even set foot on a golf course. By the 'fourth hole' in my garden, there was a big wall surrounded by a wire fence, and a swimming pool on the right. As I didn't want the balls landing in the pool and hitting the kids on the head, I had a huge fence built to stop that happening.

'Jack,' I asked, one day, 'when are you going to take me on the golf course?

'Not for six months,' he replied.

I can't pretend I wasn't disappointed, but, six months later when he took me on the golf course and we played three games, I had a handicap of eleven. Usually, people start at about twenty-eight, so I was well pleased. Then, after a year or so, I was down to about an eight, which is six over par.

Since those days, I've met so many wonderful people through golf. In the early 70s, I met the incredibly glamorous, red-haired film star Rita Hayworth, when she was playing with the singer Billy Eckstein – and I joined them in a threesome! Then, when I played a game with Rita on our own, I had to tell her she wasn't bad at all! I also met Doug Sanders, Don Cherry, Chi Chi Rodriguez and Arnold Palmer; and the day I first played golf at the Riviera Hotel was one of the very early occasions when I saw Dean Martin, whom everybody called 'Duke'. I caught sight of him in the locker room, and he was standing there staring very earnestly at the palm of his hand in which he held a business card, although it wasn't obvious to everyone.

'What are you doing, Duke?' somebody asked, puzzled.

'Reading my palm to see if I'm gonna get lucky,' he replied.

Later Doug Sanders used to invite me to his tournaments and I would get to meet other famous people, like Neil Armstrong. We've been very good friends since then, and I've often stayed with him in Houston, where he puts me up in his guesthouse. Much later still, it was through Doug Sanders that I met President Bush on a golf course when he was playing in a tournament. His wife, Barbara – and at least two hundred secret servicemen – were also there.

Doug, who was coming down the fairway in an eight-seater golf cart, with the President and some other people on board, saw me. He slowed down, put up his hand to stop me going past, and indicated that I should come over.

'Enge,' he called out, 'come and meet Mr President.'

So, taking my hat off, I crossed over to them. To my astonishment, President Bush also took off his hat before shaking my hand. Afterwards, I kept saying to people: 'The President took his hat off to shake my hand.'

That night, there was one of those formal functions where everybody gets dressed up in dinner suits, and I had my picture taken with the President and his wife, Barbara, and Arnold and Doug. Afterwards, the First Lady asked me for a signed picture of myself! And I had to say that I would send this on to her, which I did.

Once I got into the game of golf, I became as obsessed as everybody else and played whenever I could and everywhere I went. If I were playing in a tournament, I would play with different pros. In the last one – the Bob Hope Classic – I was with Alice Cooper, and Pete Sampras was also there. The number of celebrities you meet through golf really is amazing.

I now have a 'Release Me Driver' for sale on my website and people are forever giving it a hit. Well, I've never been one to miss an opportunity! After all, you do have to release your hands when you hit the ball, and thus my hit song title seemed appropiate.

In the early 70s, there was another very nasty shock in store for us. I was at home in the Pink Palace at about seven o'clock in the evening, discussing some ideas for a new show with my then road manager, Rick Piccone. At that time, my parents were staying with us and, while Rick and I were having our conversation, somebody rushed in and said Mum, who was upstairs in her bedroom, was in great pain and having a heart attack.

As soon as I heard this, I went into shock and Rick had to take over and call 911. When the paramedics arrived, they rushed Mum to UCLA Medical Center, and I went with her. It was just *awful* waiting in the hospital, while she was being treated that night – and, even more awful, when I was told she had just had another heart attack while she was being examined. I was totally distraught – *very* scared – I loved her so much that I sat there all night, *willing* her to live.

Fortunately she was a remarkably strong woman, even though she had had ten children, and she did, *thank God*, survive both those heart attacks – and another eight in the years to come.

Where is my mind at the end of a day?
Sought heavily and pushed in a turbulence of power,
Racked by an assortment of places and appointments,
An active thought –
Enthralled by the happening, but puzzled in the quantity,
So to speak . . .
Each day a laugh, a joke, sometimes a little sad,
Calendars marked with me,
With always an expression to coincide with hear, see and speak,
Eligible of tired niceness with sincerity,
A pause to dream and think, to recollect me
. . . My mind.

Engelbert Humperdinck

When I arrived in Australia in the 70s, I was feeling depressed, and I found writing poetry to be a release valve. I was getting tired of being away from Popea, and I now had three children – Louise, Jason, and Scott – who had arrived in 1968 – to miss when I was on the road. The zip had gone out of my step and my life seemed to be just one big hotel room after another! To make matters worse, I had just come from playing in big arenas and beautiful theatres and, after the comparative sophistication of venues in the UK and the US, I found it slightly difficult to adjust to Australia's smaller theatres. Since then, I've been back and forth to Australia on countless occasions and now it is one of my favourite places to perform.

Back then, though, I was obsessed with the idea that my career was regressing, and that my venues were getting smaller. Even getting to Australia was hectic and a lot of trouble because, in those days, the flight used to take between twenty and twenty-four hours – and, to top it all, the air stewards in San Francisco were on strike and the airlines were only serving oranges and apples, and no hot food. The only time we were able to eat was if we stopped off at one of the little places, like Fiji, en route. Mick 'the gig' Greene, my guitarist, was always saying in his Cockney accent, 'Oh you get a *good* cup of tea in Fiji,' because we certainly didn't get any cups of tea – or any other hot drink – on the plane. With all these bugbears to contend with, I always landed in Australia feeling exhausted and depleted.

What's more, having arrived in a vast country, where everybody – not just the koalas and the roos and their joeys – love their outdoor pursuits and, in particular, love going to the beach to swim, I *never* swam. I flatly refused to do this on account of my fear of sharks. I had listened too long and too often to stories about these creatures being as big as lorries, with dead-looking black eyes the size of tea saucers. And there was another reason – in addition to the fact that I was once very nearly eaten by a shark in the Madras harbour – why I feared them.

When I was a boy, I went to the beach in Madras one afternoon and I saw Colonel Villiers, one of our neighbours, picnicking there with his two children. Suddenly, while I was talking to them, screaming broke out at the edge of the sea and, when we all turned round, we could see that a man was being attacked by a shark in the shallow water which was lapping the beach.

Colonel Villiers leapt up, grabbed a towel, ran down the beach and, not giving a thought to his own safety, waded in. The shark was still circling around at that moment but, having bitten off the man's arm, it finally took off. Sharks, we are told, do not *like* human flesh. They simply attack, take a bite, then glide off. I do not, however, find much comfort in this thought!

As soon as the shark floated off into deeper water, the colonel pulled the man he had been cradling in his arms to safety, then, having managed to set him down on the beach, he covered the man's upper trunk, which was missing an arm, with the towel. It was a very traumatic sight for anybody to witness, let alone a young boy like me. Since those days I have been dreadfully afraid of swimming in any ocean, even the ones that the authorities claim are shark-free! People are always saying to me, 'Oh, you can swim here; there are no sharks here!' But, after my two experiences in India, I reply 'bullshit'.

The only sea I have ever risked swimming in is off Barbados. That island has a reef around it, and there has never been a shark attack in the area that we took our children to. I did some thorough research before I let our kids put a toe in the water there. I would never *ever*, however, swim in the sea off Australia because most of the fishermen who told me there was nothing to worry about were usually missing a limb.

The year 1973, when I turned 37, was the year of my huge tour of Japan – and the year when Gordon Mills nearly burned my boats. Boy, did he embarrass me with a practical joke that misfired. Having arranged for me to do all the publicity photos before I left for the tour, he got me dressed up in what he claimed was a 'traditional Japanese costume'. In truth, I was dressed in a woman's kimono.

'I want you to have your photos taken in a *real* Japanese costume,' he had said, not letting on that it was a woman's get-up – and those pictures were released and published before I got there.

It was a rotten trick, not at all funny, because everybody in the Japanese Press clearly got the wrong idea. Gordon might have thought it was a joke, but it was no joke to me. The pictures of me dressed in women's clothes were splashed all over the Japanese papers. The Japanese people didn't think it was funny either. They thought it was strange – an insult to their women. 'This is ladies' kimono,' they kept saying. 'Not for man, for a lady.'

I had to keep explaining the mistake and saying I was sorry. I was really angry with Gordon. When, as instructed, I put on that kimono, I thought I was doing something that would please not insult our Japanese hosts, but I was gullible. I had never been to Japan before and I did not know anything about their traditional costumes, so it was all too easy for Gordon to fool me. The journalists kept waving the newspapers, containing the original photos, under my nose every time I hit a new city and gave a press conference; and I was forever being asked about the costume I was wearing in the photo.

We played about eight places in Japan – major cities that included Nagoya, Osaka, Fukowaka and Tokyo. The people were marvellous, very gracious and very respectful. I even learned a sentence or two in their language, so I could introduce myself with 'Good evening ladies and gentlemen' and say 'thank you very much', et cetera. I was there for two weeks, but the promoters didn't give us much time off to appreciate the country and its customs. In those days, we used to do anything between twenty and eighty one-nighters in a row, and we were often on the road for three months at a time. Obviously, when we were playing in Japan, there were some days when we were travelling on the bullet train, which is a very interesting ride and I certainly made the most it.

Jeff Sturges was my music director and arranger at this time and I had a nineteen-piece big band, called The Universe, on 'loan' from Tom Jones. On our first journey, I arranged for the bar-car to be closed off so that we could have a little privacy. Those trains are fast – hence the name 'bullet' – but I don't think any of us could recall how many hours that ride took. I bought drinks for everybody and, later, Jeff told me the whole band couldn't believe how well I looked after them, offering them an 'open' bar and all.

'Wow,' they kept saying, 'let's stick around with this guy! He's talented on stage and wonderful to be with offstage, as well!'

On that tour, I also visited *dojos* in certain cities of Japan, where, thanks to some martial arts' lessons that I had had with a guy called Mike Stone, I managed to blend in well with the local experts. My first lesson with Mike Stone took place inside Priscilla Presley's tennis court at her home in Beverly Hills in 1973.

Without any recourse to a crash diet, nor any mucking about with eliminating this or that food group, I never looked better – and never worked so hard. He really got me into the fittest shape I had ever been in my life.

There were times, following these martial arts' workouts, when I would do two shows in Lake Tahoe, then run all the way from the venue to where I was staying, which was about six miles away but at a far higher altitude. Running in the mountains, while dealing with the change in the atmosphere, is no small accomplishment; as the miles go by the air feels so thin it's almost as if you are trying to fill your poor lungs by inhaling oxygen through a cocktail straw.

My hope was that if I learned martial arts – and got mega fit – that maybe I could play 007. Some hope! Later on, I discovered that, because he didn't think it would pay as much as the tours, Gordon had always kept me well away from any film business. I didn't find out until years later that he had actually dumped all the scripts that had come in for me. Had I known, I might have become a matinée idol like Elvis!

Although I found the training sessions with the Japanese martial arts experts very severe and demanding, at least some of the photographs that were taken counteracted the implications of the other pictures of me. Gordon's joke certainly backfired in many a *dojo*, when they found out I was quite the man in the field of martial arts.

By the end of the tour, however, the Japanese people – including their Press – accepted that the costume I had worn in those pictures was a genuine mistake. I may have been oversensitive about all this at the time, but I have never wanted to be a woman – and I think most women prefer me as a man!

I guess it is when you are missing home the most that you feel in the mood for buying another home – and this is what I did when I returned from yet another of my mid-70s' tours. When I had first come to America and started working in Las Vegas, I had met a lady there called Bea Heath, who was in the property business. She was a lovely person and I asked her if she could look for a home for me. When she said 'yes, of course', she had no idea that she was about to drop a bombshell.

'I think you might be very interested in this house,' she said when she brought over some Polaroid pictures to show us the rooms, the garden and the general layout of the property. 'It's going for the right price, and I think it would be well suited for you and your family.'

Having looked at the Polaroids displayed in front of me, I said, 'That's some home. It's really nice. Did you say who it belonged to?'

'It's called the Pink Palace,' she replied, 'and, at one time, it belonged to Jayne Mansfield.'

Stopped in her tracks by the look of shock on my face, she asked, 'What? Why are you so shocked?'

'Because I met her in England once when we were both on tour,' I replied, 'and I was supposed to visit her in that house one day.'

In fact, Jayne Mansfield, the blonde bombshell and pin-up star, who was renowned for her vital statistics had been performing in cabaret in a club in Bristol where I was on tour, and she had accepted an invitation to sit down and have dinner with us. Jayne was bright and vivacious and very interested in me and my background and we talked for a long time. Before she left, she had said to me, 'You must come to visit my home in Los Angeles.'

'I'd love to come to America,' I said, as she wrote down her address and her telephone number for me, 'and I'd certainly love to see this pink palace you live in.' I knew I could never afford to go then, but it was a nice thought!

Two weeks later she died in an horrific car crash. At that point, of course, I had no idea that one day I would still get a chance to visit the pink palace she had spoken of, and even less of an inkling that, one day, I would own it.

When I told Bea about this encounter, she said, 'Well, maybe you can visit her history instead. The least you can do is take a look at the house for yourself.'

We did and we bought it and fixed it up at an expense that totalled $1.9 million – and we went on to live in the Pink Palace for 27 years. I also bought a Deutchman piano that was in the house for $80,000.

* * *

The Pink Palace was beautiful, but very dilapidated and a little on the dark side when I first saw it. The mature trees in the grounds were unbelievably beautiful but cast too much shade. I realised it needed a great deal of attention and that we would have to put a whole lot more money into it, but I liked it. For six months after we acquired it, we had the builders in and we had to live elsewhere, first at the Beverly Wilshire, and then in a rented home on Hillcrest Avenue.

The Pink Palace was our first, glamorous American home and we loved bringing it back to its former glory. There was a beautiful, spacious living room with a 24-foot ceiling, an indoor waterfall and a heart-shaped pool outside. On the wall, going down the stairs, there were framed pin-up pictures of Jayne in all her glory, and I also inherited a naked bust of her, but unfortunately the statuette was so damaged, she was missing her left nipple! When the builders were taking down a wall in the house, they came across a lot of memorabilia and personal stuff that Jayne had stuck to the walls, which made it a fantastic piece of film history.

One of the rooms was called the 'copper room' for its ornate copper ceiling, while the ceiling in Jayne's office was covered in red leather pads. Once, when there was an earthquake, one of the pads came off and, underneath it, we discovered a hand-painted ceiling from years before. The beams in the dining room were ornately painted as well and the ceiling in the front hallway was a grand 40 feet high.

Soon after we moved in, however, we began to suspect that we were not the only people living there, but we never actually met the 'someone else' who was using our house. We used to come downstairs in the mornings and find dried, green leaves scattered everywhere and, for some time, we had absolutely no idea how they would get there. As it turned out, however, we had a guest – a tramp, who was living in the attic. Apparently, he used to come down at night to help himself to the contents of our refrigerator and, as an animal lover, he always left a sprinkling of dried catnip leaves behind him for our cat, Tommy Dorsey, whom we had inherited from Bea. At first we thought the herb on the floor was some kind of drug and we were somewhat rattled, but

Above With Patricia at my
parents' home after my show at
De Montfort Hall, Leicester

Left A trip to Paris

Below My first kiss after the
ceremony © Grace Waring

Left Celebrating Pat's fortieth birthday in Hollywood

Right With Patricia and Pat Boone at the Las Vegas Riviera after the show

Right With
Cary Grant and
Patricia, taken
at the Las Vegas
Riviera after my
show

Left At Heathrow
with Brad, aged
4½ years

Above Scott, me, Pat,
Liberace and Jason

Left Me and Pat

Top right Trap
shooting with my dad

Bottom right By the
heart-shaped pool
at the Pink Palace
(clockwise, left to right:
me, Pat, Jason, Scott,
Bradley and Louise)

Above With Sammy Davis Jr during my Entertainer of the Year Award

Left My star on the Hollywood Walk of Fame

Above Celebrating
Mum and Dad's
diamond wedding
anniversary

Right After Bob
Hope's Classic Golf
Tournament with the
lovely Dolores

Above My favourite
low-rider Harley ©
Mara Magliarditi

Left My best-known
picture around
the world © Mara
Magliarditi

our fears were groundless. It wasn't until a builder came to repair the roof that our tramp was discovered and scared off into finding himself another attic in which to live.

As well as the cat, we also inherited a dog at the Pink Palace, a huge St Bernard, who looked just like those dogs you see in cartoons with the barrels of rum strapped around their necks. We called him Zeus, but, in the end, we couldn't keep him because we were travelling too much. Fortunately, Bea's daughter took him and loved him until the day he died.

The animals and our tramp house-guest, however, weren't all that we inherited at the Pink Palace. The place was haunted. No kidding! We used to see little children dancing around the living room like they hadn't a care in the world. We never saw the spirits of any adults, just a multitude of children. Seeing ghosts, however, wasn't a new thing for us. When we shared a farmhouse with the MAM organisation in Sussex, a 1,500-acre property commonly used by the families of Tom Jones and Gordon Mills as well as ourselves, we discovered that the house had secret passages, hidden rooms and all sorts of mysterious nooks and crannies. It was a huge old mansion that was full of the ghosts of people who had lived there in the past. They were all over the place; you could just feel them there, and everybody who visited reported seeing them as well.

When Pope used to tell friends that the Pink Palace was haunted and spirit-viewing there was a near nightly occurrence, they would always ask if it frightened her. On the contrary, Pope *loved* to see the spirits and, when they disappeared one day for no reason that we could come up with, she genuinely pined for their return. They kept her company, and we never once felt there was anything to be scared of. Besides, as I have always said: 'It's not the dead than can harm you; it's the living.' But it became time to leave the palace behind when we witnessed one too many people pass from the living to the dead – right in front of our eyes.

In our 27-year tenure on the winding Sunset Boulevard, there were 49 fatal car accidents. The roads around the mansion were full of curved, treacherous bends, and we were appalled at the number of accidents that seemed to happen almost every day. When Jason was just learning to drive, a terrible accident happened just at the end of our drive and, as Patricia and I ran towards the gate, we could hear people saying, 'Oh, my God! He was so young.' Past tense! My heart almost departed from my body, but then, when I realised the dead boy wasn't Jason, my heart went out to his parents. The young guy involved in the accident had gone through the windscreen and hit our wall. He was dead the moment he landed. I am sure it was this horrific event that put Popea off the mansion and she fell out of love with the Pink Palace and, wanting more peace of mind, returned to England. I am not surprised. Even Louise had an accident outside that place when she was driving one of my cars. Thank God she was driving that hulking Cadillac; if it had been a smaller vehicle she would have been crushed within it for sure. As it was, the 1976 convertible – the last year they made this model – that she drove was rammed by the garbage truck behind her with such force the entire car went from a complete stop to a flying leap. The chassis was destroyed, but I didn't care; Louise was unharmed.

Once we were living in Los Angeles, I joined the Bel Air Club. I used to love standing around observing all the people. It was a somewhat different venue from the shabby balcony that I used for people-watching in the old days! Likewise, there were no celebrities, just regular people in the club I had belonged to in Leicester. In the Bel Air Club, however, there were people I had seen on the big screen – people like James Garner, Jack Nicholson, Joe Pesci and Carrol Shelby, the world racing car champion who had his own car, the Cobra. To this day, we often visit Carrol at his home where he lives with his English wife, Chloe. An amazing guy, he had a heart, kidney and liver transplant; and, for a man who has so many parts that were not originally his, he is one of the most genuine people I know! I remember when the singer/songwriter Don Cherry was first starting out, he accepted Carrol's generous offer to come and stay for a bit at the Shelby home in Texas. When Don asked Carrol if he could borrow his truck for a day's use of running errands, Carrol happily handed Don the keys, watched him pull out of the drive and then, smiling at his own joke, he called and reported the vehicle stolen – and had Don arrested!

When I first became a resident in Los Angeles and went to the golf club there, the other members apparently thought that I was a stuffed shirt – and a snob. I suppose this was because I am shy and I don't bound around people, saying: 'Hey, how are you doin'?' I really wish my shyness wasn't so often confused with my being stuck-up. But, when I first see someone I don't know, it's second nature for me to wait until they say hello first, then I am more than happy to reply, 'Well, hello, how are you?' The good news is that, once the people got to know me at the Bel Air, they decided they liked me after all and they didn't think I was a snob at all.

The person who introduced me to that club was a guy called Gus Brigantino, a wonderful Italian gentleman who looks like the Godfather and who I have so much respect for that I treat him as such. His friends affectionately call him Goombah, and absolutely everyone respects him. I have now known him for about thirty years. I first met him through Jack Turner and it was Gus who introduced me to Bob Tucker, who became a very good friend of mine, and I used to play golf with Bob on every occasion I could.

Every single time I played with Bob, things would proceed thus: we would go out to dinner as a foursome that included his wife and mine, or if I was there by myself he would come and pick me up and take me out. He never ever left me alone – and his wife was always saying, 'He thinks more of you than he does me. He'd rather go out with you than go out with me.' When I lost him to cancer eighteen months ago, I lost a chunk of my heart and a part of my life.

That's because we really were great friends – and that's how men are! When they get a good man friend, one they have a lot in common with, they want to spend a lot of time with that person; and, in my experience, some men can get very possessive of their friends. As we reached the mid-70s, however, it was not my male companions who were going to get me into very deep water.

CHAPTER FIFTEEN

I was in BIG trouble – the worst kind of trouble. In 1974, not long after 'Love Is All' became No. 1 in the UK charts, my illicit, extra-marital behaviour on the road finally caught up with me. The Press had discovered that I had had an affair – and apparently a child – with a woman called Diane Vincent. Diane had kept our business to herself, until the papers reported that Popea and I had a new baby – Bradley, who was born on 25 March 1974 – then I guess she went off the rails and decided to go public.

Perhaps this was because she had always believed, in her heart of hearts, that we might end up together one day and, seeing Popea in the papers, holding a brand new, beautiful baby, caused her to realise that Popea was my true love. But I will never really know what motivated her to inform the Press and why she felt the need to inform the world of our affair.

The net result, though, was that the paparazzi were after me again and, when they are in full hue and cry, there is no escape. I couldn't run away from myself, but, to avoid coming face to face with anyone who would be capable of blowing matters out of all proportion and doing even more damage to me and my family, I fled to the famous L'Hotel, in the Rue des Beaux Arts in Paris. Once there, I stayed in the Oscar Wilde suite. Since the walls were covered in mirrors, it only seemed to make me feel worse, because whichever way I looked I had to face myself.

I never left my room and had room service all the time, but the paparazzi still found me and I had to make a quick exit in the middle of the night and wait at the airport for a morning flight to make my return to England. The paparazzi can be a menacing lot, to say the least, and I totally understand the pressures of people in the public eye who suffer the agony of being hounded by them. I realise it goes with the territory if you are in the public eye, but I do not think all the slings and arrows, dirty tricks and menace are justified – and sometimes innocent people's lives are destroyed.

I am not saying, however, that I was innocent in the case of Diane Vincent, but I still do not know for sure if the baby she carried was mine. There was no DNA testing back then, and no way I really could be sure that I was guilty of all the things the Press kept laying at my door.

In the late 70s, I was also caught up in a much-aired harassment scandal. This came about when a dancer said I was sexually harassing her when, in truth, she was sexually harassing me! She used to come to my room and say, 'Well? I'm here.'

Once I'd wised up, I used to say to one of my people, 'Would you tell her I have a guest?' Then, when things did not improve, I fired her. She couldn't take that, so it became a case of 'a woman scorned . . .' It wasn't a nice situation, but I didn't lose the case. The insurance company paid the lawyers $628,000, but she got nothing.

At times like these, it is the lawyers who make the money, and too often that's what these cases are all about.

The hardest thing to bear about one's sexual misdemeanours is the realisation that your behaviour is about to produce some absolutely devastating results and potentially irreparable heart-aches. I regretted such behaviour, and it was *very* painful to know that my family would be reading the stories in the newspapers; and it hurt me so much to have to dial Popea to tell her what was about to be revealed the following day.

'You have to prepare yourself for what you are going to be reading in the papers tomorrow,' I said, choked. 'I'm so sorry. It's just something that transpired and it is unforgivable, but I hope you will try to forgive me.'

I am *not* going to pretend that there were not multiple slips between that cup and these lips, but I am fairly certain that I could not possibly have made all those women pregnant. If that were the case, my trousers would have had to be around my ankles *ALL* the time, and medical science should be conducting a few studies on me to find out where this Hump is coming from – or been!

There have been times when I have opened my hotel door and found a tape recorder sitting there. Whether its owner saw somebody enter my room and put the recorder there to try to catch some naughtiness, I can only surmise. Either way, I'd kick it to one side or say, 'You can come and pick it up now!'

When I decided to share my private life in this autobiography, Pope and I agreed that it would be best for me to be open about almost everything. Until now I have never felt the need to straighten out the erroneous tales, which, anyway, I think is an impossible task. Whatever you say, people will believe what they want – and this, we have discovered, can even apply to people who know you well. A good friend of ours, for example, from the early days recently attempted a walk down memory lane with Popea, and was talking about a night we all went out together – Popea and I, and this woman and her then boyfriend. She remembers the night as a *very* special, romantic evening, because her boyfriend proposed to her at the same time I proposed to Popea.

Try as she could, Pope could *not* convince this friend that it *never* happened, that she was POSITIVE it never happened because she knew I had never actually asked her to marry me. We chose a ring together, but there never was a starry, starry night when I got down on one knee and proposed!

Some half-truths, however, get blown up out of proportion. The Press, for example, has reported that I have made love to 3,000 women, but you should only believe half of what you read. (I'm *joking!*) My comfort is knowing that today's newspaper is tomorrow's fish 'n' chip paper.

While Popea is only too aware of all the events that could have screwed up any marriage that is not as strong as ours, there is also much we have only acknowledged without really considering it in any emotional depth. In coming to the decision to tell all, we thought this should be a cathartic experience for both of us. But we still found ourselves skirting around certain events when we were discussing things in a restaurant near our home in Los Angeles and we ended up making light of what we knew we were finding tough to discuss, by coming up with jokey titles for my book.

'How about *Before, During, and After the Lovin?*' Pope teased.

'How about a first *double entendre* line that reads: "This book is not a kiss and tell; it's a kiss and get on with it . . .?" ' was my response.

It's amazing how interesting a plate of food can be when you're finding the conversation difficult – indigestible. Pope seems far more comfortable discussing emotional roller-coaster things than

I am, and I sometimes think she understands my nature far better than I do. The way we were both raised – eating in silence and being led to believe that men do *not* make apologies for their behaviour – is significant and still makes certain things very difficult. I cannot begin to imagine what would have become of me if I had ever lost Pope – and I *never ever* wanted to hurt her.

Some people might be surprised to know that what distresses, *guts* her most is the public's reaction to my behaviour, rather than the behaviour itself; and she simply cannot stand being pitied. She is the first to understand that people are weak sometimes, and that I'm not alone in this. She also understands that, unlike many people, my life is lived in the public eye – and the press are never far away. I've been on the road for so many years and, during the forty years that we've been married, there have been so many times when I have not known what she was doing, or how she was feeling. She may have been feeling good, she may have been feeling bad, I didn't know and I never really questioned it – and she never nagged or criticised me for not questioning it!

That night, as we moved on from talking about the past to discussing what we could take home as a treat for Bradley, who was coming to visit us that evening, I asked Pope if she would like some more sauce with her dish, and a little later she handed me her serviette because the spiciness of my food was causing me to sweat. This may not appear to be a romantic moment, but I realised just then that the bond between us was absolutely unbreakable. We care far more about each other than anyone could ever truly imagine, and there's nothing past, present or future that we can't handle.

Nevertheless, I still found it an impossible task to sit opposite her at that restaurant table and engage in a conversation about what it must have felt like for her to remain by my side when my misdemeanours became news, or how she handled the days when paternity suits in my life were so prevalent that I began to get them rolled up in bouquets of roses thrown on stage. In fact, I was having so much trouble with all this, I decided I just had to invite Pope to do a kiss 'n' tell in her own words – and she agreed.

So this is her story and her words and you might be surprised to read what bothers her most.

* * *

POPEA: What aggravates me more than anything else in this world is the title I have always been given in the newspapers: the 'long-suffering wife'. I *wasn't* suffering, and if I were, it would have been the end of our marriage. I walked away during our courting days when he had a fling with a dancer at Les Arch in Jersey, and I would have done the same again if I had felt the need or desire to do so. I would have cut off our relationship if I were unhappy then – and I wouldn't stay if I were anything but happy now. But I am still here, and that's up to me, isn't it?

That isn't to say there have not been times when I found our life together difficult, but that was more because of a lack of communication about certain situations than because of the behaviour itself. I would have liked to have the chance to tell him how much something had hurt me at the time, but Engelbert is his father's son, born and raised in a time when men did not apologise for their actions, even when they might feel sorry.

Many years ago, I bought an antique handgun for Enge, which was one of a pair of models that were quite difficult to find. For a more recent birthday, I set out looking for its mate, and the dealer that sold the first to me was trying his best to help, striving to recall where he might have heard news of that model's partner up for sale. I asked him to be careful when he rang me with any news, because I didn't want Enge's surprise to be blown. So when he rang me one day to tell me that he had had success in locating the gun's match, he was not surprised to hear me say, 'I can't talk now, my husband's here. I'll have to call you back later.'

In those days you could pick up any line in our home and overhear a conversation, and Engelbert had done just that, and was quite shocked by what he had heard me say. Of course, he jumped to absolutely the wrong conclusion, hearing me tell a man I couldn't speak freely because my husband was around, and he came storming downstairs asking, 'WHAT THE HELL IS GOING ON?'

Oh, he was beyond just being upset at hearing me tell a man I couldn't talk on account of my husband being there. He was absolutely livid, really.

'WHAT'S THIS ABOUT?'

'I'm not telling you,' I said, 'but you'll be sorry for this reaction when you know the truth.'

When his birthday came and I gave him the gun, the perfect mate in a series to complete the one he already owned, he got very emotional about how he had behaved. He didn't say he was sorry, but I knew he was, because he slept with that gun under his pillow for a week. When I plumped the pillows each morning, I'd come across it and carefully put it back. I was touched by that, knowing that he felt sorry, even if it was never put into words.

So, what has been difficult for me at times is that knowing how he is means there will not be a conversation about any of our rough patches. If I were always going to him about something he'd done, I suppose he'd say something like, 'Oh no, *not* again,' and then I'd feel I was being awful. So I've let things be that have happened in the past, things I haven't thought worth bringing up again all these years later – until now when he has asked me to do just that.

The one time he really was forced to find words for his actions on the road was when the first woman went after him for paternity money, and he had to phone me to warn me about what I was about to read in the press. It must have been so hard for Enge to know that I was going to find out about it. He phoned me from Paris to warn me that the next day's papers would tell of this affair and the possible child he might have had by another woman. Then his friend Billy [LaSaplio] who I am sure meant well, came on the phone, but what he said was: 'You know, Patricia, it's like working in a sweet store; you taste one and taste another and keep on until you get sick of it.'

'That *doesn't* help,' I replied, 'don't say all this crap.'

The truth is I wasn't stupid about any of it; I never was. I had grown up a bit by then as well and, after the initial shock of that first one, the other things that popped up along the way didn't bother me the same way at all. But what I did *not* need to hear moments after news of the first one, was that Enge wasn't feeling sick of it all right then!

That first woman who sued upset me because, at the time, I had just come out of hospital with my lovely new baby. Oh, Bradley was just exquisite, he *really* was. I think this other woman simply wanted everything to hurt as much as possible, and probably intended the pain to befall Engelbert more than me. But she must have known how *I* would feel, because women who have had children know what it's like to hold your newborn baby, and how that can put you on an absolute high. And it was right then, right when the papers printed a picture of me holding my lovely baby, born on 25 March 1974, that she chose to tell her story and get it in the papers, too.

The timing was clearly intentional, as the reports said that this child of hers was already three or four years old, or something like that. And, even though I had just brought Bradley home from hospital and I knew there was about to be a bit of a circus, I started to feel sorry for the child, if it was indeed Engelbert's. It was all *very* difficult and, of course, I cried when I heard it. My mum was living with me at that time and she asked, 'What's the matter?' and I made up some stupid story about having a terrible tummy ache, just so she wouldn't worry. I was always thinking about somebody else. And that was a terrible and complicated thing to have to hide from my mum, because I didn't want to hurt her. I so wanted her to cuddle me, but I didn't want her to feel badly about Engelbert. So it was all a mixed bag of emotions and not knowing which foot, belonging to which person, to put first. So I just braved it.

Knowing nobody else would know the story until the next morning, I decided to go out on the town; I wanted to be seen dancing and having a good time of it. So Mum and I took June, my sister, out to a restaurant where you could dance and, as it was somebody's silver wedding anniversary, there was quite a festive mood in the place. Mum and June danced all night; June with one of the waiters, Mum with a guest at the anniversary table. But nobody asked me to dance! Little did they know, but that was the whole point of going out. I didn't want anyone to think I had something to hide. I figured when they read the news in the papers the next day, they'd think, 'Well, we saw her out last night; obviously she doesn't care about it, or isn't worried about anything, in the slightest.'

The next day I walked down to what was the equivalent of a small village not far from the house, knowing the papers and the news would be out, and wanting to have a look. I asked for all the gossip papers like I hadn't a care, as if what I was requesting would have all the emotional impact of a tin of tomatoes. Really, of course, I felt terrible getting the papers and seeing right away that the news was in fact there, right on top. But I still wanted everyone to think that I was OK, especially for the sake of the children.

I couldn't ever hide the bad publicity from them. They would only have found out from other school kids, who would say, 'Did you see that in the paper?' or, 'Look, I've cut this out for you.' You can't protect them, so you explain it to them in the nicest possible way, being careful that if you're saying it's all OK and that you find the news and the behaviour understandable, that you aren't in effect giving them *carte blanche* to act the same. I had to juggle with that one, had to figure out how to explain that although I wasn't feeling hurt and their father's behaviour made sense to me, that not all women would feel the same.

I remember telling my boys, 'If you ever go out with a girl and she thinks you love her – and you don't – please let her down nicely. Even if you break her heart, there is still a gentlemanly way of doing it. Don't just never see her again.'

These days I say to Scott, 'Is there a bride on the horizon?'

'No, just a bedmate at the moment,' he replies. 'And I know what you're going to say, Mum: "let her down gently".'

I know that men are different from women, especially when it comes to relationships and the meaning of a sexual act. Bradley has taught me a lot about relationships and what goes on, and sometimes he gets into trouble with his dad for what he reveals about the nature of men.

'You *shouldn't* tell your mother *that*,' Enge will say.

'What if she asks?'

'Well *don't* tell her!'

It's been educational – and sometimes funny – though none of it is altogether surprising. Sometimes I think men have no idea that women are on to them when they are, but no one should assume anything at all. For Enge, I just wish and hope he was honest with the girls he encountered. I used to worry that a lot of the other women in his life just had no idea that he was *never* planning to commit to them.

For my part, I understand how a young man could not be away from home for all that time without having sexual needs. Plus at that time he was gorgeous, with a well-known name, and these women would follow him all over the world at their expense. How could it not go to a man's head? Especially for this young kid from Leicester. All of the attention has got to affect you, and at some point you must think you're God's gift, mustn't you? What with all these people telling you that you are, and gorgeous people, at that.

I don't think the problem was the girls that just screamed for him – the thrown knickers and all. I think it was the women who were introduced to him by other stars, women who would come backstage, all of them lovely. I don't picture him going into the audience and picking one out, though that could have happened, too, of course. The only thing, no matter where she came from, is that I hoped she understood what I did, that men are so different, and sex doesn't always mean there is any love attached. Men need it. That's why I didn't give two hoots about it, as long as it was sexual, followed by an 'OK, get out of here.' But when it becomes a relationship, that's when it becomes hurtful.

I always said to myself, if ever he bought a flat or a home for someone, then that would be IT, because I would know then that the person meant a lot to him, or that the situation meant he was torn between loyalty to his wife and children and to some other passion.

If it ever came to that with anyone, I always had it at the back of my mind that I would see my children through to leaving home, or at least to an age when they were grown up enough for me to talk to them about it. It would have been awful if it had ever come to anything like that, because they love their dad so much and, through it all, I loved him, too. As long as I kept that simple reality in mind, I could deal with it. Actually, there's only one time that *really* sticks in my mind about this whole period, and that was when Louise ended up being hurt by his behaviour.

Louise was his 'princess', always was. At one point he had an affair with a dancer, and he and the dancer, as well as Louise and a couple of singers, all went out for dinner. At the meal, he called this particular dancer his princess. Louise was very young at the time, but she kept her dignity and went to the toilet to cry. *She* was his princess. The girl came in and asked, 'What's the matter?'

but Louise just glanced at her, turned on her heels, and walked out. She couldn't even talk to her. Louise had got what was going on, and the whole thing must have been very hurtful for her to deal with on her own. She clearly had a difficult time telling me, because she didn't want to betray her dad.

So that was what I felt the most pain about, because I felt sorry for her, sorry that she had to deal with it, sorry that she wasn't quite sure how to deal with it, and most sorry that for a moment she had to feel less special because of what she had overheard. Imagine, some dancer being called the same thing?

'He loves you, Louise,' I said, 'and although what he did was a very bad thing, it's just a name. For her, it was just another word like "darling", and I'm sure he only meant it that way with her. He would never want to offend you or take anything away from you. No matter what; *you* are his *only* princess.'

I have read in the newspapers that I have said, 'I could wallpaper a room with all of his paternity suits.' It's a cute little quote, so I have never bothered to correct it, but the truth is I have never said anything of the sort and have no idea who made that one up.

Where these women were concerned, you never really knew the truth of it all. It was clear that many of them were making things up, but others we couldn't be so sure about. The two women he paid paternity money to never had any DNA tests done, or actual proof of evidence, which they really should have done.

The first one he had been seeing for a long time, so it could have happened and makes a little more sense, but the other was a devout Catholic, a very religious girl, and with her I somehow just didn't see it, couldn't imagine that he would have been with that one at all. If she were so religious, *why* would she go to bed with a married man? But I guess you never know, and anything's possible; shit happens.

Obviously, a lot was fabricated. One girl used him just to get in the papers and the headline was: *Engelbert Kept Me as a Sex Slave*. Utter bullshit! Engelbert used to have to step over her in hotel hallways while she was having sex with the guitarist, whom she married, so it was obviously all a set-up.

But, like Louise, I did witness some of his naughty behaviour first hand.

One night I was at a big dinner with Enge, the kids, and the entire band in London, and this particular girl was there. I went and sat with the singers, simply because there wasn't room for everybody at one table. It just goes to show how sex and drink can take over, because I was sitting right nearby when she walked in and, as she walked by him, he put his hand up her skirt. The guys in the band didn't know what to say or how to react. I mean, if I hadn't been there they'd have laughed, but with me right there they just didn't know what to do.

When she came over to our table, she said, 'Oh, I walk around nude all the time at home. My husband just loves my body.'

'Well, you've got a lovely body.' I replied, coolly.

She then told me about her husband and how handsome he was. Finally I said, 'I hope you don't torture Engelbert like this, it will ruin his ego.' And that was all I said; I didn't say anything about how I saw through what she was doing, but she got it.

When we went back to the hotel suite in London, where we were about to leave to go to Spain on holiday, while the rest of the band went on ahead to the next venue in France, she must have phoned him because we heard him saying, 'No, I *don't* want you to go to France, *don't* do that. You can come to Spain with us.'

'What will your wife think?' she must have asked, because his reply was, 'Oh, she'll be all right about it; I'll explain the situation in some way. We'll arrange something.'

Anyway, after two days in Spain, he caused an emotional rift, manufactured some sort of argument, and walked off in a huff in the way he can do. I'm sure it was all pre-planned – he had obviously made sure she was somewhere in Spain, and he was off to see her.

On another occasion, I went to Australia on a surprise visit, and my sister Mary and I showed up backstage at the concert. I hid while Mary said hello and he kissed her, but when he saw me, he said, '*Jesus Christ!*'

'I expected something more, like you swinging me around the room as a reaction,' I said.

It had obviously panicked him to see me. And I soon discovered *why!* After the show that night, I discovered that the Other Woman had had to be told to leave his room, because they thought I would be going back to the room with Enge. Clearly, she was absolutely furious – livid. When I went to the end-of-the-tour fan party, Enge became ill and had to go back to the hotel room. He did so without inviting me along, which I would have expected him to do, and I felt very alone and sad. He obviously didn't know how to make it up to her, and that's why he fell ill and had to leave the party early.

'You've got to get your priorities right,' I said, but I didn't go on and on and annoy him, because I thought he might be actually hoping I would provoke an argument which would give him a chance to say, 'Oh, she's always on at me.'

His manager took him away in the car and, just before he did, he said, 'I'll look after him – he'll be fine.'

'Yeah,' I said, 'they said that about Elvis, too.'

It was just awful how obvious it was that they didn't want me to go back to the hotel. Enge was shit-scared! Again, he could have been honest about the whole thing and not upset me at all, but I guess sometimes men just do not know how to be honest – and it was that that used to make me mad more than jealous.

'Why the hell doesn't he tell me?' I used to think.

And, as the children were growing up then, I also thought, 'Why can't he be honest instead of lying about things?'

I couldn't bear the lies then, because I had reached a point of understanding and I thought: 'If you *know* I understand, then you should *know* you don't need to lie about it, right?'

'The thing is,' I said to Engelbert, 'if you had been honest in the beginning and said to these women, "I love my wife, and I'm not leaving her, but I don't mind having a bit of fun on the side," they would have known where they stood.' But because he didn't want to be thought a bad person and thus made up stories, they didn't know where they stood. Maybe he told them we were always arguing, or said that he was unhappy at home. Naturally, they got the wrong idea, or had false hopes, and it was all because he didn't want to be known as a bad guy doing naughty things behind his wife's back.

I suppose things could have worked out the same way for him and me in the beginning but, if they had, I would have been just fine with it if he had been open and honest. But maybe they would have wanted more no matter what he said. Once a woman feels she's got a foot in and thinks he's unhappy and that she is actually helping him, she feels she's doing the right thing. I'm not faulting them.

Likewise, I could *never* – and would *never* – say to him, 'You've got to do this, and don't you dare do that . . .'

It might have been easier if we were just starting out today. Girls used to get married so early when we were young, but these days they just go out with the condoms in their bags! Thank God for them; they save them from diseases and allow them to figure out what they really want. Back in our day, though, everything was so different. That's why I was so ashamed when I got pregnant. I mean, I was even ashamed when we kissed each other at the gates and didn't do anything, but I ended up getting aroused.

'Oh God,' I used to think, 'what would Mum say if she knew I was feeling damp with arousal?'

I was *so* ashamed that my body reacted in that way.

Nowadays, I'm sure my mum could have talked to me about anything, and she would have understood everything. But, back in those times, I was the babe, the darling, and she wouldn't have wanted her darling soiled in any way.

I have, however, been honest and open with our kids about sexual things, and they now know that I was pregnant before I got married. Louise always knew, and said, 'Thank God!' when I told her we were going to let everyone know in Engelbert's book. 'I can't keep going back a year, just to keep this secret going,' she chuckled.

We used to laugh about it together, and naturally I turned to her when the time came to inform the boys.

'How am I going to tell them?' I said.

'Oh, Mum! Just *TELL* them,' she replied.

Anyway, I think because Enge and I have known each other for so long, it feels like we grew up with each other – and that helps me to forgive what I know. Maybe it's also because we have a bond like that of brother and sister as well as lovers.

Things were different for me in relation to him. It was not as if I fell in love with an Engelbert Humperdinck. He was a nobody then. I mean, I even gave him his spending money when we were first together; I paid for everything. So it wasn't that, wasn't even the promise that something might come of what he was aspiring to do. My feeling then was that I would love to make his lunch in the morning and send him off to the factory where he would do his job. I thought he would be a singer at the weekends in a working men's club.

I *never* imagined in my wildest dreams that I would live the life I live – and I just take it for granted now. I thought I would marry a nice guy, pack his lunch when he was going off to work, and have his dinner ready when he came back. That was how I was brought up. But I have no complaints about how things have worked out, and nothing further to share than what I've written here.

When Enge decided to write his book, I urged him to be totally honest about everything, once and for all.

'You don't have to name names or be awful about anyone, but I think it's really important that you should be honest and really go deep into your life,' I said.

I've always thought it would be good for him to shake a few things loose so that they wouldn't trouble him any longer, but I was very surprised when I learned that he wanted me to comment on how his behaviour has affected my life – or explain in my own words why it hasn't. On one level, this makes perfect sense, because if I *write* about what has pained me, then he doesn't have to hear it directly, which he would have to do if he wanted to include my feelings in his book.

I know there's a part of him that tries to rebel against his upbringing – his maleness – so that he can talk freely to me about everything, but he isn't able to do that yet. And I think this is why he asked me to write my own honest account. He realised he couldn't write, 'At that time Patricia was feeling . . .' if he didn't really know how I was feeling, and wasn't willing to make unfair guesses.

At first, I thought my contribution would be inappropriate, as this is *his* book, not mine. But, as we discussed it, I began to understand how important it was to him to have my thoughts, and I found it easier to agree when I understood that this was more for us than anyone else, especially when he told me he wanted me to say absolutely anything I wanted, and he wouldn't even read what I'd written until the book was published. If that doesn't say trust, I don't know what does.

So, we've never gone through it all face-to-face, and are only now just getting our emotions out in the open with one another. It's a strange order of things, but I'm happy for the chance to let him know how I've dealt with everything that's happened thus far. At one level, I think my need to rise above it all has only made him feel worse all these years. Now, with our raw emotions spilt out and spelt out for ever, they can't hurt either of us ever again. And that's all I want to say.

As promised, I have not read what Pope has written above and I will *not* read it until the book is published. Though we won't share words on the topic, I have a feeling the Pope already understands everything about me. Without knowing what she has written, however, I just want to add the following story to finish this chapter in my life.

Over the years I chose to ignore and not to address so many things, and I must say it feels wonderful to be doing that now. By facing up to my past I feel as if I'm starting a new chapter in my life, and I feel much more comfortable in my skin. The moments I treasure most now are the quiet ones at home without worrying that there's something else I should be doing with the time to further my career.

When Pope and I first moved to our home in Leicester, our four children surprised us by collectively becoming Father Christmases. When we woke on Christmas Day, we found that they'd crept into our bedroom without us hearing them and left a stocking full of goodies at the end of the bed. Then, a few Christmases ago, Popea, being the incredibly dedicated gardener that she is, kept what she claimed was a fresh Christmas tree wrapped outside the kitchen window in brown paper – root ball attached. All I could see was this enormous brown-wrapping paper structure with a few fronds sticking out the top.

'When are we going to unwrap that tree and bring it in, Pope?' I kept asking.

'I have to keep it wrapped to protect it from the frost,' she explained, 'but we'll bring it in and decorate it tomorrow.'

Then, on Christmas Eve, when the family was gathered in the house, Louise called to me from outside. 'Dad, could you come out here a minute?'

When I went to see what the fuss was about, my son, Jason, who was sitting in my car, suddenly turned on the headlights, while Popea who was lurking in the garden pulled the wrapping paper off the tree.

It wasn't a tree at all. It was my Christmas present: one of the original, bright-red telephone boxes found on the streets of London throughout the 60s and beyond.

When I first moved to London to make it big, I left Popea – then my girlfriend – in Leicester and we used to trick the phone company by calling each other and reversing the charges, one payphone to the next, so we wouldn't have to pay for the call. I remember standing inside one of those red boxes, night after night, saying, 'You hang up first.'

'No, *YOU* hang up.'

'OK . . .'

'Are you still there?'

'Yes.'

And we'd go on like that for another hour or so, just acting as young lovers do, not wanting to end a call, yet not having anything substantial to add to the conversation.

I remember wishing I had more to share so that we didn't have to fumble about; I wanted to regale Popea with stories of success and tales of how well I was getting on in London, but I didn't yet have any of that to share. Every night, when I first walked into the phone box and shut myself inside, I would stand and listen to the ringing tone before she answered and I would make myself this promise: that before long I would have stories to share with Popea that would *really* impress her.

CHAPTER SIXTEEN

Men behaving badly, that was us, as soon as we finished a show in the mid-to-late 70s. In those days, we would be at a venue for a week at a time and, all of us, the band and I, would stay in the same hotel. When I was winding down from a show between performances, I used to get *very* mischievous and I loved playing practical jokes on everybody. Once, in the late 70s, when we were playing at the Garden State Arts Center in New Jersey and staying at a Holiday Inn hotel, near the theatre, I was in this kind of mood. I dumped a big metal wastepaper basket, filled with water, from a balcony on to the wife of one of my musicians. She, however, got her own back on me for ruining her hair. Having located a garden hose, with a really forceful jet, she turned it full blast on to me and my room! I was never really allowed to get away with anything. Band members were forever sneaking up behind me and blasting me with water hoses, or fire extinguishers and putting jam doughnuts or sticky Danish pastries in my bed.

In those days we were all drinking a hell of a lot after shows – much too much. Usually, we just took over a bar in the hotel and ended up legless and having to help carry each other back to our rooms. We never got argumentative with each other, though, or aggressive with anybody else. We were always good-natured drunks and, whatever shape we ended up in, we were always on time for the next performance. Then, having completed the show, it was a question of 'once more unto the breach, lads' and 'every man for himself' and his favourite tipple.

My guitarist between 1975 and 1976 was a Scotsman named Mike Egan, who was a natural-born prankster. He initiated a lot of the funny things that went on and we called him 'the crazy Scotsman' because he was always doing crazy stuff when we were on the road. One night in Toronto, when we were in a lift along with some very serious blokes in suits, Mike was in a very mischievous mood. He was carrying two guitars in their travel cases, which made it an even tighter squeeze in the lift, and we were all bunched up, close and personal, like tinned sardines.

Mike, who was the last one in, was also the first one out when the lift came to rest in the lobby. As the doors opened, he pretended to trip over and began to clown around, sending his two guitars flying, as he did a series of spectacular tumbles over and over on the floor. We were all in fits, tears running down our cheeks, but the men in suits were *not* amused.

On another occasion when we had just checked into a hotel in Acapulco, Mexico, Mike, who was dressed in a really nice suit and carrying a suitcase full of his clothes, left the lobby ahead of us. The swimming pool was in the middle area of the hotel, and all our rooms were just off it. As Mike was walking to his room, he started clowning around as usual, goose-stepping and swinging his arms to and fro, as if he were in a Monty Python sketch. Then he just walked fully dressed and still carrying his suitcase, straight into the swimming pool, and out the other side, as if this was the normal path to take.

Elsewhere, when we were on the road, Mike and Alan Warman, who was my road manager and hair dresser in those days, started to race each other across a spacious lobby area that had a tiled floor. They got up to such a speed in their effort to beat each other to the lift that they couldn't stop running and Mike hit the opposite wall with such a thump that he sprained both his wrists. All bandaged up, he could still play that night, but his battered and bruised, sprained wrists were excruciatingly painful and it was very much a case of 'the show must go on'!

Those were really fun, men-behaving-badly days, when people like Neil Diamond, the singer of 'Sweet Caroline' and 'Song Sung Blue' fame, who was incidentally born Noah Kaminsky, and Buddy Greco, who eventually made it into the UK charts with 'The Lady Is a Tramp', enjoyed knocking around with us. We used to love going to see each other's shows and hanging out together. It was an exciting time.

Yes, we were all *very* high-spirited and mischievous and we did behave like naughty little boys, but we never got *really* crazy like some of the pop stars and groups. We never *trashed* rooms and got banned from bars and hotels. We only trashed and damaged each other.

Once, when we were staying in the Bel Air Hotel, in Los Angeles, all our passports, which were stacked together in a pile, were stolen. This posed a real problem for us because we were supposed to be leaving on a tour the next day and it usually takes about a week to get new passports. We had to go to the British Consulate in LA, where we spent all day on the Sunday getting new passports issued. Having succeeded in that, we flew to Mexico to do a TV special from the Tabernacle Hotel, which was so luxurious it had a swimming pool in every suite! Later, I was told that Frank Sinatra had seen our show on TV and said to his manager: 'Hey – I wanna do that TV show that Humperdinck did.' That was such a compliment coming from him. I had met him in Vegas, when I went to see his show at Caesar's Palace and then gone backstage after the performance to pay my respects.

When Elvis passed away in 1977, I was performing in Lake Tahoe. At this time I used to finish each concert with what I called 'The Trilogy' – three gospel songs – which Elvis also used to sing. This was a great way to provide a really good finale for my performances. Every show had a curtain call and an encore when the curtains would close then open again to a single spotlight and there I'd be, ready to commence singing 'The Trilogy', starting on the gospel song: 'I wish I was in a land of cotton . . .', ending on the 'Battle Hymn of the Republic'.

The day I received the news of Elvis's death, however, I was SO upset, SO gutted I wasn't sure how to address the tragedy and best honour him on stage. He had always come to see my shows and I had always gone see his and, over the years, we had become close.

In the end, I decided I would say a few words when the curtain first rose, then back up these words at the end of the show by acknowledging that Elvis and I both closed our shows by singing a trilogy of gospel songs and that, from here on, I would be doing this alone.

When the curtains closed, however, and I heard the music begin, I *couldn't* speak, *couldn't* do it. I was *choked*. I just had to walk away from the mike and leave the stage and, when the curtains opened again and the spotlight flashed on, there was nobody standing in its centre. All the audience knew, by then, that Elvis had died and I'm certain they all knew *why* I'd left the stage and not returned. Although this happened as a result of my being

WHAT'S IN A NAME?

overcome by grief – and unable to speak or sing – in the end that empty space left on the stage, although quite eerie, seemed very appropriate. It also seemed incredibly apt that Elvis's songs that were in the UK charts in 1977 included the titles 'All Shook Up' – which we all were by his death, 'Are You Lonesome Tonight?' – which we were whenever we thought of him, and 'Crying in the Chapel' – which so many did the day of his funeral.

I guess it says a great deal about how deeply embedded Elvis was in so many people's hearts that he is still remembered, still talked about today as if he were here only yesterday. The same is true of John Lennon, who was so tragically gunned down outside his New York apartment block on 8 December 1980 by a deluded fan. After his murder, three of his singles, 'Imagine', 'Give Peace a Chance' and 'Woman' topped the UK charts for two months.

Mentioning Elvis has reminded me that, one day, at Gordon's behest, I shaved off my sideboards, even though I felt they were an intrinsic part of my image and had helped me to make my mark. I had grown mine in 1965 and Elvis had grown his in 1972. Way back then, what with Elvis's exact replica of my hairstyle and our matching sideboards, we looked like brothers when we had our picture taken together – and people could hardly tell which one of us was which!

'Elvis,' I once said, playfully mocking his Mississippi accent, 'I *lurve* your music and I *lurve* everything about you. You are one of my favourite people in the whole, wide world – but you *stole* my sideboards.'

'Hell, Enge,' he replied, 'if they look good on you, they for sure look good on me!'

When he was inventing his 'signature' suit, the one that had that oversized collar, he arranged for an artist to follow him around with a sketching block and come up with various concepts for new outfits that he might like to wear on his road show. To give him an idea of how he might look in the clothes, this girl made pencil sketches for him to study before he had a costumier create the actual outfits. There's a documentary that was made of Elvis at this time, during which you can see the artist handing him a sketch of himself dressed in a high-collared item and pants with flared legs, the whole bit that became his 'signature' image – and she had also added sideburns on him. On the film, he looks at the drawing, then says with a mock snarl, 'Hell, that's *not* me; *that's* Engelbert Humperdinck!'

He obviously liked the sideburn image the sketch artist had given him, though, because he grew them.

The moment I shaved mine off, I realised I should not have done it. Although, by the early 70s, many performers had emulated my look, I should *not* have agreed with Gordon that I needed to try something different. It was the mistake of a lifetime, because I was the *innovator* – I started the fashion for sideburns – but I didn't have the confidence to disagree with Gordon and keep them. Why should I have to cut them off, just because Elvis put them on? But that's how it happened. I agreed to shave them off because I was given the impression that people would think I was copying Elvis, instead of Elvis copying me. Elvis was so huge, it was easy to convince me that the public would have seen it the wrong way round, and thought that I was trying to be somebody other than who I was. I guess I just hadn't found the courage of my own convictions to do what I thought was right, regardless of what anyone else thought. Unfortunately, I still had many years to go before I would even come close to thinking in that way.

Meanwhile, I was the butt of many good-hearted jokes. The 'Amore'-singing Dean Martin once said: 'The Humper was all right, but the dink fell off and it hospitalised forty-seven people.' Bob Hope said, 'Have you *seen* this guy? His sideburns are *so* long, it looks like he's always on the telephone.' I said, 'My sideburns are *so* long, they somehow wind up on my conductor's face.' Another wisecrack was: 'His sideburns were *so* long, he tucked them into his underwear and got tickled to death!' After an earthquake in Northridge, Johnny Carson said: 'Humperdinck got shook up so much, his sideburns wound up on one side of his face.' And people used to come up to me, take one look at all my long hair and ask: 'Have you got ears?'

In the early days, I *did* have long hair, but not *that* long. Then I grew it *really* long and, during that period, I had a moustache. The reason I grew the moustache is because when the papers did those Top Ten Sexiest Men competitions, I never seemed to get a look in! The Top Ten always consisted of men like Burt Reynolds, Tom Selleck, and Robert Redford, who all had moustaches. So I grew one and, guess what, I came in at number four! Later still, in about 1989, I started wearing a ponytail. I tried lots of different looks and, when people study a montage of all the looks that I've had during the last 38 or so years, they can see just how many different styles I sported. I even had blond hair at one time, but that didn't last very long – about a year. It didn't really suit me – I'm definitely a dark-haired guy – and one that should *never* have shaved off my 'signature' sideburns!

Trouble was looming on the horizon by the late 70s and coming closer to home every day.

After many lucrative years working together, things were falling apart between Gordon and me – and we were no longer getting on.

When I paid to get out of the contract I had signed with him, an into 'perpetuity' one, which should never have existed in the first place, I relinquished everything I owned in the MAM company. This included millions of pounds of collateral. By then, MAM had marinas, hotels, Burger Kings, airplanes, farmland, jukeboxes, one-armed bandits – the spread of its financial interests was just amazing. Even the MAM office itself in New Bond Street, in London, was worth a fortune. But, no matter what, I felt I *had* to get out of the contract and move on and, in doing so, I cut off my nose to spite my face.

Even the selling of our lovely mansion in Weybridge came about because Gordon advised me that I couldn't continue to own property in the UK and owe lawyers money, which I certainly could not have afforded to pay, if I was now going to buy a house and land in America. Then, even after I sold the house, an absolutely enormous solicitor's bill cropped up, and all I got out of the selling of the house in that prime Green Belt area was £50! So there must have been some jiggery-pokery going on. Two years later, I found out that the mansion had gone on the market for £4 million – and I *really* felt I'd been stung. By then, I had sold 120 million albums and, assuming I made a pound or two per record, I should have earned more than £240 million. I was gob-smacked to find out later, though, that I had only been granted a minuscule percentage of the amount I should have received.

I am a *very* trusting person, and I trusted Gordon because he was my friend, my *BEST* friend. I trusted him with everything I had, because that's how we behave with friends – one hand washes the other. I would, if things had been different and I was given the chance, have taken care of him forever. But, as he is no longer with us and is unable to explain or try to defend himself, I really do not want to go into this sorry matter in great detail. I will only add that the problems were *not* all due to Gordon. There were many other people in the business who were bending his ear back then.

As I have said, although he was only too aware that I wanted a part in a film, he always dumped any scripts that came in for me without showing them to me and he always wanted to keep me on the road because the revenue that was generated from my one-night appearances and the selling of merchandise was astronomical. Too much time spent making movies, on the other hand, would have made a serious dent in all this. Merchandise really was important in those days (it still is) – and I can only begin to imagine how much money was generated at my massive sell-out concerts. Even recently, for instance, I played to 110,000 people in one day – so imagine the amount of money that would have been generated in my heyday.

I was *stupid* – financially naive – but I was not alone in this. Many other stars have been down the same route. Billy Joel, the platinum-plated singer-songwriter, who is a Grammy award winner, was done out of millions; in 1972, an American band called Grand Funk Railroad sued their manager for $8 million in unpaid royalties; former members of the anarchic, chart-busting group, the Sex Pistols, sued their manager, Malcolm McLaren, for £1 million in a suit that was settled out of court; and Bruce Springsteen, one of the world's biggest-selling album artists, sued his manager for squandering money. Even today, the papers are always reporting that celebrities, like Jennifer Lopez, are suing their former managers or agents for millions that are owed.

That said, I *should* have realised, right at the beginning, when I became part of the stable that Gordon was building, how things would be – how he would handle both Tom and me. It saddens me to admit it, but I think he was always more interested in Tom's career than he was in mine. What I think happened, once I became as big as Tom was that America was calling out for me and Gordon had no alternative but to send me there. At one level, it always appeared to me that he wasn't holding the reins equally between his two stars – and that, of course, was *not* to my liking. I always felt, as a result, that I had to keep abreast of what I was doing and where I was going; and I worked *very* hard on building up my own career. Basically, I did my very best to keep up with the Joneses!

Everyone knew there was a bit of rivalry and a race going on between Tom Jones and me, so none of this is hot news. But, within that race, Gordon did *not* play fair, did *not* give me the same attention and opportunities that he was giving Tom. I found out from other people that he was giving Tom first choice of all the songs on offer and only those that Tom didn't like or rejected came to me. I was, in other words, 'second fiddle' and naturally, this upset me a good deal and started the gears of my mind turning on how to get what I rightly deserved. It was all a long way away from the times when Tom and I were trying to make it in the early days and we ended up having to share a bed together at Popea's mother's house – not something I was accustomed to as I don't share a bed with any Tom, Dick or Harry!

Tom was even offered the record 'After the Lovin'', which Joel Diamond, a producer-turned-friend who I call Joel D, had offered to me, but when Joel took the song to Gordon, Gordon said, 'You know, Joel, I don't think Engelbert is right for this one, I think I'll give it to Tom Jones.' So he let Jones have a shot at it, and Jones turned it down, so it came back to me, Mr Second Fiddle!

A talent, called Charlie Callelo, did a brilliant arrangement for that song, and when Gordon tried to change it when I was about to record it, I said to Joel D: 'Take everything that Gordon did – and added – *OUT*, and let me do it the way it was.'

He did and, of course, it upset Gordon tremendously.

I gave Gordon notice in 1976, and the song was released in 1977. I am sure it only made matters worse between us that Gordon didn't think it was going to be a hit and it went double platinum!

By the time I ended my contract with Gordon, he was not the Gordon I had first met and come to know. He had changed from those days when he was playing with the Viscounts and I was doing my usual one-nighters, and we were travelling together. He was my best friend, then, and there was nothing I would not have done for him. I remember that for his wedding I borrowed one of his suits to wear and, prior to that, when I was making money as Gerry Dorsey, he borrowed *my* clothes and sometimes my car. There was give and take, but the appropriate measures of give and take got lost in time's translation.

So, in 1976, when I had had enough of this one-sided affair – when, being a provincial person with no head for business, I had gone along with everything for far too long – I split with him and, in so doing, lost a fortune. But I was too desperate to get out of a situation that had become very painful to care. The lawyers, and the contracts, had all tied me up in absolute knots and, in the end, it was doing my head in and I just couldn't handle any of it any more.

'Power corrupts' and 'money corrupts' are common sayings and can become unfortunate traits and Gordon seemed to adopt both. I could read it in his face and hear it in his words. For a long time, then, Gordon handled two giants in the world of show business, who had come out of Great Britain, but the idea 'Where would I be without them?' did not seem to cross his mind. Then, when I split, he lost fifty per cent of his clientele and his 'empire' became lopsided.

Rumour had it that Tom was also ready to part ways with Gordon as well and I suppose these events had a really traumatic impact on Gordon's ego. He was a very proud man, who had been suffering with ulcers from the time I first knew him, and the smoking and drinking really didn't help either. Gordon lived well! He drank fine wines every night, and sometimes Cognac as well. He wasn't alone in this, I loved doing that, too, but not to the same extent then.

Now, I wish that I had been strong enough to persuade him to change his ways and remember the good years we had shared in the past, but I wasn't. I loved the Mills family – Gordon's father was a great man, but his mother, as I had feared, took a dislike to me after I left Gordon's stable. I was *truly* sorry about that because I had always felt that his family was *my* family. Even then, if Gordon had come to me and said, 'Enge I'm having a problem, do you think you can help me out?' I'd have jumped at the chance.

'*Sure*,' I would have said and I would have done anything – whatever I could – to help him and to save our friendship.

'Gordon,' I'd have said, 'if you can reassure me that you'll be the person you used to be, and promise me you're willing to try to be that, I'll be so happy to have you at my side again.'

But we both had too much pride.

It's tragic that he is not around today to witness his own legacy. He's left a beautiful family behind him – and his widow, Jo, radiates a beauty inside and out. I would *love* to have him here right now, to share my success and everything else that I have achieved. I would have so liked us to grow old gracefully – or disgracefully! – together. It was a truly *terrible* end to a friendship that was worth more than any amount of money.

There were other managers and agents in Gordon's wake, some who could only be called 'thieves', but I am not going to name them. I discovered, as so many had before me, that there are as many 'sharks' on land as there are in the sea – and they come up on you with the same stealth. Such people, I have now concluded, are happy to burn you up in five years, squeeze all the money they can out of you, then drop you. They might have been in the 'industry', but they knew *NOTHING* about music or what it means to be creative and perform. Music – and being creative with it – is the lifeblood of any singer, but such people snuff something out in you, as surely as wet, clammy fingers do when pressed on burning candle wicks.

Recording and performing well on stage has always filled me with an incredible feeling of vitality; sometimes when it's only too clear that an audience has truly enjoyed my show – and is showing their appreciation in clapping and cheering – I like to tell them, 'Applause is the food of an artist; thank you for not starving me or my people'!

Eventually, after being ripped off just one time too many by poor management guys who, although they dented my spirit, never crushed the real bones of my talent, I offered the job of being my manager to my son, Scott. I knew he was a smart kid, with a good business brain, and that he would never do anything other than try to make things work for us as a team. He might have been inexperienced, but he certainly did his best and he won some great opportunities for me along the way. He also learned a great deal about being with his father on the road! We truly helped each other.

Flashing forward now to my present manager, Alan Margulies, I got to know this *dear* man through another dear friend who, at that time, was general manager of a New York hotel. Her name is Armella Steppan, although I affectionately call her The Grass-hopper. She earned this nickname from me because when she plays golf, she hops with each swing, and the grass flies absolutely everywhere. She's a wonderful person whose judgement on the character of others is always spot on, and I'll be forever grateful to her for introducing me to Alan Margulies, who also represents Ann-Margret and Burt Reynolds.

When I met Alan, I understood exactly where Armella was coming from in recommending him to me. All that was needed when he became my manager was a handshake. The nicest part about our relationship is that we hang out a lot together in restaurants and at functions and he visits my home regularly. I've never once felt the kind of anxiety with him that I've felt with other people who have held the same position in my life in the past.

When he came on board he said: 'Right – if it doesn't work out, there will be no hard feelings. Right?'

I knew then that things were going to work out between us and I was finally able to relax. But, oh boy, did it take a long time for me to get to that point in my life! It was Alan, by the way, who encouraged me to write the words that you are now reading – *not* the words about him!, the *whole* book.

CHAPTER SEVENTEEN

I was in a bad way. By the late 1970s, I was drinking Remy, lots of it, far *too* much in fact. When you become convinced that, no matter how hard you are trying, your career is headed for the doldrums – and you are also discontented with whoever is handling your business affairs – it can really set you off on a downward spiral. Each time you feel depressed or have another panic attack, you think the answer lies in the bottle, in another drink. It's a common scenario in show business and, like so many before me, I tried to dull my fears and drown my sorrows in drink.

The binges, better known as benders, left me with a lot of blank spaces in my brain. I could never remember the night before the next morning and I rarely knew what I'd been up to. The ever-helpful Press, though, were not slow in publicising my problem, and they kept hinting and printing that I had started to abuse alcohol. Then, my manager, Harold Davison who I was deeply unhappy with, tried to get me committed because he thought I was going crazy. He even turned up at the Pink Palace and tried to solicit my wife's help in this.

'You've gotta help me get him committed,' he said to Popea, 'I think he's abusing drugs as well as alcohol.'

'Do you realise you're talking about my HUSBAND?' Popea fired back. 'I know he drinks, but he doesn't use any drugs. And, as his wife, I would know.'

She was right – the only coke I was familiar with was the one with the capital C that came out of a can, and the only pills I took were an occasional sleeping pill to help me through a time change. I am not a Goody Two-Shoes but, when I walked past rooms where my band was burning incense, I thought: 'Hey! These guys are really religious.' Little did I know that they were burning incense to cover the smell of the marijuana that they were smoking. *They* knew that if *I* knew that they were indulging in drugs of any sort, it would have meant instant dismissal. So, from my days as an altar boy, incense was a familiar smell to me; and, *yes*, I really was that naive!

The saddest thing about my downhill period is that I should have been feeling on top of the world. In 1977, I had just released my 'After The Lovin' album, which went double platinum and even earned me a Grammy. It was *so* strange to be feeling depressed and to be in such bad shape right then, but the harder I pedalled, the less acceleration I seemed to have. I guess I was experiencing emotional and physical burnout, but this didn't occur to me at the time. I just felt there was nothing I wanted to do and nowhere I wanted to go, and I certainly couldn't feel excited about my current success, because I didn't feel any excitement emanating from my then-manager, who had come along after I left Gordon's stable.

One of my problems was that, despite all my success, I still lacked true, deep self-confidence and, offstage, I was still a very shy person. Nothing much had changed since I first saw my name on a billboard, for example, and stood there awe-struck.

'That couldn't be me, could it?' I had thought.

It was actually some time before I could bring myself to phone my mum and dad and say, 'Hey, guess what . . .' because I couldn't quite convince myself that it really was *my* name on the billboard and not some other bloke's who just happened to have the same name as me! When I performed in those days, I continued to do a few impressions of Dean Martin and Jerry Lewis and then Elvis. I didn't need to do this, but I felt if I just stood there singing, even after I had had hit songs in the charts, it would not be enough – that something else – someone other than me – was needed to really please and satisfy the audience. And as, after all, nobody had booed me off stage when I had done the impersonations in the Army canteen, I continued to give my lack of confidence a boost by performing in this way.

When I went to see Elvis, however, I realised the only person he ever imitated, or took fun of, was himself!

It took me a very long time to accept, though, that I could now strip myself of all those unnecessary appendages in my shows. When I finally did, I thought the shows worked so much better. Instead of trying to be a comedian and an impressionist in addition to being a singer, I just sang. I also discovered I liked taking the mickey out of myself and making fun of myself on stage. I never acted as if I really believed I was the 'King of Romance'. I never took that role too seriously, even though that was what I was now being called. The only time I was serious on stage was when I was singing a sincere ballad, then I would allow my own true inner feelings to shine through.

So, one way or another, although there was no apparent need for me to be feeling so at the mercy of my blues and fuelling myself with so much alcohol, I was.

To make matters even worse, I had started throwing up when I came off stage and I couldn't catch my breath. This was not, it turned out, because I was drinking so heavily – I had come down with an advanced asthmatic condition that was most likely caused by stress. In Las Vegas, a guy called Michael Flowers, who is now a manager and who looks after Shirley MacLaine, said to me, 'I know a doctor who deals with allergies, and I think that's what you've got.'

'Yes,' I thought, 'an allergy to bad, unsupportive business managers.'

Michael then suggested an acupuncturist, who was rumoured to be brilliant in his field, and I agreed to meet him.

Ever since then, Dr Ha has been my hero. This is not a man who promises, 'I can cure you.' He says, 'I can try to help you.'

His talent is backed by true modesty.

'Duong,' I said, when I first met him, 'I'm feeling absolutely ghastly, so anything you can do to help would make me a happier man.'

He gave me a treatment in Vegas one day, repeated the same treatment the next and, in four days, he cured me of the throwing-up and the asthma. It was like a miracle!

The *National Enquirer* newspaper got hold of this information and wanted to take pictures of Dr Ha putting in the acupuncture needles and publish a story about his amazing healing skills. I was willing to do anything to help the man who had helped me, and so it was that camera flashbulbs were popping all around me while my face was being turned into a pincushion. It *was* effective, though, and Dr Ha's business picked up pretty quickly after that feature was published.

* * *

As well as being a very supportive wife, able to tell pushy managers when to sling their hooks, Popea was also a brilliant mother. Thanks to her, our children had a great childhood. She used to take Louise to drama and dance classes, and she even once succeeded in getting Jason into a dancing class.

'You need to understand,' she told him, 'just how important it is to know how to dance before you ask a girl to dance. It'll be really great for you to learn how to waltz and tango.'

It seemed like a very good idea and she was very pleased when Jason agreed to go, but he was no Billy Elliot! His time in the class was very brief! The following week, the teacher took Popea to one side and said: 'Please don't bring Jason again – he's just too disruptive.'

So, Popea enrolled him for a kung fu class instead!

Too often left in the position of a single parent when I was away, she was forever ferrying the kids around from one place to another, here, there and everywhere. The only time she ever left them was if she came on a short tour with me. Then Grandma Healey, who they loved to bits, would come and stay with them. Once when we were on tour in Germany, Scott and Jason, up to the usual kind of mischief that boys get up to, lit a fire inside our huge garden shed, rather than outside, and up it went in flames and burned down. Our valet dealt with the matter and didn't say anything about it until Popea got back. By then, Harvey the rabbit had died – probably from shock – and he had to be buried in the garden.

One morning the two boys came rushing into the house saying to Popea, 'Mum! Harvey's *alive*! Harvey's lying on the grass. Harvey's come back to life again. Honest.'

Somewhat mystified, Popea followed them into the garden and, lo and behold, there was Harvey. For a moment she thought we should have called him Lazarus but, when she got up closer to him, she could see that he was not alive, he was very dead – to the point of decomposing! Our dog had smelt his corpse lying beneath the earth and dug him up!

It was only in recent times that Popea learned that Bradley used to go fishing in our garden pond and hook out the koi carp and the goldfish. She had always thought that their diminishing numbers was due to a crane which used to flutter in and out of the garden sometimes. But, no, it was Bradley who had gone fishing and stolen them.

'Bradley,' she said, when she finally found out from one of his friends who used to go 'fishing' with him, 'I know something about your past.'

'What's that?' he replied, keeping his cool.

'You're a bloody thief,' replied Popea.

'What on earth do you mean?' he asked, now rattled.

'It was you who used to steal the fish from the garden pond,' she said, accusingly.

'How did you find out?' he replied, shocked.

'Your old fisherman friend,' Popea retorted.

During my years in the business, I have had the pleasure of singing for members of various royal families around the world on several occasions. One of these was very early on in my career when I was performing at the London Palladium for four months; the other was at a Royal Variety Performance, which was always given on a Sunday because there were usually several acts from West End shows appearing in it and Sunday was the only time they had off and it was usually the most convenient for the other artists taking part. Given that it was for charity – usually in aid of the Artists' Benevolent Fund – and Her Majesty The Queen was the patron, every year a member of the Royal Family would attend. Also, since the idea was to raise as much money as possible, the prices of tickets were very high, so you ended up with an extremely elegant audience but probably one that wasn't quite used to letting its hair down! At the end of this performance, there was none of the usual clapping, just the muted, muffled sound of gloves patting gloves. Everybody present was so bejewelled, so done up in diamonds and emerald rings and bracelets, that they just sort of tapped their fingers very gently to avoid hurting themselves or shaking their jewels off while they showed their appreciation. It was slightly strange being on the receiving end of that.

The show I starred in also had Des O'Connor acting as master of ceremonies and introducing everyone, and Diana Ross had also come over to sing. Following the show, as was customary, all the performers were presented to Her Majesty The Queen Mother, who was representing the Queen that evening. She had such amazing presence and gorgeous blue eyes. It used to be the case that when you played in the presence of a member of the Royal Family, though, that if they didn't clap, the audience didn't clap either. That used to be protocol. Nowadays, the audience don't take their lead from the royal box, but I think they like to take a quick glance up there to see if the occupants have enjoyed the acts as much as they have.

What I remember about that occasion was feeling so thrilled when the following day there was a photograph of me in the newspapers alongside which was a caption that read: 'The Queen Mother's Favourite: Engelbert Humperdinck'.

Thank you, ma'am, I thought!

Another encounter with members of a royal family resulted in a funny situation in Monaco, when I was performing at one of the Red Cross charity events that were arranged by Princess Grace. Her husband, Prince Rainier, was going to be in attendance and so was Princess Margaret, together with a lot of other lesser royals and a great number of dignitaries.

During the daytime while I was there, we were invited to go out on a wonderful, luxurious yacht that was big enough to house a helicopter pad on the top of it and big enough to cross the Atlantic on its own. When we finally left the yacht and started strolling back to the hotel, we came across a crowd standing around the steps of it. I stood there for a while, mingling with the crowd and looking at everybody else, then, unable to resist, I tapped a man on the shoulder and said: 'Excuse me, what are you waiting for?'

Turning to me, he said in a loud, excited whisper, 'Engelbert Humperdinck is in the hotel!'

He didn't even recognise me!

A bit later, I decided to go to the beach, where there were all these colourful changing rooms. I was sitting outside one of these, having a long, cool drink, when a lady, who was wearing a huge hat and who I subsequently discovered was a countess, came along. Covered with emeralds on her fingers, wrist and neck, she went into the cabana, threw aside its curtains, took off her hat, put it on to a table, and then began to strip off all the rest of her clothes in front of me. Soon, all she had on were the emeralds. Then, just before she walked off down the beach, still naked, with only a little towel wrapped around her, she sat down at my table and, with a wicked wink, said in a very posh voice 'H-e-l-l-o there, Engelbert.'

The audience, which attended Princess Grace's charity gala that night, was also dripping in jewels and, again, when they applauded they just brought their fingers together ever so carefully, so that they wouldn't shake off any of the sparklies. As a performer, you couldn't hear any applause. We just did the show, and walked off stage to the sound of our own footsteps. It was hysterical! There was me working my arse off, and hearing nothing – not even a single posh, plum-in-mouth 'bravo'.

After the concert, Princess Grace invited us back to the Palace, and we went there to have cocktails with the royal couple and the owner of Coca-Cola and Heineken.

When I was in Kuala Lumpur, I was invited to a party at the palace by the King of Malaysia, and there were three young princesses, standing in the line-up.

'Will you dance with the princesses?' the king asked me.

'Yes, Sir, I will,' I replied, obediently. I know my place!

Turning to the pretty princesses, he said: 'Now stand in line, await your turn, and Engelbert will dance with you one at a time.'

John Smythe, who was travelling with me, was also present, and the king said to him: 'You can dance, too.'

'I can't dance,' John replied in a panic. 'I've never learned . . .'

'You will dance,' the King insisted.

'Oh? Well, yes, Sir, I will,' John said, getting the message.

The princesses were not the king's daughters and I never discovered whose daughters they were. I was much too busy dancing with one after the other! The first one took my breath away by doing the sort of dance with me, where hips and faces are glued together. It took some doing in that situation to maintain courtesy and protocol, but I remembered my manners and managed!

* * *

As the 70s came to an end, it became clear that they were never going to be as lauded by the Press as the free-for-all 60s, but they were not the boring decade that some people tried to make them out to be. There were plenty of excitements and dramas, some good, some not so good. Sadly, my old buddy Jimi Hendrix died at the tragically early age of 38; it was a great loss to the music world. On the positive side, though, George Harrison's concert for Bangladesh proved that rock could raise millions, a forerunner of the Live Aid concert in the early 80s. And the Iron Lady, Maggie Thatcher, entered Downing Street as the first woman Prime Minister; while the phenomenon of Punk, exemplified by Sid Vicious and the Sex Pistols entered the scene and nearly wrecked a BBC studio!

It was hardly a dull decade and, on the career front it was a good ten years for me, even though I hit the bottle and lived through some pretty down-and-out, rough times.

I had decided by that time that one of the best investments I could make was to buy property and as I was giving up our house in Las Vegas, Popea and I decided that we wanted a base in England. We had two choices: London or Leicester. London was obviously convenient for business, but we had, and still do have, strong family ties with Leicester, and the property in that area also offered another important factor in choosing somewhere to live: space – for my fourteen Rolls-Royces!

The house is actually an old manor house that was formerly owned by the Duchess of Hamilton and which was frequented by royalty when they were hunting. I remember that when we moved in, there was no heating and the children arrived before Popea and me and we had to huddle together in sleeping bags to keep warm. I refurbished the entire place myself in order to make it habitable and what were once the servants' quarters are now luxurious rooms for guests who might present themselves at odd times. We've made it into exactly what we want from a home and in it I have my own quaint, typical, English, countryside pub. It's all very olde-worlde, and there's a dartboard there. In fact, I've become a very good darts player, who's scored a lot of maximums, played a lot of dart professionals – and beaten them! All my sporting photographs are on the walls of the pub and we often have a barbecue at family get-togethers, and when my band are on tour here, they come for a barbecue and an English beer or two! They think that's quite something – because the beer in America is so different from the real ale we get in England.

My friend Dave Spradbury enjoys telling the story about how, when he visited us there a few months ago, Popea and I picked him and his wife up and went out for a drive around the Leicestershire countryside. He couldn't get over the fact that, although I tour all over the world, I hardly ever get to see my home county of Leicestershire! But that's how it is. We had a lovely meander through all the lanes and I booked a table for Sunday lunch in a village pub. Very excited, I said to Dave: 'We can have roast beef and Yorkshire pudding.'

My mum always cooked that for our Sunday lunches and I couldn't wait to go back to my old eating roots! I *really* was homesick for the food that I grew up on.

Each time I come back home, I have my private moments in the cemetery where my dad and mum are buried. When Dave was in Leicester with us, two years ago, I said: 'Do you think you can help me, Dave? I've got to go down to the shops and buy my Mrs a new iron. I'm also going look for a new telly for the bedroom.'

'Sure,' Dave said, and we drove to the local shops and walked into this massive electrical shop and bought the iron and the new television. I love doing ordinary things like that. There's always somebody who comes up and says hello and that's really nice. I'm very proud of coming from Leicester, and I like to believe what I'm told, that I've been a great ambassador for that city and for England.

When people come up, they say: 'Engelbert, it's *wonderful* to see you, how are you?' and things like that. Or they say: 'My auntie worked with your sister'; or 'My brother used to work in the same factory that you worked in when you were a young man'; or 'Your dad used to go down to the pub with my dad'; or 'We used to go and see you in the working men's club' – it's as if, one way or the other, I am personally linked to everybody who stops me – and their cousins, uncles and aunts. It's really great.

I have my own favourite charities, of course, and, last year, when I put my name behind a golf charity event for cystic fibrosis sufferers, our local club in Leicester raised a vast amount of money, and some of these funds, I recall, came from my own fan club, whose members are always amazing me with their generosity. A fan club in the US helped me raise a quarter of a million pounds for leukaemia research, and I presented the cheque to the Lord Mayor of Leicester, who in turn gave it to the Leukaemia Research Fund.

The 80s, when they arrived, began very dramatically with a Turkish assassin taking a pot-shot at the Pope (not my wife, mind you) in St Peter's Square, in 1981. Fortunately, although the Pope was wounded, he survived.

Soon after this, Popea's mother was staying with us in our house in Leicester. One morning at breakfast, she suddenly announced that she had seen some UFOs out of her bedroom window the night before.

Popea and I didn't react and just went along with it, but we were saddened, fearing that this was a sure sign that Granny was getting on in years and that her mind might be getting a bit soft around the edges.

'Well, if you see the UFOs again,' I said, gently, not wanting to give her the idea that she might be 'losing it', 'wake us up, so we can have a look, too.'

The next night she came into our bedroom, and, shaking me by the shoulder, she said: 'Quick, the pair of you – *get up*. They're out there again.'

So, feeling we had no choice but to indulge her, Pope and I got up and followed her to the window. *What a shock!* I am *not* kidding. It was like a scene from *ET* out there. Strange lights were darting about, lighting up the night sky and hovering, from time to time, over our garden, right above the geodesic spaceframe that covered our swimming pool. As always happens on these occasions, I discovered that there was no film in my camera, and none to be found anywhere else in the house. As Pope and I scrambled round trying to get the best view of the 'visitors' from outer space, we kept bumping into each other and into Granny. Finally, having rubbed our eyes and had another look, we rushed to the phone to call our local radio station to ask if they knew what it was all about. Naturally, not wishing to be thought a looney, I didn't identify myself when I asked the question.

'We don't *really* know what they are,' came the response, 'but you're not the first to call us with this enquiry. We've been getting quite a few calls, including one from Bob Monkhouse, saying that there are UFOs hovering over Engelbert Humperdinck's place.'

We never did discover what those lights were. Perhaps they were UFOs, after all! They disappeared so fast into the sky, it was like a scene from a comic book.

After my father died in 1984, I was feeling very overwrought and emotional about everything. One night, when the band and I went to a Japanese restaurant after a show, a strictly private dinner just for me and my entourage, which consisted of about fourteen people, we ended up consuming 96 bottles of Sake. Between sips, still feeling *very* raw about my dad, I kept breaking down and crying my eyes out. Sake, I've been told since, can have that effect on you. And that really was one of the most memorable alcoholic binges I have ever experienced. I have to admit that I got so drunk, four of the guys – including Mike Stone, my karate teacher – had to carry me out of the restaurant, lower me into the limousine and then, when we reached the hotel, carry me up to my hotel room.

The next morning one of the guys said: 'D'you know how heavy you are when you're legless?'

My dad was always a very strong-willed man and he was in hospital when Popea was going away for the weekend to visit her girlfriend, Carol. He said, 'Don't go this weekend.'

'I've got to go, Dad,' she said. 'It's John's birthday, and I've promised, 'but I'll be back before you've even missed me.'

Dad, who was 91, died that weekend.

When Popea went with my mum to see Dad's body, Mum just stood there repeating, 'Oh, my shepherd'.

It was *so* sad. She couldn't believe he had gone, but she was very grateful that they had had such a long and happy life together. We really didn't know how she was going to bear up at the funeral, but she was *wonderful* – heartbroken, yet so dignified even when she broke down and cried.

When my mum became terribly ill in 1985, I had called Dr Ha right away. I wasn't quite sure what to say, or how to describe what was wrong, or even how to say out loud that my mother had a heart condition and I was sure she was slipping from my life, but then I burst out: 'They've only given my mother six months to live, Duong. Please help – they've only given my mother six days to live.'

Duong's response was so typical of him: 'I'll be on the next flight,' and he flew out with his brother and treated my mum for two days.

'I'll be back in three months,' he said as he left.

That sounded like a *very* long time to wait. It was, after all, half of mum's predicted life span. When Dr Ha came back in three months, however, she went on to live for another three precious years. She was blind when he arrived – had been for some years – but, and this was a totally unexpected gift, he brought partial sight back to her. He never mentioned, by the way, that he had delayed his honeymoon just to fly from Los Angeles to Leicester and offer a helping hand. After treating her, he turned to me and said, 'Enge, your mother's got six months.'

It was better than six days: when that's all you've got, you don't have time to prepare for death.

Dr Ha said that he would return in three months, and with his three treatments, along with the almost daily care from Mum's local doctor, Dr Jarvis (my grateful thanks to you, Dr Jarvis), my mother went on to live for three more years.

Despite the time gained, however, my mother's final illness left me totally distraught. She was seriously ill for much of the last year that she lived and even ended up in a coma. When Pope phoned to tell me she had lost consciousness and was comatose, I cancelled my current tour and got a private plane from Valley Forge to Leicester.

When Pope called, she said, 'You need to come home, mother is not well.' She didn't tell me mum was in a coma – she didn't want to upset me – but from the tone of her voice I knew something serious was going on.

'*Put mother on the phone*,' I demanded. 'I can't,' replied Pope, 'she's resting.'

My mother must have, somehow, overheard the conversation and knew Pope was talking to me. She came out of her coma, sat up, and said, 'Give me the phone.'

'You take care of yourself, my son, my son,' she said, into the receiver.

'Mum, I'll be home tomorrow and . . .'

'Keep the family together,' she requested. And those were the last words she ever spoke.

When Irwin and Louise came to meet me at the airport, they told me, as gently as they could, that she had passed away. Inconsolable and out of my mind with grief, I cancelled the concert tour I was about to commence in England. But when my wife and my sisters heard that I had done this, they said, 'Oh, no! Mum wanted you to sing for her,' and she then told me that our mother had once specifically stated that, after her death, she wanted me to keep singing to her from the stage, and that it would upset her if I abandoned or cancelled any of my shows.

So, I honoured Mum's wishes and re-instated the tour I'd just cancelled. But it was hard, very hard, performing in a raw, grief-stricken state. I was close to tears on stage and I bawled my eyes out every single night when I came off. There is no question in my mind that performing then was the hardest thing I have ever done in my life, even though I knew it was what Mum would have wanted.

At that time, Tony Cartwright was managing a violin player named Gary Leviney who agreed to play 'Ave Maria' at my mother's funeral in Leicester. I knew that she would have loved to hear him play this. On the day of the funeral, it was raining in Leicester and, the moment I got up, I somehow knew that everything had gone wrong with this plan. Apparently the night before, Gary had phoned Tony and said, 'I've broken my arm – and I won't be able to play at the funeral.'

Tony, knowing how much it would mean to me to have him play the violin – the same instrument my mother used to play – said: 'Gary, whatever happens with the arm, you have to play at the funeral tomorrow. Engelbert will be absolutely gutted if you don't.'

'But Tony,' Gary replied, 'I can't move my arm!'

'Just come down tomorrow, anyway,' Tony said firmly, 'and we'll sort something out.'

So, despite the broken arm, Gary practised playing 'Ave Maria' in the least painful position and decided that he would play it, come what may, at the funeral because he knew how much it would mean to me – and to my mother.

In the end, it was a very special moment at the funeral. Everyone in the congregation was crying, not just because of the sad nature of the occasion, or because Gary had a big plaster of Paris on his arm, but because he was somehow showing us that we have to keep going in spite of life's traumas. I have never forgotten that moment. I know it sounds like a little thing, but it wasn't. It was an important and beautiful moment. When he played, I closed my eyes and let the tears just flow.

After the funeral, one song that I could never sing again on stage was 'How Do I Stop Loving You?' I stopped singing it altogether because each time I tried to sing it, I could never make it through the whole number because my body was wracked by sobs.

I loved my mum so much, it was a truly terrible time for me, however hard I tried to move on. She had had eight heart attacks before she died and images of all those days and nights that I had sat by her bed when she was ill and thought unlikely to recover, kept running through my mind. For reasons unknown to me at those times, I had often felt compelled to place my hands beneath her bed and hold them there. It was as if I was trying to hold her up. It was not until later that year that I learned that what I'd been doing, absolutely instinctively, was using my power as a healer. I'd been asking God to take my strength and give it to my mother. Holding my hands thus, I was channelling my healing powers from me to her.

After she died, I kept recalling so many special things, like the time she gave me a ring that had a green stone set into it. I lost that stone so many times and I was forever breaking into a cold sweat when I noticed it was missing its jewel yet again. There I would be, crawling around on my hands and knees searching for it and, on one occasion when I was in a club, I had every employee – including the owner – on their hands and knees, searching for this stone with torches. Finally, after saying innumerable times, 'My mother gave this ring to me and I must find the stone,' someone found it and carefully placed it back into my trembling, outstretched palm.

I was always having to have the stone put back in its setting, but the wretched thing continued to fall out no matter what. And, as the ring only had sentimental value, I thought I might be overreacting somewhat when its greenness, as I called it, kept popping out and causing me endless anxiety attacks.

Just after my encounter with tuberculosis, I went to see a psychic lady in London, a doctor's mother known to be gifted in the paranormal and a very wise woman. Having ushered me in, she instructed me to open my hand so she could examine my palm. As she did so, she suddenly announced, 'I need a drink,' which is *not* something you want to hear from someone who's about to reveal what's in store for you. Anyway, while I sat there feeling somewhat concerned, she got herself a drink, and then returned to examine the open palm of the hand on which I used to wear that ring, which I had stopped wearing because the stone kept falling out.

'You're going to get on,' she said, a note of conviction in her voice. 'You're going to *really* make something of yourself.'

She had no idea what business I was in, or hoping to be in, and I was hanging on her every word.

'You will become very well known here in England, but you will also spin around the world. You will spread around the globe like wildfire.'

I could have kissed her.

'There's also going to be a big change,' she added.

At the time I assumed she meant a big change in my fortunes – in my bank account – as I had no idea I was soon to change my name. But she was right on all counts: my first hit was not only a hit in England, it went around the world, was indeed 'global' – and I changed my name.

Towards the end of the reading, she put her hand on my chest and said, 'You've had a nasty pain right here'. Her hand was resting on what I called my tuberculosis spot, right in the place where I once had a tube keeping me from death. At that point, I must have lost my ability not to react to her predictions.

'Don't worry about it,' she said soothingly, 'it will never come back. It will disappear like you've never had it.'

Now, when you have had TB, you are usually left with scar tissue, but I do not have a single scar.

I was feeling giddy as I absorbed all her promises. 'When will all this happen for me?' I asked as I was leaving.

'Be patient son, be patient.'

And as I went out, she cautioned, 'Don't ever lose that ring with the green stone. It's a very expensive one.'

At first, I just assumed that she meant the loss would be costly for me because it had so much sentimental value, but then I couldn't help it, I decided to put the psychic's words to the test. I took the ring to a jeweller's to get it valued.

I was in for a shock!

The ring contained a real emerald, and it was a very valuable heirloom. Even my mother hadn't known this. Afraid of the responsibility and disturbed by the warning that I had better not lose it, I gave the ring to my father to look after. He got so sick of losing that stone, too, however, that he fashioned some sort of sticky adhesive underneath the stone and, at last, it remained fixed in place.

In 1988, I was very honoured when I was invited to perform during the Olympics in Seoul, in South Korea. I had brought along Alan Warman, my road manager, and my public relations person, a brilliant man named Clifford Elson, who was referred to as the 'Godfather', and my minder Brian Walters, who's still taking care of me to this day.

When we arrived at Customs, it was a bit frightening, to say the least. There were about a thousand troops and militia people hanging round the place, armed to the teeth. The event's organisers were very worried about these games because the location was so close to North Korea, and they were aware of the possibility that the North Koreans might bomb the stadium. The memory of the terrorist attack on the Olympic Games in Munich, in 1972, was in everyone's mind, and it was clear that Seoul had no interest in suffering a similar tragedy and the resulting world headlines. So, they ran a very tight ship and security was so rigid it had the opposite effect on us, and made us feel *insecure*. There's nothing like seeing men, wearing frowns and firearms, to remind you of the ever-present potential for real danger. We couldn't move from one hotel floor to the next without alerting the security guards and arranging an escort for the lift.

There were all these photographs on the walls of the hotel, and I said to a PR lady who was taking us around, 'Are these all film stars?'

'No,' she replied, 'they're all wanted men – gangsters from North Korea.'

The venue for the show was unbelievable. The auditorium held about 8,000 people and I performed with a hundred-piece orchestra for ten days in a row. They transmitted the performance live, so Americans saw it at something like five in the morning. It was the first time a Chiron had been used, which enables the words of a song to be printed on the screen while you sing. It was an historic event all round. The top Russian singer performed, and a Chinese woman who was the equivalent in her country of Madonna in America. It was quite cosmopolitan, but my chief memory of it was the omnipresent security.

My own security man, Brian, never left my side – never has done, really! Every time I travel anywhere, he is always there as my minder. If anyone were to judge his character over the phone, they would deem him a kind, sweet, docile gentleman. In fact, every time I phone to tell him I'm coming to the UK on a long tour, and ask if he'll be able to look after me, he always replies: 'It would be my pleasure, Enge, absolutely any time you need me, I will drop anything to work for you.' He is an extremely polite, courteous man, who is willing to lend a hand and help me with anything I need, even a clue on a crossword. As a matter of fact, while writing this book, I have often had to ask Brian to fill in the blanks for me. He doesn't drink or smoke, and his antennae are so sensitive, so finely tuned that he is aware of all the minute detail of every scene and situation. There have been quite a few times in the past when he has suddenly gone very quiet in public places and, whenever I've asked, 'What's on your mind, Brian? What is it?' his answers have always reassured me that, as long as he is around, my back is more than safe. He just doesn't miss a trick.

On a recent tour in Bristol in June 2004, Brian and I went out for a nice Chinese dinner on a much-needed night off. Seated near our table was a large group of loud young men, who were getting rowdier with every sip of alcohol. Although they stayed at their table and I never felt the least bit threatened, they kept calling out, 'Please Release Me! Hey, Engelbert! Please Release Me!' and, every time a new person entered the restaurant, one of these fellas would stand up and set everybody off again by pointing me out to the newcomers.

'Hey hey! Have you noticed Engelbert Humperdinck is in the restaurant? Look there – *release* us – it's Engelbert!'

Although I enjoyed my meal, Brian hardly touched his. He had both eyes locked on the Irish table in the corner. 'It's OK, Brian, they're harmless,' I said. 'Stop worrying and have some chili prawns and help yourself to the crispy beef.'

As I said this, the loudest one in the group stood up again, boxed his mates about their ears, and called out another hello and release me greeting to me.

'Really, Brian,' I added as he tensed again, 'I'm not worried about that kid.'

But he is such a professional, he still didn't take a bite to eat.

What is it about me? Why was I was always being taken into custody?

OK, I know this only happened twice, but, for the majority of the population, it doesn't even happen once.

I was going to Russia to film a small role in a movie in which Louise had the leading role, but when Bill Strasburg and I left Los Angeles we still hadn't got our visas. Having been told, however, that by the time we got to Frankfurt someone would meet us with our visas and provide all the proper paperwork we needed to continue on to Moscow, we set off so that I could take my place in front of the camera lens.

When we touched down in Germany, there wasn't anyone there to meet us as planned and, although we waited for as long as we could for an official to arrive, ultimately we had to board the next plane and continue on to Moscow empty-handed.

Once at Moscow's Sheremetyevo Airport, we waited in the

queue with the other travellers, but we did not get to leave via the same exit!

When the immigrations officer found we didn't have the correct documents – just our passports – he led us outside and instructed us to stand against the outer wall of the building. Bill and I were speechless – and not because we don't speak Russian – we thought we were going to be shot!

We were: the officer shot our pictures!

Back inside the terminal, we were escorted to baggage claim to collect our cases, and then taken out of a side door where a slightly decrepit school bus was waiting for us. We had no idea where we were going, or what was going to happen next, but when soldiers are prodding you with guns, you don't stop to ask questions!

Almost an hour later, we arrived at an old building with many steps, which turned out to be a former hotel that was then being used as a detention centre for anyone attempting to enter Russia illegally, or without the proper paperwork. It turned out we weren't the only ones. The place was absolutely crawling with people who were waiting for formalities of one kind or another to be ironed out. The average length of stay, we learned, was ten days.

Our stay, thank God, was not so long – and we actually ended up having a great time there. There was a bar and, as the barman was keen on pocketing American dollars, he just loved us. While we were sitting having drinks, one bloke got word that his documents had been processed and he was free to go, and the entire place erupted into one big celebration with everyone buying him drinks and loudly toasting his freedom.

Our documents, we then learned, were on their way; and phone calls placed to the British and US embassies were successful in getting us released after just over four hours. Having said fond farewells to our newfound friends, we caught a flight at two-thirty in the morning to Samarkand, near the Afghanistan border. That flight felt so primitive! There were even cardboard boxes stacked in front of the emergency exits, and a flight attendant pushed a rickety trolley of enormous, cracked soup tureens down the aisle to offer us our supper.

When we landed, Bill and I were accidentally separated, and I was taken to the hotel in a car provided by the embassy, while Bill was stuck in a spluttering taxi that seemed about to break down at any moment.

The hotel floors were comprised of pressed earth, and the shower was situated just a foot or two from the toilet. In my suite there was just one channel on the television. Still, we were treated very well, and the director of the film was wonderful to us.

When Bill became quite ill from a serving of homemade Kim Chee he had purchased at an open-air market, the director recognised that he would have a very difficult time using the portable toilet on set, and arranged for a KGB car to take him back to the hotel for a little privacy and comfort. Driving such a car was quite a symbol of authority and status there, especially when you keep in mind that many – if not most – of the locals got themselves from A to B in the back of a cart pulled by a donkey. At times in the KGB car it was really amazing. Every other driver recognised it when it approached and pulled over to let it pass. Bill used to joke afterwards that they moved out of the way not because they were shit scared, but because they were scared of shit!

On my last night there, the KGB man who was keeping an eye on the situation kindly invited me to his modern home for a feast, and I remember riding in a KGB car, watching the cars parting in front of us like a giant zipper being undone. I felt like Moses as the waters parted in the Red Sea! At his home, he had a table on the verandah for twenty people and a table inside as well. You could have any drink, any food – *anything* you wanted, and we had the best of everything.

To be honest, at the time I just took things for granted. I didn't really pay any attention to the razzamatazz and fanfare, because I was there to do my job. That's how it was then – and it's why, today, I make sure I have time to enjoy things. I am making up for all the things I missed then. I take time to stop and stare, and to notice things. I also get up, go out and play golf or tennis.

Even though I was always a bit of a playboy as far as having a drink after a show goes – sometimes far too many – I always did my martial arts practice in the mornings. Mike Stone, who trained me, was a world champion and credited with 92 undefeated bouts in the ring. My personal thanks to him for training me was never to neglect my practice, even if it was only for fifteen minutes, with a hangover, in a hotel room.

I have never ever become blasé about honours, compliments and awards and, when I was told that my name was to be added to the Hollywood Walk of Fame 7,000 block, I was thrilled. My entire family – Popea, Louise, Scott, Jason and Bradley – were present to share this prestigious moment with me on 21 October 1989. It was a marvellous day and we were greeted by Johnny Grant, the Honorary Mayor of Hollywood and Chairman of the Walk of Fame Committee. Johnny Grant made a welcoming speech, saying very nice things about me and then I was given the opportunity to respond and thank the committee for choosing me to join such an illustrious group of people. Then, I was asked to uncover the terrazzo stone which contains the brass, star-shaped plaque with my name on it. It's situated on the same block as the stage-and-screen legends Tom Hanks, W C Fields, Errol Flynn, Meryl Streep, Johnny Depp, Sidney Poitier, Sonny & Cher, Reba McEntire, Samuel L Jackson, Walt Disney, Mary Tyler Moore, Morgan Freeman, Nicolas Cage, Paul Newman, the Beatles and Stevie Wonder. So, I really am in very good company!

There could not have been a more thrilling end to the 80s than that and I was really looking forward to the next decade, even though I had no way of knowing then that, before the end of the 90s, I would be re-entering the UK charts with 'Quando Quando Quando' at No. 3.

CHAPTER EIGHTEEN

No more kisses. From my early years and all the way up to the 80s, I used to have two girls come up on stage during my performances when I was singing the sexy song 'You Make My Pants Want to Get Up and Dance'. Having sung that song to them, I would kiss them passionately. One night, though, one of the girls who made it up on to stage could only answer me in a very hoarse whisper.

'You're *not* well,' I said after I had leaned into her and kissed her. 'You sound *really* ill. You've obviously got a dreadful illness and you really shouldn't have come up on stage when you're as sick as this.'

'Oh, no, I've just lost my voice because I was screaming earlier,' she croaked. 'I'm OK, really.'

But she wasn't and it was too late for any of my grumbles. I'd already kissed her, the kind of kiss that the girls who came up on stage expected from me and, lo and behold, a couple of days later I got a viral infection – one that took four and a half months to heal and stumped five doctors when it came to its diagnosis. Prior to this, I had been working very hard, burning the candles at both ends and my immune system just hit the deck.

When I got the viral infection, I had just finished a string of performances in Las Vegas, where it was 110°F outside, but I was all bundled up in a thick sweater and still shivering and shaking and feeling absolutely freezing. I would come off stage, looking for a blanket! This was so strange. Usually, having worked my arse off out there, I would exit, sweating from head to toe. Now it was the complete opposite, I was shivering. When we went on to Germany, I was also due to be making an album for the German market with a producer called Leslie Mandoki and, while I was in the recording studio, I kept complaining that the air conditioning was making my teeth rattle, and that it was just too much for my present condition.

'You *really* must turn it off,' I kept grumbling. 'I'm absolutely *freezing!*'

'Turn it off! You *must* be joking!' the studio engineers kept exclaiming in return. 'You *can't* expect us to work in this heat!'

'I'm sorry, but I can't have the air conditioning on; I'm *very* cold – dangerously cold.'

Making records in those days was a very expensive business, and I was paying for the entire production. The cost was about £200,000 – not an amount I wanted to waste on catching a chill on top of a viral infection! And, as I was paying all the bills, they had no choice but to respect my wishes. The perspiration then rolled off them, but I was much more comfortable and able to keep up the singing.

I had already consulted specialists in New York, Los Angeles and England – all to no avail, but one day, while I was in Hamburg on this grand European tour, I met two astrologers, Mauritania Turnia and her husband, who told me they knew of someone, an iridologist who was involved in holistic medicine.

'He has a tremendous reputation as a healer,' Mauritania said. 'Would you like us to take you to him?'

I know for many people the idea of holistic medicine, or herbal remedies for the curing of disease is little more than preposterous, but by then I was desperate. I didn't know anything about holistic medicine, but I was willing to try anything anyone suggested, and I jumped at the chance to see somebody who might be able to help me.

'That would be *really* kind of you, thank you,' I said. 'I'm willing to take my chances with him; it can't do me any harm or make matters worse. Right?'

So they drove me and Pope to where he lived and worked in a little bungalow one hour outside Hamburg. The whole place had a Jekyll-and-Hyde feel about it. There were all sorts of bottles in different shapes, sizes and colours, which contained strange-looking potions. The shelves themselves looked as if they had grown out of the walls and there seemed to be no rhyme or reason to the order that the bottles were placed in; and I couldn't begin to guess what was ground up in the various pestles and mortars. It was, though, a breathtaking array, which says something, considering I hardly had any breath to spare!

After making the introductions to the holistic practitioner, Charles Beaulieu, the astrologers left us there on our own, and

Pope and I just stood there like lemons, unsure where to look. It was really odd standing there, looking round this place, with the wide eyes of an Alice who'd just come through the looking glass and didn't know what was what, or which way was up. When I noticed Charles was missing one of his legs, my mind wondered if this was a war wound, but I saw no sign of malice at the sight of an English face.

Please, sit down,' Charles Beaulieu instructed me a few moments later in fairly decent English, 'and let me check you out.'

As I sat down, he beckoned for me to move and sit in front of him so he could look into my eyes with an iriscope. He gazed into them for all of twenty seconds, before declaring brusquely, 'You have a viral infection that is going to take two years to heal.'

'WHAT? Oh, no!' I groaned.

'But I will work with you on that,' he added. 'I'll give you some holistic medication to take, and I'll tell you what to do with the yolk of one egg every morning. I want you to follow my instructions to the letter for a month, then come back to see me in two months' time.'

'Very well,' I replied meekly, hoping that's exactly how I would feel when I returned.

I did follow the cure to the letter. I did the 'toxic cleansing' every morning, taking a dessert spoonful of sunflower oil, then swishing an egg yolk around my mouth for fifteen minutes before spitting it out. I'm not kidding when I say that the yellow yolk was drained of all its colour by the time I had finished with it! Truly, it went in yellow and came out clear! I also had to use an eyedropper and squeeze a few drops of a remedy into a glass of water and drink it, every morning at seven.

It proved to be a miraculous cure! In two weeks, the viral infection was gone – totally gone – but I continued the detox for four weeks and, after two months, as instructed, I went back to Germany to see Charles Beaulieu once more. Popea and Scott came with me.

While I was there, he looked into one of my eyes and affirmed what I had hoped – that the infection had left my body completely.

'Oh, *thank God* for that!' I exclaimed, relieved. 'And *thank you* for making me well – for fixing me.'

'You know, I have two healers,' he said.

'Oh? Would you like me to see one of them?'

'Not at all,' he replied, smiling. 'I want you to know that you are better than both of them.'

'I'm sorry,' I said, puzzled. 'I *really* don't understand.'

'*Really*? Well, I can tell you that you have the kind of aura that reveals you have the capability to heal people. Your vocal tones have healing qualities, but you're capable of much, much more. I can spend some time with you teaching you how to use this gift, if you wish.'

I was intrigued and, having nodded my head, I followed him upstairs to another room to be told more.

'You have healing powers within you that could be *very* helpful to other people,' he said at one moment; and he showed me some simple healing techniques. Suddenly what he was demonstrating made complete sense of what I had felt compelled to do with my hands when my mum was ill. I now understood that I was somehow attempting to have the power of healing pass through me to her.

I hope nobody will mistake what I have just said as egocentric, and think that I am implying I have some sort of unearthly magical powers, or that I see myself as the second coming or anything like that. I really am just a vessel, an instrument through which healing can be channelled – and hopefully passed on. I'm the hypodermic needle, the medicine comes from above.

I don't know whether it's been coincidental or not, but the results have been positive a surprising number of times. I have learned how to close my eyes, but still 'look' at a person and be able to see the dark spots of illness, or discomfort, within them.

'Start with your family and friends, Charles said, 'and practise a little bit whenever you can. You can do this in public, you can do it in private, or you can even do it *en masse* if you like.' Then he added, 'You can make money by performing healings, and even if you haven't an interest in charging for your services, sometimes people will insist upon paying to show their appreciation of your skills. If that occurs, just donate the money to your favourite charity.' Which is exactly what I have done.

After leaving him, I was still sceptical that I would be able to help anyone, but I decided to give it a go when one of my backup singers had been suffering from a migraine for three days.

'Why don't you come with me to my dressing-room?' I suggested one day.

She had obviously picked up that I had a reputation as a womaniser.

'Hm . . . oh . . .'

'No – NO, I am not suggesting *that*,' I said. 'It's all above board. I just want to say a prayer over your head.'

Once in the dressing-room, I was still wondering if I was performing the healing correctly when she suddenly opened her eyes and said, 'What did you do then?'

'What do you mean?' I asked, concerned that I'd done something wrong.

'It's *gone*,' she replied. '*My migraine has gone.*'

That was quite a moment!

Anne Oliver, who owns a dance school in Leicester, used to stretch me out whenever I was in town. During my British tours, I used to take the band to her studios because there was ample space to rehearse. I remember when she was highly pregnant, how funny it was to see this big-bellied woman trying to do the splits!

As a dancer, she developed bad knees and assumed that she was destined for surgery. I performed a three-minute treatment on her, and am thrilled to say it worked. What was wrong, I do not know, but what helped was the grace of God. To this day she's still fine and maintains the poise of a well-trained dancer.

Just a few months ago, I performed what is likely to be the most splendid healing I will ever have the satisfaction of performing. It wasn't only wonderful because of the outcome for a dear friend, but also because my whole family was gathered around this man whose pain we all felt, and whose suffering was eased right in front of our very eyes.

I met Miguel Torres in the early 70s when I visited a disco he owned in Acapulco. We then stayed in touch and remained friends when he moved to Las Vegas, and again when he settled in Nashville just a few years ago. Recently, he had suffered a debilitating bout of Bell's Palsy, and he woke up one morning with his face frozen and contorted in such a bad way that he assumed he had suffered a profound stroke during his slumber. He couldn't close his right eye – and had to tape the lid down in order to sleep at night; and the left side of his mouth curled up so high that all his teeth were exposed as if he were constantly snarling. It was clear from a single glance that this man was deeply miserable about the way he looked.

As it happened, due to my current US tour schedule, Pope and I had arranged to celebrate our wedding anniversary in Nashville; and, as Louise lives there, she very kindly said she would organise a supper for us. That night, before we left for the restaurant, as we were sitting at her dining table – an ornate one with cherubs holding up its glass top, inherited from our home in Las Vegas – she told us that, as a special treat, she'd invited Miguel to join us. At the restaurant, just before Miguel arrived, in walked Bradley, who had made the trip from Los Angeles to celebrate our anniversary with us. Less than a minute later, in walked Jason, fresh off a flight from Las Vegas, holding a wine menu in his hand, pretending to be our sommelier. We were absolutely *thrilled* and, as Popea and I were rejoicing that we had almost every member of our family with us, in walked Scott, all the way from Australia wearing a stetson hat that he had borrowed from his hotel room (some Nashville hotels have stetsons on offer/for purchase in every guest room). We were *overjoyed*. Suddenly there we were re-taking our seats at a surprise family reunion dinner that our children had planned for us. Only parents who have watched the children they have raised leave the nest for various cities, states or countries, will really know how much that evening meant. Popea and I felt it was one of the most enchanted evenings of our life. The thought that all our children would make such an effort to come together to celebrate our wedding anniversary was *very* special. We couldn't believe our eyes, which had promptly filled with tears at the surprise of it all. We then surprised them by divulging our long-kept secret when we confessed that we had been expecting Louise before we got married and that it was, therefore, our fortieth anniversary, *not* our forty-first!

When Miguel arrived, our hearts sank and our jaws dropped. His poor face was so badly affected by the palsy and, just sitting beside him, I could feel how tense and uncomfortable he was.

'Let me give you a treatment before dinner,' I suggested gently 'it only takes three minutes.' He agreed.

Through clenched teeth, he then told me that his doctor had warned him that sometimes Bell's Palsy keeps its grip for three months, sometimes for six, and sometimes, unfortunately, the effects last forever. There and then, we all decided that we should say a healing prayer before dinner; and, with the family gathered around, I conducted a prayer for his health, using my hands to take away his sickness.

The effect was unbelievable.

Popea, Louise, Bradley, Scott and Jason watched as the muscles of Miguel's face began slowly to return to their rightful position; and, after just three minutes, all that was left of the Bell's Palsy was a tiny twist of the lip.

Overjoyed, I told him we'd do another healing the next day in the hope that we could heal that as well.

A few days later Miguel called me and left a very grateful message on my cell phone, and it's one voicemail I have chosen to save. 'Enge, it's Miguel,' he said. 'I just wanted to say *thank you* again for how you helped me; I still can't believe it. You are a great man and a great friend. I love you – God bless you.'

These days I always perform a silent, healing prayer for the audience at my shows. I've never told anyone when this healing is taking place, but a few of my fans say that they can tell from the way my hands are positioned when this is happening. And, as I said, I also never tell a person when I catch sight of a dark patch within them. All this is because Frank Sinatra got *so* upset with me.

'What's wrong with your hip?' I asked him one day when I caught a glimpse of a dark patch in that area of his body.

'Who *told* you there was anything wrong with my hip?' he snapped.

'*Nobody*, Frank,' I answered.

I could see that he was really upset and I regretted mentioning it.

'I just have this ability to sense sickness,' I added placatingly. 'I don't know how I'm able to, Frank, but . . .'

It was too late. He wasn't listening. He just stormed off to the nearest telephone to curse whoever he believed had shared the secret of his ailment with me. At that moment, I vowed never to speak of my 'gift' again. What Beaulieu had not taught me was that not everyone would be amenable to hearing what I had to say.

I didn't blame Frank for his reaction, I was just embarrassed and mortified to have upset him.

'Nobody's supposed to know about my hip,' he kept muttering to no one in particular.

At this time, Frank's afflictions often received unwelcome press attention, and Sammy Davis Jr was also in the papers for seeing multiple doctors about his own joint troubles. I had told Sam about Dr Ha, but he had said, 'Hey, man, I don't wanna see any more doctors, man. I've seen enough of those cats to last me a lifetime.'

It was quite clear that Frank didn't want his hip problem to reach the journalists – and, from then on, I figured I should keep my mouth shut. Of course, if someone actually brings up their ailment in conversation, I am always happy to suggest a treatment.

The hoarse girl I kissed on the stage was the last one I ever kissed when I was performing. I didn't want to transmit the viral infection to somebody else, and I certainly didn't want to risk getting any other ailment myself. I suppose it was lucky that I never caught anything else during those years when I had performed that particular ritual. Some of the girls used to get really turned on and passionate on stage, and their tongues would become *very* adventurous and busy! It was a shame to have to give it up because everybody, including me, used to look forward to that moment when I sang, 'You Make My Pants Want to Get Up and Dance'!.

In addition to the 'no more kissing rule', there were also a few superstitions people had to keep in mind when around me. One of these was the time-honoured, English show business superstition of 'no whistling in the dressing-room. And if you *do* whistle by accident, go out, turn around three times, swear, kick the door and only then can you come back in again.' The superstition came about because, in olden times, stagehands used to whistle a signal for somebody up in the wings to drop the sandbags that changed the scenery and if you were unlucky enough to get hit, then the consequences could be dire. Over the years, I have had to send an awful lot of people out of my dressing-room to perform the anti-whistling ritual.

Hank Schoknecht, who was a captain at the Riviera Hotel showroom in Las Vegas, used to take the kids and me skiing at Lake Mead. He had a boat and we all loved going out on that, too. Until he left Las Vegas in 1988, he was like family, like a big uncle to my children. When he was leaving Vegas, he mentioned that, although he was retiring, he wanted to find something else to do, and I went fifty-fifty with him in buying a hotel in Mexico. He put my name on this and called it Posada de Engelbert.

In 2001, Jeff Sturges and I went to La Posada, which is built in the old-time Hacienda architectural style, with lots of tiles. We stayed for about four days, and it was great. It's not a large place by any means – about fifty rooms – but a lot of actors and actresses used to go there in the old days for their vacations – Desi Arnaz and Lucille Ball, John Wayne, and people of that ilk.

There was a general, a three-star one in the Mexican Army, who used to come to the hotel and he loved my singing. One day, he gave me a badge, which I've now lost, but when I had it, I used to be allowed to go straight through customs the moment I showed it to whomever was on duty. It was a mystery to me, but it certainly had some pulling power!

A lovely getaway, set in the wilds and right on the beach, we have to take dirt roads to get there. While Jeff and I were there, we sat around all night, drinking margaritas and listening to some of my earlier recordings. It was hard to tell on those recordings when I took a breath because my phrases were so long. These days when I go Posada de Engelbert with Jeff to work on arrangements, I find we can put things together so much more easily there because it's so quiet. Nobody bothers us, and we can just sit around or carry on, have a beer, and do our own thing.

Performing and recording is what energises my life, and the fans are the ones who provide the necessary fuel.

My audiences are not fleeting ones. The fans come back over and over again, and each time they come back they get more enthusiastic, which only makes me feel stronger. In many places, I see the same faces in the same seats, night after night. In Las

Vegas I would play two shows a night for four weeks in a row at the Riviera, and the fans who would sing along with me from the ringside seats were the same people who were there the show before, the night before, and the week before as well. They obviously paid the maitre d' a lot of money to hold those top-dollar seats for them, and it was an amazing sight for me to see such dedicated, loyal, familiar faces looking up at me. It was, to say the least, *invigorating*!

This phenomenon of the returning fan has occurred in many more localities than Las Vegas. I remember shows throughout the 1970s all over New York state, especially in Westbury, Long Island, and Westchester County, where entire chapters of my fan clubs would arrive in a city or town ahead of me and my band to set up elaborate banquets and parties for grand celebrations after our last night at a particular venue (at the end of every year there were closing night parties).

At these events I would sit at the head of the table, with my music director, Jeff Sturges, next to me, and the legendary musicians of my band seated on the other side, or opposite me. Sometimes members of our families would be there with us and, together with the managers and agents of the time, we would all gather on the dais, with the fans and fan-club presidents sitting at banquet-style tables (the host of the party would sit in the middle with me), or in big groups of circular tables, and we would all enjoy the food and festivities together. Those were fantastic times.

These days, every time I arrive at a venue, a different chapter of a fan club takes the time to come in and decorate my dressing-room for me, and the time and dedication they devote to the task is astonishing. It really recharges my batteries and provides the first buzz of excitement I feel when I am about to do a new show. Hundreds of new chapters of fan clubs have formed over the decades, and even those established in the early years are still going strong.

It all started with Bill Mills and his wife, Lorna, who established my very first fan club. Then came Hilda Shadwick, a sophisticated, educated woman, who wrote thousands of poems to me – or about me. One of them was titled 'Portrait of Engel', in which the last stanza read:

If we all shared the characteristics of this gentle, talented, happy man, God would smile a tender smile, and the Devil would put his tail between his legs, and jump into his fire!

She handed on the baton to Janet and Peter Synnott of The Engelbert Humperdinck Appreciation Society, which has been doing a wonderful job ever since. From there, along came Judy Kay and the Starlite Club, and we now have the Union Jacks Club, too.

I am still in awe of my fan clubs, because somehow, from the very first, the members generated interest all around the world for Engelbert Humperdinck, and I now have two hundred chapters in America, as well as fan clubs in Canada, Australia, New Zealand, South America, South Africa, Jamaica, Asia, Hong Kong, Taipei, Singapore, Jakarta, Kuala Lumpur – not to mention the whole of Europe. And, if I've missed out any countries or fan clubs, I can only apologise.

These people are my spark plugs, my cheerleaders, and it is unbelievable what they are prepared to do for me. In addition to decorating my dressing-rooms, they meet me at airports and wait for me at the stage door. With so many cell phones around, it's hard for me to find a way out of a building without one of them alerting the others, who then tell me how much they appreciate what I do for them. They've got all the corners covered, which is exciting, to say the least. I really do have a bit of a cult following. They are very strong, and there are militant fans among them as well. If somebody in the audience dares to make a distracting sound, or say anything derogatory about me, these people jump on them.

'*Shut up! Let's hear him sing!*' they snarl.

Once, at a show in Texas, a woman hit her unappreciative husband over the head with her handbag, then dragged him out of the auditorium! And, more recently, I heard of a man who told his family and friends that he wanted to remain a fan of mine when he moved on from this life to the next. Apparently his favourite pastime was listening to my songs in his Ferrari, so when his time came to pass on, he wanted to be buried in his beloved Ferrari, with 'Release Me' playing through the speakers of the car's cassette deck.

His request was apparently honoured.

I've also had the pleasure of getting to know some of my fans as close friends. One is Franck Namani from Paris, who became a devoted fan when he was a boy of eleven and, after following my shows and success for close on two decades, he sent a note of introduction to me backstage one night, via my maitre d', Peggy, with whom by then he had become quite familiar.

On that particular night, I was feeling *really* tired, so I broke the news to Peggy that I wasn't seeing anybody, but she should give me his telephone number and tell him that I would be happy to call him later. Moments later, she returned and said that he had replied, 'That's quite all right, but do me a favour and give him this tie.'

His name was printed on the back of this beautiful silk tie, one of the luxury items that could be found at Namani's stores in Paris, Brussels and Geneva. He was such a polite gentleman.

'Peggy, go and get him,' I said.

She did, and Franck and I have been friends ever since. This man knows my music – the writers and composers and musicians involved – like the back of his hand. If I say, 'Franck, what song . . .?' he always knows the answer. He will also fly anywhere in the world to come and see me – and after the Hard Rock Café opened in Acapulco in 1989 and I was asked to donate an item of memorabilia – a $10,000 beaded suit – and make the trip to present my donation, Franck flew out for this occasion. We treat one another with a profound respect. I call him Mr Franck; he calls me Mr Enge.

Obviously, the fans and friends who support me in these ways make everything I do worthwhile – and where would I be without them?

That said, there have been a few fans along the way that my family and I could have done without. Some were mere fanatics who got carried away and blurred the lines between my private life and theirs; others wanted to take their lives – or mine – altogether.

The first time I was summoned to a police station on account of a fan was in America. There sat a young, tear-stained, red-faced girl.

'I'll commit suicide if you don't let me meet him,' she had told the police.

And they believed her.

Whether I believed her or not was irrelevant. When the police ask you to accompany them to the station, you follow.

For the most part, these girls were so drained after what they'd put themselves through to meet me, they were close to exhaustion by the time I walked in to offer some comfort, sign an autograph and sit with them awhile in a holding cell. In fact, by then, they seemed more relieved than excited to see me.

Others devised far more personally frightening ways to get to my side. They made threats on Patricia's life and, to this day, there are some shocking letters on police files from women who are so certain that we belong together that they'll do whatever it takes to be with me. Or they have somehow come to believe that they're married to me – and that they own me. They are deluded people who have created a fantasy in their own mind, and who are trying to make it reality. There are still people I've never met who write letters to my office, saying, 'When are you coming home? The children are waiting for you!'

I am obviously pleased to have made a profound impact on so many lives and to have been able to touch audiences and listeners all over the world, but some of the people who try to contact me are touched in a different sense of the word!

When we were living at Jayne Mansfield's ex-house, the Pink Palace on Sunset Boulevard, a woman, loaded down by six suitcases, arrived one afternoon at the front gates, which happened to be open because my son Bradley, who was about twenty-five at the time, had just come in. Bradley must have sensed there was something odd about the scene because he had the presence of mind to lead her to believe he was the janitor.

'May I help you?' he asked politely.

'I'm here to move in,' she stated.

'Who are you?' he asked, his curiosity aroused.

'I'm Engelbert's wife, stupid.'

Bradley, of course, became a bit rattled at this point and asked her to leave.

When she refused, he said he'd get Heiko, our big German Shepherd dog to come out and chase her away and, on hearing this, she set down her bags and kicked him hard, right in the shins. Closing the gates, he went inside, got the dog and phoned the local police department.

She was still carrying on about being my wife, calling Bradley all sorts of names and insisting that I would never have anyone as untidy as he was working for me, when the police arrived to arrest her.

Some fanatics have threatened my life, usually in angry letters, but a few have gnashed their teeth at me over the telephone. One time, when I was performing in Las Vegas, a call that prompted me to call Security right away, came through on the hotel phone.

'*YOU'RE MESSING WITH MY WIFE.*'

'Pardon? Who is this?' I asked.

'*I KNOW YOU'RE MESSING WITH MY WIFE, AND I'M GONNA BLOW YOUR HEAD OFF.*'

'Look, I don't know who you are or how you've got hold of this idea, but you've definitely got something confused here, pal,' I said and slammed the phone down.

The police got involved in this one and they must have taken his threats seriously because the next thing I knew the FBI showed up and told me that I needed to start wearing a bulletproof vest.

For the next three years, my martial arts instructor and I wore these wretched vests almost everywhere we went. But, for some reason, which must sound daft, I never felt the need to wear mine on stage. I did, however, always have a minder checking the crowd and keeping an eye out for loose cannons; and the security guards, realising that the most unlikely looking fan could be out to get me, took extra precautions with the crowds.

Once, before a performance in New York, a guard came backstage and dropped the most beautiful dagger on my dressing-room table. The handle was covered in splendid jewels, and it really was exquisite.

'Is this for me?' I said, picking it up.

'Well, it *WAS*,' he said. 'So you might as well keep it.'

'What do you mean?'

'Someone was planning on sticking you with it.'

'Really? He was?' I said, looking at my reflection in the blade.

'No. *SHE* was. I took it off a woman.'

Incidents like these are why I never walk into an audience. I give the impression I do – that's one of my tricks – but I never actually leave the stage and never have done. I have learned to be cautious.

During the heyday of the 'After the Lovin' fame, I noticed many of my golf caps had gone missing. One day this girl approached Billy Boy [Bill LaSaplio] who was waiting outside a rehearsal at a venue, and handed him one of these caps.

'Would you please see if Engelbert will sign this for me?' she said.

'Let me see what I can do,' Billy answered, thinking that the cap looked very familiar.

Sure enough, when he brought it to me, I recognised that it was one of my own and, although I autographed it for her, I asked him to find out where she got it. It turned out that I had an untrustworthy limo driver that week, who was stealing my caps from the boot after picking me up from a round of golf, then selling them to girls for $200 a time. The girl won her prize of a signed item of mine – and the driver lost his job.

Another driver, who faced a far more serious interaction with me, was present for one of the worst frights I have ever experienced in my career. This occurred when I was on holiday in Las Vegas in the late 70s. The driver was taking me back to the house when *BOOM!* Someone had taken a shot at me. The bullet came in one window and flew out the other, just barely missing me as it flew in and out. The driver's reactions were not quite what I expected. He braked and brought the car to a halt.

'*NO!*' I yelled. 'Put your bloody foot down! *Go! Go! Go!*' – and he did.

As we took off, I kept staring at the hole the bullet had made right next to my face. I had never imagined that something like that could happen to me, and I realised that I had to be very careful when I was out in public. This happened during an emotional roller-coaster period of my life and, if I had to guess, I'd say that the attempt on my life was fuelled by jealousy – and it was probably jealousy that was justified.

I am not making excuses – or justifying any of my bad behaviour – but girls of all ages, bless them, were always an occupational hazard in my business. I've had girls who have passed out cold when I've bent down from the stage to kiss them;

they used to shake like a leaf and go apoplectic when I went anywhere near them, then pass out. This didn't happen just once, it happened many times.

In the early days, guys would sit in the audience yelling for me to choose their wife for the 'You Make My Pants Want to Get Up and Dance' kissing routine.

'Take my wife . . . Come on, *take her*. She's up for it. She wants you to,' they would keep calling out.

And, if it wasn't their wife on offer, it was their girlfriend.

What was I? Foreplay?

But, at one level, given I was nicknamed the 'King of Romance', *that* was my job. If my singing made people feel sexier and more seductive, happy to fall into the arms of their partner, I am pleased about that. But I always had to remember that there were a lot of jealous people out there, and sometimes I did wonder – and get scared – about whether any of them would succeed in blowing me away – killing me.

Realising that my status as 'Mr Romance' could be thought to justify acts of violence from Mr or Ms Jealousy was not a happy situation; and sometimes I wondered if such threats came from the very men who had wanted their wives or girlfriends to have their picture taken with me, or come up on stage. Perhaps they then changed their minds when they witnessed their partner's reaction and, at the very time I thought I was making someone happy, jealousy might have been rearing its ugly head and turning a sweet experience sour.

The aggro could also have been prompted by jealousy over my lifestyle, or a woman feeling jealous about Popea being the one I really wanted in my life, or even a man's jealousy that I had the ability to make his wife or girlfriend swoon in a way he did not. Maybe some of the blokes just got fed up watching girls queuing for hours on end for my autograph, or waiting until I left a restaurant so that they could run in and nick my used serviette. Perhaps some just couldn't stand witnessing the shirts being ripped right off my back. Whatever the cause, there have been a good few who found the fame I enjoy tough to handle – and I may be lucky to be here still and able to tell the tale.

* * *

Golf is still my great passion and I love playing as often as I can. Sometimes I smile when I think back to my beginnings in the early days. Golf clubs, then, were *very* snobby places and the people who owned or ran them were very particular about their membership. They were 'old' money who hated 'new' money, and they certainly did *not* like show business folk. Just before I made it really big, I applied for membership at our local club, but they turned me down because I was in show business. After I made 'Release Me' and I was making some real money, I wrote to the secretary of the club, saying, '*I realise that you don't approve of show business people, but I can assure you I have a clean slate, and there is nothing wrong with my character. I just want to say, if the club is up for sale at any time, please make sure that I am the first to hear of it.*'

I just couldn't resist doing this! The gate on our property actually went as far as the fourth hole of that club and, since then, we've had another home on the fourth – our home in Las Vegas is positioned there as well!

When I did eventually become a member of the golf club – at a time when I had become used to appearing in front of hundreds of thousands of people – I was too shy to go into the changing room of the golf club! The club was a bit intimidating and, I preferred to take my golf shoes from the boot of my car and change before hitting the course.

Sometime after I had achieved my success, I bumped into the host of the television programme *Opportunity Knocks*.

'My God!' Hughie Green said, obviously embarrassed. 'I suppose I should *never* have turned you down, should I?'

'No, you *shouldn't*,' I replied, smiling. Then I added: 'I guess you were a little *short-sighted*.'

I could afford to say that then, but I said it in a fun way, without any sarcasm.

OK, so, thanks to Hughie, it took me a little longer to get established when I failed that audition, but I have no regrets. Looking back, I wouldn't have missed those years for *anything*. Despite all the struggles, trials and tribulations, Popea and I were very happy, and when I look back on my life, that's what counts.

EPILOGUE

The good thing about having a great career, a career that takes off and fulfils all one's dreams and brings financial security after so many lean years, is the knowledge that your wife and family will no longer have to experience the 'hungry years' for the sake of your art! I used to think, 'As long as I can keep my head above water, and ensure that the kids have a roof over their head, clothes on their backs, food on the table, and comfy shoes to begin their walk through life – and, hopefully, a dad to be proud of on school open days and sports days – all will be well.

The problem with that rosy picture, however, was that I was *never* there for their special days at school and I missed out on what most dads, who take their paternal duties seriously, take for granted and are then able to reminisce about.

In our home in Leicester, there are photographic albums that are full to bursting with captured memories of little ones, dressed in neat English school uniforms or fancy-dress clothes, or on school trips or in plays that would bring tears of joy to any parent's eyes, but I only feel a deep sense of emptiness and loss of days gone by when I look at them. Those are days that I can't rewind so that I can take *my* place in those pictures. I was so busy living my dream, working on a future, that I missed the blessings of the present! I just had to learn to live with the distance, the endless miles between us, and the time spent away, and hearing my children grow up over the telephone is not something I would ever want to do again.

The problem was I didn't want to lose the dream and all the good things of life that it could offer me – all of us – so I stuck to the plan and worked my arse off. But, no doubt about it, all those years on the road led me to some very lonely, dark places that could not be filled by my on-the-road family, or the kind folks who stayed backstage when I was riding the adrenalin highs that followed shows and who remained until whatever hour it was time to pack up and move on.

I look at some of the luxurious tour buses that today's stars use and I feel deeply envious – and I wish that they had existed back in my 'missing years' days. If they had, I would have loaded my whole family on board, teachers and all, and led them out for the best kind of adventure and learning that I know – travel. There would have been room enough for their friends during the school holidays and tons of space for growing up – and even for our grandchildren when they eventually came along. Popea would not have had to play dad as well as mum – and be the bad guy with the black book. If I'd been around, there might never have been a need for a black book for making notes on naughty children. And, of course, we would have piled the dogs in, too. We're a family whose lives have always revolved around our canine companions. They keep us humble and bring us great happiness.

One thing I know for sure, then, is that I wish there were a lot more pictures in those photo albums of me as a doting dad but, like the song says, I just have to settle for the fact that, however great the distance between us, they were *always* on my mind.

That horrible sense of loss all changed, of course, when my children grew up and, of their own free will, gathered round me and, one by one knocked on the door to my road . . . and, oh, how gladly I opened it.

Louise worked for my set-up for years, but she wasn't the first to jump on board my tour bus! After I left Gordon Mills and MAM's perpetuity contract, giving up properties worth millions and millions of pounds, I needed a tour manager and Scott, who was always a streetwise guy, and who had an ambition to travel and learn the ropes, took on the job. I think he was really up for it for a couple of years when the hole first appeared in the management chair, but he basically got on with it for ten years! In that time, he saw many of his ' way out' ideas come to fruition and the marks of their success are still hanging on my walls – like *The Dance Album*, the *Beavis and Butthead* soundtrack on which I sang the tender love ballad 'Lesbian Seagull', and my connection with the Universal record label, which I am still with today.

When I realised that Louise would shine a whole lot brighter if there was a spotlight on her, I started to get her to mess around with me by singing at rehearsals. Her shyness, though, was far beyond anything that even I had felt as a lad when I was performing for my parent's friends from behind doors and under coffee tables. The microphone in her hand seemed to amplify her every insecurity and doubt. But I saw beyond that, picking up on the yearning that she was hiding within, the yearning of a creative entertainer's soul. I can't remember now how she went from not being able to finish a song without breaking down and criticising herself to stepping out on to the Hollywood Bowl stage to sing, with a hundred musicians behind her, but she did it – and it was one helluva a stage to learn on and the experience was enough to keep her hooked for the next seven years.

Bradley was always a bit of a surprise. He was the youngest of our litter and the hungriest to be on stage. His business acumen and personality were already bringing flocks of people to his merchandise stall on tour, where he sold T-shirts using the town-crier voice of those who sold apples and pears in Leicester market. Having done so, he'd pose for pictures and sing a few notes of a song to tease and test the water. It wasn't until my millennium tour dates, though, when we were aboard a ship off Malaysia that I first recognised that he had a real talent for singing and, having listened with new ears, I was so proud of him.

There he was, in the karaoke bar of the ship, singing 'Bed of Roses' and, almost without realising it, I started telling the very merry men and women in the bar: 'That's my son! That's my son . . .'

Apparently he had been hinting for quite a while that he could sing and would sing whenever and wherever and, one day in Glasgow, when he was handing out charts for a song called 'Angels', I crept up to him and said, proud as Punch: 'You're going to start by singing in two of my shows.'

That was all he needed to hear! His face wreathed in smiles, he fled the merchandise table, grabbed hold of the mike and went on to sing for a whole year at my performances.

Jason is the only one I wish I could have helped in the same way and stolen more time to be with in his early adult years. He really wanted to be an actor, but I didn't know just how much because he was never in my face quite like the others. He was a quiet one with loud ambitions, but it was as if I had the stage monitors up and ringing in my ears and I couldn't hear him; and he wasn't one to admit that he needed help. Popea used to take him around Los Angeles to auditions for films, and he had a lot of my stubborn pride that eventually led him down a neon path, straight past Hollywood to Las Vegas, where it was easier to make a life for himself and his family. I wish his taste for being on camera, though, had led to more than it did; and I wish I had been able to open some doors in that world but, again, those are days I can't rewind.

There have been many times on the road, when I've been flicking through the television stations, and caught a glimpse of Jason in a show or film that he has landed for himself, such as *Pretty in Pink* and several Tom Cruise projects, in which he was the star's stand-in. He definitely has the good looks for movie stardom and maybe now, with the years of searching for the right path behind him, and the lessons learned in the raising of two boys of his own, he may venture off once more to find the camera lens and make it into the limelight.

The bridge on the road is an image that always comes to mind when I think of the times I shared with my family while we were all working on our own things. Those were always occasions when we reconnected through our common bond and became a force to be reckoned with. Popea and the kids were my watchdogs, fierce as could be when it came to protecting me, and I always tried to return the favour and do the same for them. They, however, always had more sense than I did of who *wasn't* 'good news'; and I wish I had listened more. If I had, I would have saved myself lot of headaches – and money – from fighting foes in court battles.

Louise always says that she wishes she had listened more, too. She was always too busy worrying that she was bugging the band with her rehearsals, or stepping on the background singers toes by stepping centre stage. It wasn't until a few years in that she had her Sally Fields' moment of awakening and realised that, not only the band but the audiences liked her, *really liked her*, and her songwriting.

Bradley, who had a natural stage presence that always got him great reactions and earned him his own posse of faithful fans, was born to be the leader of the band, and that's what he's doing now. Scott was the easiest to bring on and the hardest to set free, but I felt that if he stayed with me, he would not have the kind of versatility and drive that is needed to be a top-management contender in a tough business. I wasn't the easiest person to manage, but my concert tour dates were steady and would take care of themselves, so it was time for him to spread his wings and work with up-and-coming talents who could feed off of his strengths and strengthen his weaknesses. He actually spread his wings all the way to Australia, and the time we had spent together made his departure there a little easier somehow. Looking back, I am so glad I had that time, sharing my career with my own flesh and blood.

I always made the kids strive to improve themselves, and this often entailed them staying for every minute of my famous two-to-three-hour rehearsals and sound checks – and sitting in on the bollocking that followed a rehearsal that wasn't up to scratch. We were around each other a great deal and I like to think that they learned a lot about the pursuit of perfection. They certainly learned from watching how Popea and I were with our families. We call each other all the time, check in, check up and double-check that we haven't missed an important moment in a morning, a day – any moment that may have passed while we were not with each other.

Everyone is getting on with their own dreams now, but I'd be willing to bet that there's an audience out there who would love to see the Dorsey Dincks – our family nickname – take the stage again, with Scott pacing around backstage and watching the quality of sound like a hawk, and Jason sitting there studying a scene for some upcoming, slightly off-centre role in a film.

A few years ago, when I recorded *The Best of Engelbert* album, which sold 600,000 copies, I included one of Louise's songs in this and Scott put it all together. It was a real *family* affair!

Popea, my angel of a wife, used to melt my heart totally by telling her friends that I was *more* than handsome when she first met me, I was *beautiful* – *gorgeous*.

'I used to ride on the back of the motorbike with him,' she was fond of saying. 'And he had this glorious head of hair. I just thought, oh my God, he's absolutely *gorgeous* – and I was always so pleased when everybody else took to him, too.'

Once, in those days, when Popea stayed at some digs with me, the dragon of a landlady said: 'There's *no* hanky-panky allowed here', and Popea had to get into bed with a woman she had never met before! Apparently, this woman was wearing all sorts of weird and wonderful undergarments and she kept taking off layer after layer. The ritual seemed to go on for hours.

No youngster would have that kind of trouble now!

I still occasionally play the big places. I played to 250,000 people, for example, in Australia a couple of years ago, but the places I prefer to play now have seats for 2,000–5,000 people. The casinos, where I do many concert performances, are smaller with about 1,500–1,800 places, but that's fine. I love singing in those. Supper clubs are few and far between now, but I never really liked performing in those. When I did, in the early days, they paid me a lot of money, but I would always say: 'I will only go on if there is no service, no food or wine being served at the tables, while I am on. Things like that were such a great distraction, and I wanted the audience's undivided attention.

I'm also delighted that my songs are still reaching so many people through my albums. The years 1999 and 2000, when I hadn't had any hits in the UK charts since 1973, were very special years. There I was again with 'Quando Quando Quando' for forty weeks and 'How to Win Your Love' for fifty-nine weeks. Then, following this resurgence, I produced four albums between 2000 and 2004. The first album went to No. 1, the second and third albums sold very well, and the fourth album, *Greatest Love Songs*, which has 24 songs on it, also rose to No. 1.

I can't begin to remember how many gold and platinum albums I have managed to get during my long career. Managers always get to keep their copies, it seems, but I always put mine up for charity auctions where people can bid for them and charities, like Children In Need or children's cancer organisations, can put the money raised to good use. I've never ceased to be surprised at how big the bids are for those albums.

Sometimes, when I recall that I have been around for so many decades and that I'm still achieving new successes, I feel like wandering around saying, 'Would you believe . . .?' And I love that Burt Reynolds story that people are always telling me. Apparently, Burt was doing a commercial for LensCrafters and, while he was in a store, a woman went up to him and said, 'Oh, Mr Humperdinck, I have all your records!' And Burt looked straight into camera, like this was something that happened to him all the time!

As for new merchandise, I've been thinking about putting some women's G-strings or thongs out there – Engelbert Humperdink G-strings or thongs. They would have printed words on them, such as 'After the Lovin'', or 'There Goes My Everything' or 'Please Release Me', or 'Am I That Easy to Forget?', and I could just add my signature. After all, who's going to see them? Two, three – maybe four couples?!

When I was living in Madras I loved hearing the myths, fables and fairy tales. As a bit of a dreamer, I found that the fantastical tales, the idea that anything can happen, that nothing is quite as it seems, both thrilled and frightened me, although I never knew exactly why. I think I just loved hearing the tales, but was too young to understand that there was a moral to the stories.

One of my favourite fables was about an insecure nightingale who took part in a songbirds' contest, held by a king in some faraway kingdom. None of the birds knew exactly what the prize was, or how it was that they were to be judged, but all the birds in the kingdom had to compete. Before the contest, the nightingale, a plain, brown-feathered bird, became very nervous that he could not possibly win the contest due to his bland appearance. The peacock, the swan and the parrot all seemed to mock his simple feathers as they prepared themselves for the grand event, cleaning their gorgeous plumage with their curved beaks. As they did so, a scattering of their feathers fell out and came to rest on the ground. Seeing these vibrant, beautifully coloured feathers, the nightingale picked each one up, and tucked them behind his wings, hoping they would give him a more beautiful – if borrowed – appearance.

When the day of the contest arrived and the nightingale appeared before the king, the other birds immediately recognised their own feathers tucked behind his wings, and they swooped down upon him and plucked them all away. Ashamed, the nightingale stood looking at the ground and did not move until the king spoke.

'Why is it you have not begun to sing for me, bird?' asked the king. 'Do you not understand the kingdom is awaiting your song? Your feathered friends have only disappointed my throne; the peacock can only spit, the swan can only honk, and the parrot only repeats what I have already heard. I do hope when you open your beak, you will offer something worthy of my kingly ears.'

On hearing that, the downtrodden nightingale sang his song, which was the most beautiful song the king had ever heard.

The nightingale won the competition, earning himself a bounty of food, the golden opportunity to sing for the king's royal guests, and a lifetime of appreciation for what only he was able to offer.

Looking back on that tale now, I feel I've come to an understanding of why it struck me so forcefully when I was a boy. Long before I'd even begun to call myself an entertainer, at my father's parties, I needed to make a little cocoon for myself in the living-room curtains before I could comfortably open my mouth and sing for his guests. The less of my exterior that was seen, the more comfortable I felt about what was coming from within. And, of course, as I've described, in later years I costumed myself with the songs of other singers, the moves of other performers, or the jokes of other entertainers. I never truly believed that what was on the inside of me, or the voice I had to offer, would be enough on its own.

In show business you have to change your image from time to time, and in hindsight I think I may have got caught up in doing so. I wore the long sideburns so well that at one point there was even an Engelbert doll, complete with jet-black hair, which was made for my fans to take home with them. And I enjoyed being a show-stopper in that white suit, in 1968, at the Leopardstown Horse Races in Ireland. It caused such a stir that the promoter Jim Aiken had to come and tell me to hide myself, as the stadium seats were emptying because people were rushing towards the paddock to have a look at the man in the white suit. Apparently, I was holding up the races. Years later, I grew a moustache because I never seemed to get a place in the 'Top 10 Sexiest Men' competitions, featured in various publications, like Burt Reynolds and Robert Redford did. As soon as I grew mine – I got in at No. 4.

Over the years I grew confident enough to shave the hair – and shed the props I hid behind, from the sax to the names: Gerry,

Casanova, King of Romance. I maintained my sense of humour on stage, because I still believe it is important to deliver something to make an audience smile, and that you have to have a sense of humour to survive in this world. I've been telling one-liners – just as a Dean Martin or a Johnny Carson would – for as long as I can remember. In the past, I used to have a scriptwriter who would come in to write little jokes for me to say on stage, and in the years I was wearing such close-fitting trousers that there was no room for pockets, my joke became: 'Girls always comment on how tight my trousers are, asking, "How do you get into them?" "Well," I'd respond, "you start off with a kiss . . ."'

Then I'd sing a song, giving an old tune a new treatment, like 'I Hope You Dance', 'The Nearness of You', or 'My Way', and in between numbers, I'd do a few impressions, and take the mickey out of myself with a few more jokes. I always had something to mock – the latest situation, the latest dress, the latest craze – that I could toss out at the audience, hoping they would laugh at it, which they always did. I can't tell you how many times people would come backstage after a show and say, 'Great show! You were really funny tonight!' And so I kept it up.

It took me many, many years to realise that I wasn't taking a compliment from comments like those any longer; there was an insecure little boy's voice in my head that always wanted to ask, 'What about my vocals? Did you like my new version of that song?' And the shy side waited and waited, never having the courage to say, 'Thanks for your appreciation of my Elvis impersonation, or my Peter Falk bit – but did you enjoy my singing?' I always privately, secretly, hoped someone would compliment my vocals.

A few years back, I concluded I wanted to be known as a singer more than a funny man on stage, and realised – as I was singing 'My Way' – that by giving each song I sing my own treatment, that I had truly developed *My Way* of performing, and didn't need to hide behind anything at all. Ironically, in all my years of ending my show with my version of Sinatra's song, various managers and producers have suggested I record it, and I've never agreed. Until now. Though I've been singing it all along, I've never recorded it, never thought to make my rendition a permanent one, and I think

I'm ready now. Just as I've lived all the experiences in this book but never written them down, I'm finally ready to reveal who I am, and I must say it feels wonderful to be starting a new chapter in life by showing the world exactly what it means to do things *my* way.

There may be a lot of gaps and empty spaces within these pages: some are caused by vacant slots in my memory due to years of mismanagement; others may be moments that have slipped from my mind simply because they are too painful to remember. And as my life continues on and continues to unfold, there are many more stories that should be – and will be – shared, and gaps that will certainly be filled.

Many people have come and gone in my life, and I feel blessed that to this day I still have faithful fans, friends, and family members who follow me and my career, and that I'm well enough to continue to get up on stage and sing for everyone. Each day I become more comfortable about opening up my heart and sharing the contents of my mind.

I now feel I've reached a new stage in my life, and am ready to continue to convey my thoughts and experiences. As the saying goes – and as with every great film – 'there will come a sequel'. When the time comes, I will fill in the spaces on these pages, and regale you with many more stories. I look forward to doing so, another time, another place.

DISCOGRAPHY

SINGLES
Here is the UK chronology with the year of release and the chart position. Engelbert spent many years recording before the huge success of 'Release Me'. Here for an historical perspective are those single releases.

GERRY DORSEY

1959
Crazy Bells
I'll Never Fall In Love Again

1961
Big Wheel

1964
Take Your Time

1965
Baby Turn Around

ENGELBERT HUMPERDINCK

1966
Stay
Dommage Dommage

1967
Release Me. No. 1
There Goes My Everything. No. 2
The Last Waltz. No. 1

1968
Am I That Easy To Forget No. 3
A Man Without Love No. 2
Les Bicyclettes De Belsize No. 5

1969
The Way It Used To Be No. 3
I'm A Better Man (For Having Loved You). No. 15
Winter World Of Love No. 7

1970
My Marie No. 31
Sweetheart No. 22

1971
Santa Lija (Sogno d'amore)
When there's no love (export only).
Our love will rise again
Another Time Another Place No. 13

1972
Too Beautiful To Last. No. 14
In Time

1973
Only Your Love
    I'm Leaving You
    Love Is All No. 44

1974
Free As The Wind

1975
Precious Love

1977
I Believe In Miracles
Lovers Holiday

1978
Loving You Losing You

1979
After The Lovin'

1980
It's Easy To Love It's Not Easy
    To Live Together

1984
To All The Girls I've Loved Before

1987
Love Is The Reason (duet with
    Gloria Gaynor)

1988
Nothing's Gonna Change My Love
    For You
How Do I Stop Loving You

1999
Quando Quando Quando No. 40

2000
How To Win Your Love No. 59

2004
Release Me No. 51

2010
Tell Me Where It Hurts

2012
Love Will Set You Free

ALBUMS

The recording career of Engelbert Humperdinck spans six decades. During that time he has recorded for numerous record companies and many of his recordings have been re-issued many times over on different labels with the same track listings and different album titles. On some occasions the original long player album releases have been superceded by the CD format to include extra tracks. There has been a steady stream of compilations over the years which duplicate preceding releases. If the content is exactly the same, then they have not been included. Many albums have been released in the US, only some of which have been available in the UK. All chart albums are included whether they duplicate other releases or not.

Here is the UK Album chronology with the year of release and chart positions where applicable.

1967

Release Me No. 6
Release Me/ Quiet Nights/ Yours Until Tomorrow/ There's A Kind Of Hush/ This Is My Song/ Misty Blue/ Take My Heart/ How Near Is Love/ Walk Through This World/ If I Were You/ Talking Love/ My World/Ten Guitars.

The Last Waltz No. 3
The Last Waltz/ Dance With Me/ Two Different Worlds/ If It Comes To That/ Walk Hand In Hand/ A Place In The Sun/ Long Gone/ All This World And The Seven Seas/ Miss Elaine E. S. Jones/ Everybody Knows/ Nature Boy/ To The Ends Of The Earth.

1968
A Man Without Love No. 3
A Man Without Love/ Can't Take My Eyes Of You/ From Here To Eternity/ Spanish Eyes/ A Man And A Woman/ Quando Quando Quando/ Up Up And Away/ Wonderland Tonight/ What A Wonderful World/ Call On Me/ By The Time I Get To Phoenix/ Shadow Of Your Smile.

1969
Engelbert No. 3.
Love Can Fly/ Love Was Here Before The Stars/ Don't Say No/ Let Me Into Your Life/ Through The Eyes Of Love/ Les Bicyclettes De Belsize/ The Way It Used To Be/ Marry Me/ To Get To You/ Your Easy To Love/ True/ A Good Thing Going.

Engelbert Humperdinck No. 5.
I'm A Better Man/ Gentle On My Mind/ Love Letters/ A Time for Us/ Didn't We?/ I Wish You Love/ Aquarius-Let The Sunshine In/ All You Gotta Do Is Ask/ The Signs Of Love/ Café/ Let's Kiss Tomorrow Goodbye/ Winter World Of Love.

1970
We Made It Happen No. 17
We Made It Happen/ My Cherie Amour/ Raindrops Keep Fallin' On My Head/ Love Me With All Your Heart/ Words/ Something/ Everybody's Talkin'/ Love For Love/ Just Say I Love Her/ Wandrin' Star/ My Wife The Dancer/ Leaving On A Jet Plane

1971
Sweetheart
Sweetheart/ California Maiden/ Woman In My Life/ I'll Be Your Baby Tonight/ Take Me For Love Now/ The First Time Ever I Saw Your Face/ Santa Lija (Sogne D'Amore)/Live And Just Let Live/ For The Good Times/ Put Your Hand In The Hand/ When There's No You.

Another Time Another Place No. 48
Another Time Another Place/ Help Me Make It Through The Night/ Our Love Will Rise Again/ Talk It Over In The Morning/There's An Island/ Revivin' Old Emotions/ Nashville Lady/ Morning/ Twenty Miles From Home/ Days Of Icy Fingers/ I'm Holding Your Memory.

1972
Live At The Riviera Las Vegas No. 45
Intro-Around The World-Till-Around The World/ My Prayer/ A Man Without Love/ Help Me Make It Through The Night/ My Wife The Dancer/ It's Impossible/ Just A Little Bit Of You/ Hit Medley-Am I That Easy To Forget?-There Goes My Everything-The Last Waltz-The Way It Used To Be-When There's No You-Les Bicyclettes De Belsize/ You'll Never Walk Alone/ Love The One Your With/ Release Me.

In Time
Baby I'm A Want You/ Day After Day/ Too Beautiful To Last/ (They Long To Be) Close To You/ Without You/ Girl Of Mine/ Time After Time/ In Time/ I'm Together Again/ Life Goes On/ I Never Said Goodbye.

1973
Engelbert King Of Hearts
My Summer Song/ I'm Stone In Love With You/ Do I Love You/ Somebody Waiting/ The Most Beautiful Girl/ I'm Leaving You/ Will You Be Here When I Wake Up In The Morning/ Eternally/ Only Your Love/ That's What It's All About/ Songs We Sang Together.

My Love
You Are The Sunshine Of My Life/ And I Love You So/ Photograph/ Free As The Wind/ My Love/ Catch Me I'm Falling/ Killing Me Softly With His Song/ Show And Tell/ Thankful For You/ Second Tuesday In December.

1974
Engelbert Humperdinck – His Greatest Hits No. 1
Release Me/ A Man Without Love/ The Way It Used to Be/ Quando Quando Quando/ Everybody Knows(We're Through)/ There's A Kind Of Hush(All over

the world)/ There Goes My Everything/ Les Bicyclettes De Belsize/ Winter
World Of Love/ I'm A Better Man (For Having Loved You)/ Ten Guitars/ My
World/ Am I That Easy To Forget/ The Last Waltz

1975
The World Of Engelbert Humperdinck
Release Me/ Do I Love You/ Just Say I Love You/ Let's Kiss Tomorrow Goodbye/
Call On Me/ Killing Me Softly With His Song/ Ten Guitars/ You Are The
Sunshine Of My Life/ Didn't We/ Take My Heart/ I Never Said Goodbye/ Love
Is All.

1976
After The Lovin'
After The Lovin'/ Can't Smile Without You/ Let's Remember The Good Times/
I Love Making Love To You/ This I Find Is Beautiful/ This Is What You Mean
To Me/ World Without Music/ Let Me Happen To You/ I Can't Live A Dream/
The Hungry Years.

1977
Miracles
I Believe In Miracles/ Goodbye My Friend/ Look At Me/ From Me To You/ The
Only Thing To Do/ Loving You Losing You/ Peace Of Mind/ What I Did For
Love/ You Are There/ Summer Of My Life/ Put A Light In Your Window.

Christmas Tyme
Silent Night Holy Night (Stille Nacht Heilige Nacht)(Gruber)/ White Christmas/
A Night To Remember/ Silver Bells/ Christmas Time Again/ The Christmas
Song/Sing-A-Long Tyme(We Wish You A Merry Christmas-Deck The Halls-
Rudolph The Red Nose Reindeer-Santa Claus Is Coming To Town)/ Carol
Tyme(Oh Come All Ye Faithful-The First Noel-It Came Upon A Midnight
Clear-Hark!The Herald Angels Sing-Joy To The World-We Three Kings-On
Holy Night)/ Home Tyme(There's No Christmas Like A Home Christmas-
[There's No Place Like Home] Home For The Holidays-I'll Be Home For
Christmas)/ Jingle Bell Tyme(Jingle Bell Rock-Winter Wonderland-Let It Snow
Let It Snow-Jingle Bells).

1978
The Last Of The Romantics
The Last Of The Romantics/ Just The Way You Are/ Love Me Tender/
You Light Up My Life/ What You See Is Who I Am/ Love's In Need Of Love
Today/ When I Wanted You/ Sweet Marjorene/ This Time One Year Ago/ Love
Is All.

Love Letters
Love Letters/ Three Little Words/ Call On Me/ What Now My Love/ You Love/
That Promise/ Yours Until Tomorrow/ Let Me Into Your Life/ I Wish You Love/
Funny Familiar Forgotten Feelings/ Come Over Here/ Those Were The Days/
When I Say Goodnight/ Stay.

1979
This Moment In Time
This Moment In Time/ First Time In My Life/ You're Something Special/ Maybe Tomorrow/ Can't Help Falling In Love/ Lovin' You Too Much/ A Much Much Greater Love/ I Believe In You/ You Know Me/ Travelin' Boy.

Engelbert Sings The Hits
I Can't Live A Dream/ Baby I'm A Want You/ You Are The Sunshine Of My Life/ My Cherie Amour/ The First Time Ever I Saw Your Face/ And I Love You So/ Leaving On a Jet Plane/ I'm Stone In Love With You/ Raindrops Keep Falling On My Head/ (They Long to Be) Close To You/ Can't Smile Without You/ Help Me Make It Through The Night/ Something/ My Love/ Killing Me Softly With His Song/ The Most Beautiful Girl/ Wandrin' Star/ Without You/ Words/ Just The Way You Are.

1980
Loves Only Love
Love's Only Love/ Best Times Of My Life/ Just Tell Me You Love Me/ A Chance To Be A Hero/ Don't Cry Out Loud/ Please Understand/ Unforgettable/ Any Kind Of Love At All/ Don't Touch That Dial/ If You Love Me(Really Love Me).

A Merry Christmas With Engelbert Humperdinck
O Come All Ye Faithful/ Have Yourself A Merry Little Christmas/ Blue Christmas/ Away In A Manger/ O Little Town Of Bethlehem/ Trilogy, (a) We Three Kings Of Orient Are, (b) The First Noel, (c) Silent Night Holy Night/ Winter Wonderland/ Mary's Boy Child/ God Rest Ye Merry Gentleman/ The Lord's Prayer.

1981
Don't You Love Me Anymore?
Don't You Love Me Anymore?/ Stay Away/ When The Night Ends/ I Don't Break Easily/ Say Goodnight/ Maybe This Time/ Baby Me Baby/ Heart Don't Fail Me Now/ Come Spend The Morning/ Till I Get It Right.

1982
Loving You Losing You
You Light up My Life/Close To You/And I Love You So/ Love Me with All Your Heart/ Just The Way You Are/ My Love/ Forever And Ever/ Sweetheart/ Can't Help Falling In Love/ The Last Waltz/ Release Me/ There Goes My Everything/ Without You/ Most Beautiful Girl/ Am I That Easy To Forget/ Loving You Losing You/ Help Me Make It Through The Night/ After The Lovin'/ A Man Without Love/ Killing Me Softly.

Misty Blue
Spanish Eyes/ Misty Blue/ Yours Until Tomorrow/ Didn't We/ I Wish You Love/ Can't Take My Eyes Off You/ This Is My Song/ Let Me Into Your Life/

The Shadow Of Your Smile/ From Here To Eternity/ By The Time I Get To
Phoenix/ Funny Familiar Forgotten Feelings/ Love Letters/ What A Wonderful
World.

1983
You And Your Lover
Who's At Look In Your Eye/ Perfect Love/ Till You And Your Lover Are Lovers
Again/ What Will I Write/ Yellow Moon/ I Don't Know How To Say Goodbye/
Beautiful Baby/ Patiently Waiting/ You Look Good to Me/ Two Lovers.

1985
Getting Sentimental No. 35
As Time Goes By/ Red Sails In The Sunset/ In The Still Of The Night/ I Don't
Want To Walk Without You/ More I See You/ You Belong To My Heart/ Very
Thought Of You/ Moonlight Becomes You/ Lovely Way To Spend The Evening/
Stardust/ You'll Never Know/ Embraceable You/ I'll Walk Alone/ Harbour
Lights/ Far Away Places/ Getting Sentimental Over You.

1987
Remember I Love You
Our Time/ Love Is The Reason(Duet With Gloria Gaynor)/ Just For The Love
Of You/ How Do I Stop Loving You/ After You/ You Made A Believer Out Of
Me/ I Bid You Goodbye/ We'll Meet Again/ Nothing's Gonna Change My Love
For You/ Are You Lonesome Tonight/ Love Is All.

The Engelbert Humperdinck Collection No. 35
Release Me/ There Goes My Everything/ A Man Without Love/ You Walked Into
My Life/ After The Lovin'/ Portofino/ Spanish Night Is Over/ Am I That Easy To
Forget/ Power Of Love/ The Last Waltz/ My Heart/ Les Bicyclettes De Belsize/
Love Life/ Goodbye Maria/ Dorero/ Hearbeat/ Way We Used To Be/ Dream Of
Me.

1989
In Love
This Time Tomorrow/ Alone In The Night/ Love You Back To Sleep/
Radio Dancing/ Aba Heidschi Bumbeidshi/ Second Time/ I Can Never Let You
Go/ One And One Made Three/ Natural Love/ Tokyo Tears/ One World.

1990
Step Into My Life
Red Roses For My Lady/ You Are So Beautiful/ I Get Lonely/ Step Into My Life/
Sentimental Lady/ You Are My Love/ Sweet Lady Jane/ I Wanna Rock You/
You're My Heart And Soul/ Dancing With Tears In My Eyes.

1991
Engelbert – Heart Of Gold
I'm Gonna Dream Our Dreams For You/ Take Away The Sorrow/ Always On
My Mind/ Sorry Seems To Be The Hardest Word/ Tell It Like It Is/ Our Love

Is Forever/ You Are So Beautiful/ Fashion Magazine/ Heart Of Gold/ California Blue/ I Wish I Could Be There/ Someone To Love/ Something's Gotten Hold Of My Heart/ I Am In Love Again/ Here We Are/ Let's Fall In Love Again.

1992
Hello Out There

Hello Out There/ We Dance The Night Away/ Right Thing That We Do/ Only Love/ Release Me/ (Everything I Do) I Do It For You / Take It To Heart/ After The Lovin'/ Fiesta Europa/ Spread A Little Sunshine/ Till The Right One Comes Along/ The Last Waltz/ Reach Out/ Hearts In The Dark/ Falling In Love Again/ We Fell In Love.

1993
Love Has Been A Friend Of Mine

Coming Home/ Golden Girl/ What If I Try/ Magic Night/ Spanish Eyes/ Loving Guitar/ Acapula/ Marlene/ As Long As I Can Dream Of You/ Blue Bayou/ Tropical Sunshine/ Woman Woman/ You Are The Reason/ Victim Of Love/ Love Has Been A Friend To Me/ Touche D'Amour.

1995
Engelbert – Sings The Classics

Close To You (They Long to Be)/After The Lovin'/ Much Greater Love/ Something/ Can't Help Falling In Love/ Most Beautiful Girl/ A Man Without Love(live)/ Release Me(live)/ Photograph/ Just Say I Love Her/ We Made It Happen/ Santa Lija(Sogno D'Amore)/ Catch Me I'm Falling/ Another Time Another Place/ Here You Come Again/ Everybody's Talkin'/ Love Me Tender/ Leaving On A Jet Plane/ Love Is All/ You Light Up My Life.

Love Unchained No. 16

Too Young/ Secret Love/ Unchained Melody/ Answer Me/ Sittin' On The Dock Of The Bay/ No Other Love/ Stranger In Paradise/ I Apologise/ Smoke Gets In Your Eyes/ Such A Night/ Love Me Tender/ Love Is A Many Splendored Thing.

1996
Live In Japan

Intro/There's A Kind Of Hush/ All I Ever Need Is You/ Il Mondo/ A Man Without Love/ Stripper/ Impressions/ I'll Be Your Baby Tonight/ Another Time Another Place/ Rlease Me/ Love Is All/ Without You/ I Can Help/ I Never Said Goodbye/ The Last Waltz/ Quando Quando Quando/ There Goes My Everything/ Spanish Eyes/ Les Bicyclettes De Belsize.

After Dark

Love Me Like We'll Never Love Again/ If I Could Love You More/ Once In A While/ I Could Get Used To This/ Healing (with Louise Sarah Dorsey)/ Answered Prayers/ Stay With Me/ Great Divide/ Slide A Little Closer/ I Know You Hear Me/ There's No Song Like A Slow Song.

1997
Engelbert Humperdinck – The Collection.
Release Me/ To All The Girls I've Loved Before/ Bella Italia/ Les Bicyclettes De Belsize/ There Goes My Everything/ One World/ The Last Waltz/ On The Wings Of A Silverbird/ Portofino/ Spanish Night Is Over/ Under The Man In The Moon/ I Can't Stop Loving You/ I Can Never Let You Go/ Are You Lonesome Tonight.

1998
The Dance Album
Quando Quando Quando/ This Night/ Release Me/ Gotta Get Release/ Mano A Mano/ A Man Without Love/ Spanish Eyes/ After the Lovin' / Am I The Lover/ The Last Waltz/ When Love Finds Your Heart/ Cuando Cuando Cuando(Spanish Mix-bonus track)/ Spanish Eyes (Spanglish mix-bonus track)/ Mano A Mano (morning mix-bonus track/ This Night (reprise-bonus track).

1999
The Best Of Engelbert Humperdinck (The Best Of Engelbert/Live At The Royal Albert Hall)
Acapulco/ Feelings/ Woman Woman/ California blue/ Spanish Eyes/ Blue Bayou/ Love Has Been A Friend To Me/ Touche D'Amour/ Tropical/ Put a Light In Your Window/ Summer Of My Life/ I Believe In Miracles/ Red Sails In The Sunset/ In The Still Of The Night/ More I See You / Lovely Way To Spend The Evening/ Getting Sentimental Over You/ As Time Goes By . . . all the following with The Royal Philharmonic Orchestra . . . Lovely Way To Spend The Evening/ I'm So Excited/ Hello/ After The Lovin'/ Mona Lisa/Unforgettable/ Lazy Hazy Crazy Days Of Summer/ Ramblin' Rose/ Too Young/When I Fall In Love/I Walk Alone/ I Just Called To Say I Love You/ I'll Walk Alone / Help Me Make It Through The Night/ Come A Little Bit Closer/ Release Me/ This Moment In Time/Les Bicyclettes De Belsize/ Am I That Easy To Forget/Quando Quando Quando/ A Man Without Love/There Goes My Everything/Spanish Eyes/ The Last Waltz/Love Is All/Please Release Me/ If We Only Have Love/If You Love Me (I won't care).

Original Gold
Another Time Another Place/ Can't Take My Eyes Off You/ Leaving On A Jet Plane/ Love Me Tender/ Help Me Make It Through The Night/ Let's Kiss/ Everybody's Talkin'/ Can't Smile Without You/ In Time/ Without You/ And I Love You So/ My Cherie Amour/ Just The Way You Are/ What I Did For Love/ Just Say I Love Her/ After The Lovin'/ Love Me With All Your Heart/ Close To You/ Killing Me Softly/ I'm Still In Love With You/ Baby I'm A Want You / Love Is All/ Forever And Ever/ Something/ Funny Familiar Forgotten Feelings/ You Are The Sunshine Of My Life/ Raindrops Keep Falling On My Head/ Can't Help Falling In Love/ I Can't Live A Dream/ Most Beautiful Girl

Live At The Royal Albert Hall
Lovely Way To Spend The Evening/ I'm So Excited/ Hello/ After The Lovin'/ Mona Lisa/Unforgettable/ Lazy Hazy Crazy Days Of Summer/ Ramblin' Rose/

Too Young/When I Fall In Love/I Walk Alone/ I Just Called To Say I Love You/ I'll Walk Alone / Help Me Make It Through The Night/ Come A Little Bit Closer/ Release Me/ This Moment In Time/Les Bicyclettes De Belsize/ Am I That Easy To Forget/Quando Quando Quando/ A Man Without Love/There Goes My Everything/Spanish Eyes/ The Last Waltz/Love Is All/Please Release Me/ If We Only Have Love/If You Love Me (I won't care).

The Engelbert Humperdinck Collection
Release Me/ There's A Kind Of Hush (All over the world)/ Yours Until Tomorrow/ If I Were You/ Come Over Here/ Stay/ My World (Il mondo)/ Dommage Dommage/ When I Say Goodnight/ How Near Is Love (Ay ay ay)/ Ten Guitars/ Walk Through This World/ Misty Blue/ Quiet Nights/ Take My Heart/ What Now My Love/ This Is My Song/ There Goes My Everything.

2000
At His Very Best No. 5
How To Win Your Love/ Strangers In The Night/ Dance The Night Away/ Sometimes When We Touch/ Nothing In This World/ Little Bit More Time/ Don't Tell Me You Love Me/ You're What Love Should Be/ Release Me/ Way It Used To Be/ A Man Without Love/ Spanish Eyes/ Quando Quando Quando/ There's A Kind Of Hush(All over the world)/ Les Bicyclettes De Belsize/ There Goes My Everything/ Ten Guitars/ Winter World Of Love/ Am I That Easy To Forget/ The Last Waltz.

2001
Love Songs
(They Long To Be) Close to You/ After the Lovin'/ Something/ Most Beautiful Girl/ A Man Without Love (live)/ Release Me (live)/ Photograph/ Just Say I Love Her/ We Made It Happen/ Santa Lija (Songo D'Amore)/ Catch Me I'm Falling/ Another Time Another Place/ Everybody's Talkin'/ And I Love You So/ Leaving On A Jet Plane/ Love Is All/ Too Beautiful To Last/ For The Good Times/ Can't Smile Without You/ Time After Time.

It's All In The Game
Dancing The Night Away/ It's All In The Game/ Strangers In The Night/ Sometimes When We Touch/ Nothing In This World/ Dancing In The Rain/ Blame It On The Rain/ Hopelessly/ How To Win Your Love/ Maybe The Feeling Will Go/ A Little More Time/ You're What Love Should Be/ Release Me(And let me love again)[live]/ Quando Quando Quando[live]/ A Man Without Love[live]/Spanish Eyes[live]/After The Lovin'[live]/The Last Waltz[live].

I Want to Wake Up With You No. 42
I Want To Wake Up With You/ True Love At Last/ Angels/ Penny Lane/ It's All In The Game/ She/ Dancing In The Rain/ Blame It On The Night/ If/ How Slow We Go/ Maybe The Feeling Will Go/ Love Me/ Hopelessly/ This Guy's In Love With You/ Brazil.

Red Sails In The Sunset
More I See You/ Getting Sentimental Over You/ Lovely Way To Spend An Evening/ Far Away Places/ I'll Walk Alone/ My Foolish Heart/ Very Thought Of You/ You Belong To My Heart/ I Wish I Knew/ Embraceable You/ Red Sails In The Sunset/ You'll Never Know/ I Don't Want To Walk Without You/ As Time Goes By/ Long Ago And Far Away/ Stardust/ They Say It's Wonderful/ Harbour Lights/ I'll Be Around/ But Beautiful.

2002
You Belong To My Heart
Unchained Melody/The Very Thought Of You/ They Say It's Wonderful/ You Belong to My Heart/ If I Could Love You More/ I Don't Want To Walk Without You/ You'll Never Know/ Red Sails In The Sunset/ The More I See You/ There's No Song Like A Slow Song/ A Lovely Way To Spend The Evening/ Too Young/ Love Is A Many Splendored Thing/ Moonlight Becomes You/ Smoke Gets In Your Eyes/ I Apologize/ Love Me Like We'll Never Love Again.

A Night To Remember
Spanish Eyes/ Can't Take My Eyes Off You/ Don't Want To Walk Without You/ You Belong To My Heart/ Harbour Lights/ In The Still Of The Night/ Stardust/ Red Sails In The Sunset/ As Time Goes By/ Night To Remember/ Love Story/ Getting Sentimental Over You/ More I See You/ Long Ago And Far Away/ I'll Walk Alone/ California Blue.

The Gold Collection
You Are The Sunshine Of My Life/ Close To You/ My Cherie Amour/ Can't Smile Without You/ And I Love You So/ Love Me With All Your Heart/ Leaving On A Jet Plane/ Something/ Love Is All/ Help Me Make It Through The Night/ Raindrops Keep Falling On My Head/ Everybody's Talkin'/ Another Time Another Place/ Killing Me Softly/ When There's No You/ Forever And Ever/ In Time/ Eternally/ I'm Leaving You/ Most Beautiful Girl.

2003
Definition Of Love
Definition Of Love/ I Want To Wake Up With You/ How Slow We Go/ I Don't Want To Miss A Thing/ If Tomorrow Never Comes/ Nothing A Little Love Won't Cure/ Angels/ Love Me/ Volare/ Brazil/ Penny Lane/ This Guy's In Love With You/ True Love At Last/ If/ She.

Engelbert Humperdinck Live
Overture/Love Is A Many Splendored Thing/ Can't Take My Eyes Off You/ Stranger In Paradise/ Per El Amor De Una Mujer (I know that we have loved before)/ Nothin' A Little Love Won't Cure/ Portofinoz/ Sittin' On The Dock Of The Bay/ Release Me/ Shadow Of Your Smile/ I Apologise/ Too Young/ Secret Love/ No Other Love/ When I Fall In Love/ Quando Quando Quando/ After The Lovin'/ Such A Night/ Yours/ Unchained Melody/ Ave Maria.

2004
Engelbert Humperdinck- His Greatest Love Songs. No. 4.
Release Me/ There Goes My Everything! The Last Waltz/ Am I That Easy To Forget/ A Man Without Love/ The Way It Used To Be/ I'm A Better Man (for having loved you)/ Winter World of Love/ Sweetheart/ Another Time Another Place/ Too Beautiful To Last/ Quando Quando Quando/ There's A Kind Of Hush (All over the world)/ Spanish Eyes/ I Want To Wake Up With You/ She/ This Guy's In Love With You/ True Love At Last/ If/
Can't Take My Eyes Off You/ Misty Blue/ Les Bicyclettes De Belsize/ What A Wonderful World! Stardust.

Always Hear The Harmony
Always Hear The Harmony/ Old Rugged Cross/ At The Cross/ Sending Me you! Take My Precious Lord! How Great Thou Art/ Our Wedding Song! What A Friend We Have In Jesus/ It Is No Secret/ Nearer My God To Thee/ In The Sweet By And By/ Amazing Grace.

Love Songs and Ballads
In The Still Of the Night/A Lovely Way To Spend An Evening/ They Say It's Beautiful/ Harbour Lights/ I Don't Want to Walk Without You/ Embraceable You/ More I See You/ Moonlight Becomes You/ I'll Walk Alone/ Very Thought Of You/ You Belong To My Heart/ I'll Be Around! Getting Sentimental Over You/ My Foolish Heart/ Far Away Places/ But Beautiful/ Yours/ I'll Be Seeing You/ Red Sails In The Sunset/ You'll Never Know/ I Wish I Knew/ Stardust/ As Time Goes By/ Long Ago And Far Away.

2005–2010
Best of Englebert Humperdinck: The Millenium Collection (2005)
Totally Amazing (2006)
An Introduction to Englebert Humperdinck (2006)
Greatest Hits and More (2006)
The Winding Road (2007)
Legacy of Love (2007)
My Love / King of Hearts (2009)
We Must Make it Happen / Sweetheart (2009)
Released (2010)

Researched and compiled by Brian Justice.

INDEX

Dorsey, Jason (son) 62, 73, 112, 139, 153–4, 186, 203, 209, 224–5, 226
Dorsey, Louise (daughter) 61–2, 68–70, 73–4, 111–12, 136, 137, 139, 154, 164–5, 168, 171, 186, 200, 203, 209, 223–4, 225
Dorsey, Mervyn (father) v–vii, 1, 2–4, 6, 9, 10, 79, 110–11, 193
Dorsey, Olga (sister) 1, 39
Dorsey, Olive (mother) 1, 2, 3, 11, 27, 50–1, 67, 110–11, 146, 193–6
Dorsey, Pat (sister) 1
Dorsey, Patricia see Healey, Patricia (Popea)
Dorsey, Peggy (sister) 1
Dorsey, Ronnie 34
Dorsey, Scott (son) 62, 112–13, 139, 163, 182, 186, 203, 209, 223, 225–6
Dorsey, Tilly (sister) 1

Eckstein, Billy 144
Ed Sullivan Show, The 84–5
education 4, 11
Egan, Mike 100, 172–3
Elson, Clifford 198
EMI records 41
Engelbert Humperdinck Appreciation Society 214

Faith, Adam 44
fatherhood 61–2, 68–70, 73–4, 111–14, 140, 154, 156, 159, 163–5, 182, 216, 222–6
finance 10, 11–12, 32, 33, 37, 39, 40–2, 45, 52, 58–9, 66–7, 70–2, 81–2, 141–2, 177–8
Flowers, Michael 185

Gallo brothers 96–7
Garner, James 159
Garrison, Greg 90

Gentle, Johnny 58
George, Corporal Johnny 18
Giaconda Café, London 45
Gibb, Barry 101, 111
golf 142–4, 154–5, 191, 220
Good, Jack 42
Grable, Betty 106
Grand Funk Railroad 178
Grant, Cary 106
Grant, Johnny 203
Greatest Love Songs 227
Greco, Buddy 173
Green, Hughie 220
Greene, Mick 100
Greenslade, Arthur 77, 100
Groby Road Hospital, Leicester 51–4
Grosvenor House Hotel, Park Lane, London 36, 37

Ha, Dr. 185, 194, 211
Harrah, Bill v
Harrison, George 75, 190
Hart, Ronnie 27–8
Hartman, Stella 40–1
Hawaii 135–8
Hawkins, Jack 144
Hawn, Goldie 142
Hayworth, Rita 144
Healey, June 30, 120, 162
Healey, Mary 62, 68, 166
Healey, Patricia (Popea) 10, 29–30, 33–4, 48, 52–3, 58, 60–4, 79, 110–14, 117, 119–20, 135–6, 138–9, 140, 153, 156–71, 183, 186–7, 190–2, 203, 209, 224, 225, 226–7
healing powers 207–11
health
 asthma 185
 loss of voice 101–3
 TB 50–4, 197
 viral infection 204–6
Heath, Bea 150–1
Hendrix, Jimi 108, 109–10, 190

McGrail, Dr Simon 102
McLaren, Malcolm 178
Melbourne Road School for Boys and
    Girls, Leicester 11
Merv Griffin Show 91
Mike Douglas Show 91
Miller, Bill 86–7
Mills, Bill and Lorna 213
Mills, Gordon 45, 57–8, 61, 64, 65,
    68, 75–8, 80, 84, 90–1, 101,
    110, 123, 127, 142–3, 148–50,
    176, 177–81
Mills, Jo 58, 64, 65, 68, 181
Morrel, Harry 83–4
Mr Music Man 44
My Way 230
Myers, Sidney 38, 39–40

Namani, Franck 215
National Enquirer 193
National Service 17–28
New Zealand tour 130
Newell, Norman 41–2
Nicholson, Jack 154

O'Connor, Des 187
Oh Boy 42–4, 46
Opportunity Knocks 38, 220
Otley, Captain Dick 21, 39

Paige, Jimmy 108
Palmer, Arnold 144
Parker, Colonel 115, 116
Parker, Mr (saxophone teacher)
    10–11
Parlorphone 44
Parnes, Larry 46–9
Pesci, Joe 154
Piccone, Rick 131, 134, 146
Posada de Engelbert 212
Power, Duffy 58
Presley, Elvis 21, 85, 115–17, 174–6,
    184
Presley, Priscilla 114, 115, 149

Pride, Dickie 58

Quando Quando Quando 203, 227

Reed, Les 44, 55, 56, 64, 87
Release Me 72, 80–1, 83, 219, 224
Reynolds, Burt 227–8, 229
Richard, Cliff 43
Richards, Keith 45
Robinson Crusoe 84
Rodriguez, Chi Chi 144
Rolling Stones 91
Ross, Diana 107, 193
Rowan & Martin's Laugh In 91, 142
Royal Army Service Corps 17–28
Royal Variety Performance 187–8

Sampras, Pete 145
Sanders, Doug 144, 145
Savile, Sir Jimmy 80
Schoknecht, Hank 212
Selleck, Tom 136–7
Seoul Olympics, South Korea 198–9
Sex Pistols 178, 190
sexual encounters 23–6, 37–8, 47–9,
    60, 156–70
Shadwick, Hilda 213–14
Shelby, Carrol 154
Silvers, Phil 126
Simmons, Percy 34
Sinatra, Frank 135–6, 174, 210–11
Smythe, John vi, 189
Song Parade 39–40
South African tour 128–30
Spence, Johnny 117
Spooner, John 100
Spradbury, Dave 191
Springsteen, Bruce 178
St Kevin's School, Madras 4
Starlite Club 214
Stay 75, 80
Steele, Tommy 43
Stellman, Marcel 77–8, 79
Steppan, Armella 182